HALDANE
1856–1915

THE RIGHT HON. R. B. HALDANE, SECRETARY OF
STATE FOR WAR, BY FIDDES WATT, 1908

HALDANE

1856–1915

The Life of
Viscount Haldane of Cloan
K.T., O.M.

by

Major-General
SIR FREDERICK MAURICE
K.C.M.G., C.B., D.Litt.

IN TWO VOLUMES

VOLUME I

GREENWOOD PRESS, PUBLISHERS
WESTPORT, CONNECTICUT

Originally published in 1937
by Faber and Faber, Ltd., London

First Greenwood Reprinting 1970

Library of Congress Catalogue Card Number 72-110857

SBN 8371-4524-4 (Set)
SBN 8371-4525-2 (Vol. I)

Printed in the United States of America

PREFACE

This volume takes the story of Lord Haldane's life down to the time when he was driven from office by popular clamour in the spring of 1915. It covers, therefore, the period in which he did that public service by which he is best remembered, and describes those of his actions which were the subject of the attacks upon him.

In fact, however, the six and a half years which Lord Haldane spent at the War Office were but an interlude in his career. His chief interests throughout his life were his philosophy, higher education, and the law. He provides one of those rare examples of a philosopher who ventured into public life to apply his principles to public affairs. His philosophical studies, and in particular his study of German philosophy, led him to be critical of our somewhat haphazard methods of government, and as he gained experience of public affairs it became increasingly his object to base the organization of government and national development on general principles. He sought the means to that end in the development of higher education, to foster which he used every possible opportunity.

⌈He was impressed by the way in which we 'muddled through' the South African War. It was this which first turned his mind to the task of applying general principles to our military organization and made him jump at the chance of going to the War Office when Campbell-Bannerman told him that no one would touch it with a pole.⌋ He was an idealistic philosopher, and as such always hoped and worked for the best, while preparing for the worst. In that spirit he used his knowledge of Germany and of Germans to smooth relations between the two countries during the critical years which preceded the Great War, while at the same time he applied himself, with his characteristic avidity to face difficulties, to making our organization of defence as effective as possible. The story of these efforts and their result is here told.

I must express my obligation to Miss Haldane for her care and arrangement of her brother's papers, which have saved me much labour, and to the many friends of Lord Haldane who have entrusted me with his letters.

F. MAURICE

September, 1937

CONTENTS

CONTENTS

CHAPTER V

UNIVERSITY REFORM

The London University Bill—success of Haldane's speech in support—opposition of Irish members—the Irish University problem—Haldane visits Ireland—drafts Irish University Bill—first contact with Edward, Prince of Wales—differences in the Liberal Party.

CHAPTER VI

THE SOUTH AFRICAN WAR
THE GIFFORD LECTURES

Campbell-Bannerman becomes Liberal leader—the crisis in South Africa—Haldane's reason for supporting Government—plans reform of Supreme Court of Appeal—presses Rosebery to lead Liberal Imperialists—General Election of 1900—breach with Campbell-Bannerman—interest in Army reform—Imperial College of Science and Technology—becomes Privy Councillor—Chamberlain's Tariff Reform—the Gifford Lectures—the first full exposition of his philosophy.

CHAPTER VII

THE LIBERAL REVIVAL

Haldane's views on Free Trade—Attempts at Army reform—the United Free Church of Scotland and the Wee Frees—foundation of the University of Liverpool—weakness of Balfour's Government—Haldane confers with Asquith and Grey—the Relugas Compact—Balfour resigns—Campbell-Bannerman as Premier—Haldane and Grey's doubt—they accept office—Haldane goes to the War Office.

CHAPTER VIII

CAMPBELL-BANNERMAN'S GOVERNMENT
THE MILITARY CONVERSATIONS WITH FRANCE

The Liberal triumph of 1906—Haldane's opinion of his Cabinet colleagues—decides to take time to consider Army reform—The

CONTENTS

CONTENTS

ILLUSTRATIONS

Chapter I

THE PERTHSHIRE HALDANES

'Our lives', wrote George Eliot, 'make themselves a moral tradition, and to have acted nobly once seems a reason why we should act nobly always.' This is as true of families as it is of individuals. *Noblesse oblige* and the tradition of a family commonly puts its stamp upon the character and actions of its members. Certainly this is the case with the Perthshire Haldanes. The traveller from Euston to the Highlands will usually find his train stop at Gleneagles, for there, upon a lower spur of the Ochils, the railway company has built a somewhat incongruously sumptuous hotel and has surrounded it with two excellent golf courses. But if to the Southerner Gleneagles is known for its golf, it was known to those who cared for the history of Scotland long before the railway came up Allan Water on its way to Perth. The Castle of Gleneagles stands with its lovely little chapel in a quiet vale fronting the exit from the Highlands, which leads down through Crieff to the Ochils, and has seen adventures in the rougher days of Scottish history, while the lairds of Gleneagles have from early times taken their part in the public affairs of their country. I need not for my purpose dig deep into the past. I will begin with John Haldane[1] of Gleneagles, who, as one of the four barons of Perthshire, sat in the last Scottish Parliament and was one of the forty-five Scottish members of the first Union Parliament, which met in October 1707, a

[1] I commend those who desire further information of the Haldane family to General Sir Aylmer Haldane's scholarly *The Haldanes of Gleneagles* (Blackwood & Sons).

I

fact which gave him the nickname in the family of 'Union-Jack', and set an example which was to affect seriously the fortunes of the family. His two surviving sons, Mungo and Patrick, who in turn succeeded to the estate, both became members of the Union Parliament. Of Mungo an old tenant of the estate told a story which is typical of the Haldane stock. It had become the custom of the packmen to assemble in the churchyards of country parishes on the Sabbath and as soon as divine service was over to make the day a market day. 'The Baron of Gleneagles, however, was of a race who, in troublous times, had risked much for the cause of religion; and, regarding such doings as a profanation of the day of rest, made up his mind to put a stop to them. Accordingly, being a justice of the peace, he gave orders that all Sunday trading in Blackford churchyard should immediately cease and determine. Accustomed to have his orders obeyed he thought no more of the matter till, on seeing, the following Sabbath afternoon, one of the servants returning from church, he asked him if the packmen had again made their appearance. Being answered in the affirmative the old laird said not a word, but, pressing his lips and drawing up his large proportions, like one who resolves on a great effort and is determined to accomplish it at any hazard, he sullenly stalked into the house. Next Sabbath the laird was up betimes, and looked as if he had more in his head than sermons. In the afternoon the churchyard was again in a bustle, with packmen and worshippers driving bargains with wonted keenness, when suddenly, to the consternation of all, Gleneagles was among them, frowning terribly and waving round his head a flashing broadsword. In a moment packmen and worshippers were in full rout, pressing and tumbling over one another in their eagerness to escape. Even decrepit old age, on that memorable occasion, exhibited such activity that in less than a minute the only living being in the churchyard was the baron himself, who deliberately tossed the whole of the merchandise into a ditch, and then, sheathing his sword walked slowly home. This summary proceeding, it is said, had the desired effect, for with that afternoon Sunday trading ceased in the parish of Blackford.'[1]

Mungo died in 1755 and was succeeded by his brother, Patrick, a man of exceptional ability and forceful character, but an adept in the 'gentle art of making enemies'. At the age of twenty-two he received the largest number of votes for the appointment of Professor of Greek in the University of St. Andrews, but was not selected. Affronted by this he took the matter into court, when the election was annulled by the Lords of Session and he was appointed, an incident typical of his career, for he was continually fighting against opposition, much of which he seems to have created himself. Two years later he was appointed Professor of Ecclesiastical History in the New College of St. Andrews. After a few years in that post he went to the University of Leyden to study law, which thenceforth was to be his career, and he was admitted advocate in 1715. He at once jumped into prominence, and in the following year became successively Commissioner of the Equivalent, one of the posts resulting from the Act of Union, member of Parliament for the Cupar Burghs, Provost of St. Andrews, and commissioner for the disposal of the estates forfeited by those who had followed Charles Stuart in 1715. This last post was not likely to endear the most tactful of Commissioners to Scots, and Patrick's handling of it called down on his head a storm of hatred and abuse. In 1721 he was nominated by the King to be a Lord of Session, whereupon his enemies at once set to work to prevent his appointment, and after protracted suits and disputes the Government yielded to the opposition and the nomination was withdrawn. As some compensation he was made in 1724 a commissioner of excise in England, a post which he held until the death of George II. He was caught in the storms of the '45 and was present at the battle of Fal-

[1] *The Haldanes of Gleneagles*, pp. 132-3.

kirk, and in the following year was made one of the two
Solicitors for Scotland, in which position he served until he
succeeded to the Gleneagles estate in 1755. The costs of law-
suits, of elections, and of maintaining houses in Edinburgh
and London had greatly embarrassed Patrick's fortune and he
was looking to his son George to retrieve the position of the
family when, in 1759, he received the news of his death without issue in Jamaica. George Haldane had entered the 3rd
Guards, in which he had a distinguished career. He was
severely wounded at Fontenoy, and after the peace of Aix-la-
Chapelle he followed the family example and entered Parliament, as member for Stirling Burghs. He too found the cost
of elections and of a house in London, added to the expense of
an officer in the Guards, a heavy drain on his income, and he
sought preferment. Eventually in 1758, as brigadier-general,
he was appointed Governor and Captain-General of Jamaica,
but he died of fever before the considerable emoluments of
those posts could make good his debts, which were all that he
had to leave his father. Patrick now found himself faced with
the disposal of the family estate by sale as the only means of
meeting his embarrassments. Fortunately a younger half-
brother, Robert, a son of John Haldane by his second wife,
was able to come to the rescue. Robert, who was born on
March 16, 1705, was baptized in the chapel of Gleneagles, and
this is the last religious ceremony recorded as having taken
place there until the burial of Viscount Haldane of Cloan. He
entered the service of the East India Company, and at a comparatively early age became captain of a ship of the company,
and in that position he acquired a considerable fortune. He is
said to have made £70,000 on one voyage. He came home in
1755, and three years later, when his nephew George vacated
his seat in Parliament on becoming Governor of Jamaica, he
followed him as member for Stirling Burghs. On hearing of
Patrick's financial troubles he purchased the Gleneagles estate
and also that of Airthrey, near Stirling. He had no children,

and he left the Airthrey estate to his nephew James Haldane, who had, like himself, entered the service of the East India Company, and was the son of Lieutenant-Colonel James Haldane, of the 1st Life-Guards, and of Margaret Pye, of whom more anon. The Gleneagles estate he entailed upon the male issue of his two sisters, and thus it eventually devolved upon Admiral Viscount Duncan, son of Helen Haldane, who had married Alexander Duncan of Lundie.

Captain James Haldane of Airthrey had, it would appear, distinguished himself in the service of the East India Company, for he was on the point of being elected a director when he died. He had married a cousin, Katherine Duncan, and left two sons, Robert and James. It is with James, born in 1768 that we are chiefly concerned. The family had, through Robert Haldane, a third interest in an East India Company's ship, the *Melville Castle*, and on the advice of his uncles, Colonel Alexander Duncan and Captain Adam Duncan, later to become the famous admiral, he was destined for the East India Company's service. Both his parents had died while he was still a boy, and it was his uncles who looked after his early training, and they saw him off on his first voyage to India at the age of seventeen. While he was still in the junior position of third officer of the *Hillsborough* an incident occurred which shows his character. Amongst the passengers was a former captain of the Dragoons, well known as a bully, as an expert shot, and a successful duellist. Indeed, it was his exploits on these lines which had caused his retirement from the army. This fellow proposed to make James Haldane party to a trick upon an irritable invalid, who, as it turned out, was actually at the point of death. On receiving an indignant refusal he publicly insulted Haldane, at dinner that evening, by flinging the contents of a glass of wine in his face. James rose at once and hurled at his assailant a heavy ship's tumbler, which just missed him but poured its contents over his face. A challenge followed, and this, seeing the dragoon's record, James could with honour have refused. But, doubtless considering that the captain's reputation as a duellist might have been held to influence his decision, he determined on a meeting, which took place when the ship reached St. Helena. The night before the duel he made his will, wrote a letter of farewell to his brother Robert, and then slept so soundly that he did not wake until he was called.

The next evening the opponents, having landed, were placed twelve paces apart and were to fire at a given signal. As Haldane raised his pistol he breathed, as he himself told later, a prayer, 'Father into thy hand I commend my spirit,' and without a tremor, on the signal being given, he pressed the trigger. His pistol burst, a fragment wounding his face, while his adversary's pistol missed fire, and honour was declared to be satisfied.

In 1793, at the age of twenty-five, James was given command of the family ship, the *Melville Castle*, and was well on the road to emulate the example of Captain Robert, for the captain of an East Indiaman was also a trading agent of the company, and his normal profits on the round trip were from £7,000 to £8,000 and frequently amounted to much more. With his future assured James proposed to marry and sought the hand of Mary, only child and heiress of Major Joass of Colleonard, great-grandson of the second Lord Banff. Mary had as uncles two distinguished soldiers, Generals Sir Ralph and Sir Robert Abercromby. Sir Ralph, the future hero of Aboukir Bay, was at the time engaged in the siege of Dunkirk under the Duke of York, and he wrote, on hearing of the proposed marriage, to Major Joass very sensibly: 'If your daughter likes Mr. Haldane there is no difficulty. They have and will have abundance. He is a young man in a profession which will command a fortune, and allow me to say it is a better match for real happiness than if Miss Joass had married an idle country gentleman, let his character be as it may.' Robert Abercromby was equally approving of the match, and the marriage took place in September 1793. James joined the *Melville Castle* at Portsmouth in the following January, but adverse winds and other circumstances delayed the sailing of the fleet of East Indiamen. For some time the crew of one of the ships of the fleet, the *Dutton*, had shown increasing signs of discontent, for which there appears to have been good reasons, and by the middle of March the spirit of the men had become definitely mutinous and the captain applied to His Majesty's ship *Regulus* for help. On the evening of March 19 a lieutenant with a boat's crew from the *Regulus* came alongside and demanded the surrender of the ringleaders, whereupon the men got up round-shot on deck and threatened to sink the first boat which came alongside. The lieutenant of the *Regulus* then withdrew and the captain of the *Dutton* left his ship, under the impression that this would quiet the men, who on the contrary grew more and more excited, and their officers lost all control of them. At this moment, when the men were threatening to blow up the ship, Captain James Haldane of the *Melville Castle* appeared alongside in his boat, to be greeted with shouts of 'Keep off or we will sink you'. Undeterred Captain James took his boat round by the stern, and in a few minutes he had scrambled up to the quarter-deck. There his first act was to restore confidence to the officers, his next to refuse to lead an attack on the mutineers. Instead he began to reason calmly with the men, asking what they imagined they could do in the presence of twenty ship of the line. This had an immediate effect, but seeing that there were still signs of confusion and uneasiness amongst the men, he learned that some of the ringleaders were still bent on blowing up the ship. He went down at once to the magazine, and there found two men, both drunk and both swearing to send themselves and their comrades either to heaven or hell. One of them was in the act of wrenching the iron bars from the door and the other had a shovelful of live coals ready to throw into the magazine. Haldane put a pistol to the head of the man at the door and told him that if he stirred he was a dead man. Calling at once for irons, as if disobedience was out of the question, he saw them placed on both men and the mutiny was quelled. The reputation which James acquired for this act of daring and his conduct in the duel enabled him to avoid any further personal encounters in an age when these were of common occurrence, and later in life he took a leading part in the suppression of duelling.

Shortly after his adventure in the *Dutton* James left the service of the East India Company. He had for some time been urged to this step by his elder brother Robert, and his marriage has doubtless some influence on his decision, but the deciding factor was that both brothers had come under the influence of the Evangelical movement, then spreading rapidly in England and beginning to cross the border into Scotland. Some years later James wrote to a friend: 'My giving up the sea at the time I did was, I believe, thought strange by many; but I have never repented it, nor do I find my time hang heavily on my hands. . . . I never was acquainted with solid rational happiness till my attention was turned to religion. My former merriment was really like the crackling of thorns under a pot. I was governed by passion, and under such a guide no wonder if I missed my road. Although I believe I had as few qualms of conscience as any one, being completely unconcerned about religion and eternity, my own mind was not altogether satisfied. I knew I must die, but it was a subject I banished from my thoughts. The peace of mind I enjoyed did not arise from any good reason. I had to hope either that I should be happy or be annihilated after death, but from total inconsideration, like a person who should stop his ears and shut his eyes when danger was approaching, and then fancy himself safe. My present peace of mind does not arise from any vision or supposed new revelation I have received. I had a book by which, from prejudice of education, and not from any rational conviction, I called the word of

God. I never so far surmounted the prejudice of education as to profess infidelity, but I was a more inconsistent character. I said I believed a book to be a revelation from God, and treated it with the greatest neglect, living in direct contradiction to all its precepts, and seldom taking the trouble to look into it, or if I did it was to perform a task—a kind of atonement for my sins. I went on thus till, having much time on my hands when the *Melville Castle* lay at the Mother Bank, I began to think I would pay a little more attention to this book.'

In 1795 Robert designed to sell the estate of Airthrey and to devote the proceeds to a mission, which he proposed to lead himself, to the East Indies, but this project was vetoed by the East India Company, and so it came about that both brothers decided to give themselves to the service of God in their own country. At this time the Church of Scotland was as much in need of the stirring of a revival as was the Church of England, and it was commonly said that her ministers were without a lively faith and her churches half empty. This doubtless influenced the decision of the brothers. In any case, three years later Robert sold his estate that he might have more time and money to devote to the service of religion in Scotland, and to that service both brothers devoted the remainder of their lives, James being chiefly distinguished as a missioner, Robert as a theologian.

James died on February 6, 1851, in his eighty-third year. He married twice and had no fewer than fifteen children. Of these it is with Robert, his third son, that we are concerned. His eldest brother James died unmarried at the age of thirty-two and the second brother Alexander eventually succeeded to the estate of Gleneagles. Robert was born at Edinburgh on January 27, 1805, and was first educated at the Edinburgh High School and at Geneva, whence he came back to Edinburgh to study law at the university and become a writer to the signet. He was a man of energy and ability, and he prospered in his profession. His family connections and his own sterling qualities brought him many trusteeships and the management of numerous estates. He married, in 1841, Jane Makgill, daughter of John Makgill of Kemback, County Fife, and by her had six children. She died in childbirth in February 1851. In that year Robert purchased the estate of Cloan, in the hills hard by Gleneagles, and overlooking Auchterarder, and though his work kept him for the greater part of the year in Edinburgh the family usually spent some months of each year at Cloan, which became their real home. On July 27, 1853, Robert married, as second wife, Mary Elizabeth, daughter of Richard Burdon-Sanderson of West Jesmond, Northumberland. Mr. Burdon-Sanderson had been a close friend and admirer of James Haldane, and in 1848 a son of his had married a half-sister of Robert's, so that the two families were already closely connected. Mr. Burdon, as he then was, had a distinguished career at Oxford, where he won the Newdigate in 1811 and became a fellow of Oriel. His uncle, the first Lord Eldon, then Lord Chancellor, made him his Secretary of Presentations, but he was so disgusted with what he saw of the abuse of clerical patronage for political purposes and of the traffic in advowsons that he resigned his post and severed his connection with the Church of England, while maintaining a deep and sincere interest in religion. Ere this he had married, in 1815, Elizabeth Sanderson, the only child of Sir James Sanderson, who was twice Lord Mayor of London, and who made it a condition of the marriage that he should add the name of Sanderson to his own. Mr. Burdon-Sanderson moved to West Jesmond in 1826, and there settled down to a quiet contemplative life, and was much concerned in seeking a faith which would satisfy him. There he was visited in 1837 by the Honourable Paul Methuen, who, a Plymouth Brother, after much talk with his host and long studying of the Scriptures, prevailed on him to join that persuasion, and Mr. Burdon-Sanderson and his two daughters were baptized by immersion.

Mary Elizabeth was delicate, and eventually it was decided that the climate of Northumberland did not suit her or her father, so in 1848 a move was made to Devonshire, where Mr. Burdon-Sanderson took a house about five miles from Plymouth, the choice being influenced by the fact that nearby lived a friend of his, the Reverend J. Harris, who had, like himself, left the Church of England and become a Plymouth Brother. In 1852 Robert Haldane came to Plymouth on a visit to his sister Mary, married to General Eckford, who had retired from India after the Sikh War and settled down there. Naturally enough Robert called on his father's old friend, and fell in love with Mary. Mr. Burdon-Sanderson found in Robert one who had inherited much of his father's active interest in religion; indeed it had become his regular practice, when riding about to inspect the estates with which he was concerned, to hold services in the villages, and at Cloan he used a barn as a meeting house for fortnightly services which he conducted. He therefore welcomed the match, but his wife doubted the wisdom of a marriage with one who had but recently become a widower and had five children. Robert was however, a persistent wooer and overcame all objections.

The first child of the marriage, a boy, died in infancy, the second, Richard Burdon, was born at 17 Charlotte Square, Edinburgh, on July 30, 1856.

The background which the youngster had inherited has here been sketched in. Looking at the gallery of Haldane portraits we see a succession of men, big physically, with strong determined faces, men from whom one would expect courage, character, and originality. Looking at the story of their lives we find a tradition established by them of service, whether public service, such as that of 'Union Jack' and his immediate descendants, and, in a later generation, of Admiral Duncan and of the many Haldanes who had entered either the King's service or that of the East India Company, or private service, such as that of Robert and James Haldane, who gave themselves as unstintingly to the service of their fellows as other Haldanes had to the service of their King. We find high courage, both moral and physical, a characteristic of these men, and with it, and perhaps naturally the consequence of it, a readiness to face difficulties and even a peculiar joy in facing them. These were serious-minded men; even the least attractive of them, Patrick, if he lacked kindliness and discretion, was according to his lights earnest in the King's service. This seriousness of mind made it a family tradition, observed by most Haldanes, to give duty to God and to their fellow men a first place in their lives. Both of young Richard's grandfathers had given up for conscience' sake positions which promised wealth and worldly success, and both had won the respect and affection of their fellows. If young Richard was not born heir to great possessions, he could look back with pride on the story of his family and say joyfully: 'The lot has fallen unto me in a fair ground; yea, I have a goodly heritage.' Certainly family pride had its part in the shaping of Haldane character.

Chapter II

YOUTH

1856 to 1879

Robert Haldane's house in Edinburgh was one of the large Adam houses in Charlotte Square, with fine reception rooms but indifferent accommodation for a large family of children, and it is not surprising that the young people looked forward eagerly to the four months of summer and autumn usually spent at Cloan, which at Mrs. Haldane's suggestion was renamed Cloanden, though later the old name was revived. There young Richard acquired something of his father's love of animals and learned to ride and shoot. He became a really good shot and always loved a day on the moors with his gun. He used often to accompany his father on his visits to neighbouring estates and to the Sunday services which he held in the Perthshire villages. In this way the two became real friends. There was considerable difference in age between the two families, and most of the elder family before long married and went their ways, which made life in Edinburgh less congested. Mr. Haldane had by the time of his second marriage made for himself a high reputation in legal circles, and had built up a large business. He was very hospitable and the Charlotte Square house had many visitors. While he loved country life and country ways and thoroughly enjoyed planting and improving his property, his real interest outside his profession was religion. He adhered, amidst the doubts and religious storms of the times, to the simple faith of his father. The effect of the 'Disruption' of 1843 in the Scottish Church was still fresh, and to a great extent divided

Edinburgh society. Mr. Haldane's profession naturally brought him into close touch with the leading lawyers of Edinburgh, while his religious sympathies were rather with the seceders from, than with the followers of, the Established Church. The former were in the main adherents of the establishment, and their philosophy, that of what was called 'the common-sense school', derived from Hamilton. Mr. Haldane felt keenly that these lacked what he regarded as an essential of salvation, a lively faith, but at the same time he was not attracted by the somewhat unctuous piety of many of the adherents of the free churches. His friendships were therefore with the less extreme members of both parties and his house a meeting-place for them. From this it is clear he was no bigot, a fact which helped greatly to keep sweet the relations between father and son when, as happened before long, differences in religion developed between them. In keeping the family together Mrs. Haldane's influence was paramount. She had in her youth much experience of religious doubts and perplexities, which helped to endow her with an understanding mind and a wide sympathy, but, as her mother had foreseen, she had no light task in taking charge of five children who had been left motherless for two and a half years. At Cloanden and in Edinburgh the children had a tutor, but next to their parents the greatest influence in the life of the young people was their nurse, Betsey Ferguson, a remarkable woman, who, having had little education, felt the need of it, and impressed upon the children the importance of it, and of aiming high. She was always ready to talk about questions of public interest with the children, and, herself one of a large family brought up by a widowed mother, turned their minds to consider the problems of the poor. It was tacitly agreed in the nursery that Richard should go to the English Bar, and Betsey made up her mind that he should follow his great-uncle Lord Eldon and be Lord Chancellor. When Richard was six she took him to London to visit his grandfather, Richard Burdon-Sanderson, and with him paid a visit to the Houses of Parliament. In the House of Lords she popped him on to the woolsack, saying: 'The bairn will sit there some day as of right.'

Mr. Haldane, whose religious faith was the form of Calvinism preached by his father and uncle, had a dread of episcopacy and he refused to send his boys over the border for their education, as was even then the common practice of the Scottish gentry. At the age of eight Richard was sent to a preparatory school in Edinburgh, which was decidedly rough, and, after a couple of years, to the Edinburgh Academy. There the influence on his mind was that of Dr. Clyde, a fine scholar and a Stoic philosopher. One of Dr. Clyde's tasks was to teach Bible history, and while honestly seeking not to disturb the faith of his pupils he could not conceal from quick-witted lads that he did not believe in the literal truth of the Old Testament stories. So in Richard's mind was first sown the seeds of religious doubt. His early boyhood had not been that of a happy, light-hearted child. He felt his position as the eldest of the second family and was by nature seriously minded, a trait which the elder family did not understand, and this threw him into himself. His parents rarely had other than elderly visitors and these were mostly of a type which regarded any form of frivolity as mischievous. He therefore made few friendships with boys of his own age and tended to be precociously introspective. Hell was an ever present reality to the children.

At the age of sixteen the boy entered the University of Edinburgh on the Arts side. There he was influenced chiefly by Professors Sellar, Masson, and Blackie, particularly by Sellar, who taught him Latin and introduced him to the philosophy of Lucretius, which Wordsworth had transmuted into his sonnet:

> *The world is too much with us: late and soon,*
> *Getting and spending, we lay waste our powers.*

This the young student made his creed, but, if it gave him a line of conduct, it did not resolve his religious doubts, which, as his reading increased, increased also. It was becoming more and more difficult for him to be satisfied with the simple fundamentalism of his father, and he was passing through a difficult adolescence, made the more difficult by his very real affection for his father and mother, between whose faith and his own he saw a widening gap. In his perplexity he turned to philosophy and became a member of the University Philosophical Society, where he made many friends, in particular Andrew Seth, afterwards Professor Seth Pringle-Pattison, but he could find no real guidance or help from the coldly practical school of Hamilton then fashionable in Edinburgh, and he took his doubts to Professor Blackie. Blackie understood and sympathized with his difficulties, and found a way of resolving them. He persuaded his parents to send him to the University of Göttingen, where Professor Lötze, one of the most spiritual of modern German thinkers, was at the height of his fame. So in April 1874, three months before his eighteenth birthday, Richard set off on his adventure.

Soon after his arrival he wrote home: 'I am now attending lectures before having matriculated, which one need not do at once. I called yesterday on Lötze, the Professor of Metaphysics, who was delighted to hear of his dear friend Professor Blackie, whose Greek letter of introduction puzzled him to make out at first, the writing being rather indistinct. I had a very pleasant conversation with him about metaphysics, and he asked me, as I was going away, to come and see him often in the course of the session. He could, or did, speak only German, which cramped the flow of conversation a good deal. The German students I have met with study well, but not so much as they get credit for with us, but every one is well educated, even the servants, and the soldiers have occasionally stripes on the shoulder to indicate that they have passed an examination in Greek or Latin which exempts them from two years' service. . . . I read the First Epistle of Peter every night before going to bed, and have to-night read the 6th to 10th of the second chapter, 5 verses, so I think we are going on all straight and reading together, which is nice, as it makes me feel nearer home having this in common.' Hanover in 1874 had not succumbed to the aggressive spirit of Prussia, nor had the great industrial development of Germany, which followed on her victories of 1866 and 1870-1, more than barely begun. Life in the small university town was still simple, even primitive. Richard had rooms in the house of a furrier in the Zindel Strasse and this is his description of them:

'The street is rather narrow, and among other objections the windows are so large that the dwellers on one side of the street can see plainly the whole of the abode of that opposite through the large windows, and one is accordingly not quite in such privacy as one could wish. Secondly the room opens right into the large common stair, and callers here walk straight into the sitting-room, and, not finding you there, proceed further into the bedroom, as I found the other day, when I was awakened early in the morning by two German students, whom I do not know very well, standing at my bedside and proposing a walk before breakfast. . . . The street reminds one of the Canongate except that it is quieter and is disturbed by fewer horses, the dogs and cows which really draw the carts making little noise. . . . Only about twenty students attend each lecture, the lecture rooms being indeed very small and numerous; the number of professors is in the ratio of one to every ten students. The professors for the most part look as if they had seen more books than soap or tailors' shops. The most of them are men of about 60, wearing coloured spectacles, broad Tyrolean hats, with dirty, badly shaven faces and their clothes almost tumbling off. They sometimes lecture in Latin, sometimes in German, it being much the same to the students. The students, however, do not work nearly as much as I expected, some of them rarely going to the lectures, and drinking beer and smoking all day. However, most of them have learned a great deal at the Gymnasium (a School) where they always stay till they are twenty-one and where they learn far more than we do at our Universities. Even an ordinary student laughs at four out of five of the working students who come from Oxford or Cambridge. My youth excites much surprise, as I am eight years younger than the average and am working at metaphysics, which they take last of all. I have had to contradict a report that I am preparing material for the history of Ancient Philosophy, not an uncommon thing here, where all the better students make books, but which I should prefer *not* to undertake yet, especially as I am by two years the youngest in the University—at least they say so. There are no such things as examinations in the classes, and much less anything as contemptible in the German eye as prizes—a great improvement upon us and I think this accounts for the fact that the Germans are so much better informed, since they do not cram things as with us, but really learn them.'

Lötze set him to read Fichte and Berkeley and a little later introduced him to Kant, strong meat for a lad of seventeen, but he evidently digested it, though before long he began to grieve for the fresh air and cleanliness of the Perthshire hills, for he found his rooms dirty and bugs were not infrequent visitors.

Of another talk with Lötze he wrote: 'I spent a very pleasant afternoon with Professor Lötze on Monday. I had a long conversation with him on the relation of Philosophy to religion, on materialism, the immortality of the soul, and so on. He said that a lifetime's reflection on these subjects (he is 65 and about my father's build, and like him very active) had convinced him that no ascertained truth in philosophy clashed with religion. Speculation might, but time had shown that speculations were untrustworthy till proved in accordance with facts, and he said that he was convinced that none of the schools even of Mill or Bain had ever succeeded in bringing a single *fact* forward against Christianity. He did not believe that philosophy and Christianity had much in common— they were not necessary to each other's existence, but the reason of this was that their spheres were different. Philosophy could never perform the functions of Religion, and as an example Mill might be cited. Materialism, he was sure, was a mere speculation and his research had convinced him that it was unscientific. He lent me a very rare book to read, and told me to come and see him very soon again. He was so very sociable and pleasant that one could scarcely realize that one was speaking to the greatest living metaphysician. He seldom sees people, as he lives a sort of solitary life in the country where his home is, about half a mile from Göttingen, and is looked upon as unsociable.'

At Cloanden he was a great walker and he and his younger brothers used to tramp for miles over the hills. Walking without a definite purpose was not regarded as a sensible occupation by most of the German students and Richard seized the opportunity of joining an expedition arranged by the Professor of Geology at Whitsuntide in the Harz Mountains. Of this he wrote to his father:

'I returned with the Professor of Geology and the rest of the party from the Harz Mountains last night, after a very pleasant tour. The Harz are a little like the Grampians when seen from a distance, but are not as steep, and are all covered with woods in which live thousands of roe deer and wild boars. They are very beautiful in some places, but are not to be compared with the Highlands. We geologised the most of the day and I found a curious "bellamite"[1] the like of which had never been found in North Germany before, the Professor said, and which he asked me to present to the University, which I did. We left Göttingen early on Friday morning by train and reached a little town in the Harz in a hour. Thence

[1] After a particularly adventurous climb which astonished the German students.

we walked all day and slept at a wretched little inn amongst the hills, from which we set off at five in the morning for the Brocken. . . . On Saturday night the whole fifteen of us had to cram into another lonely little inn where we slept. The next day was Sunday, but the Professor said we must walk to Goslar in order to get food and lodgings, on the road they all went to hammer rock for specimens, and I walked on to Goslar as I did not like this way of spending Sunday at all, and ordered beds and eatables. After supper I went to bed early as we had to be up early next morning and on Monday night we arrived here. . . . I feel the want of Sunday very much, for the day does not exist here. I shall be very glad when the time for coming home arrives, which it will in about 8 weeks' time. I should like to be in the loft at the fortnightly meetings and was thinking that you would be preaching as we came to Goslar on Sunday. Are Moody and Sankey gone to London or back to America? If there is an account of their last visit to Edinburgh in any paper I should like to see it very much and also should like a report of the great cricket match.[1] I am not at all comfortable to-day on account of the hot weather; my room is literally swarming with bugs. I have caught several in my clothes, found one in my milk basin and have to rise every now and then to kill them. I had a nice letter from Mother and a weekly *Scotsman* giving a full account of the Assemblies. I am reading through the Romans and through John's Epistles with Candlish's sermons. The weather is intensely hot and I have a swim in the river every morning. Everything is green and beautiful but it is not home and I long for Cloanden.'

About a fortnight before leaving Göttingen he wrote to his mother of another talk with Lötze: 'I have just returned from a visit to Lötze who invited me to come and sit for a while with him. I had an exceedingly pleasant time and a long

[1]The match between the All-England Eleven and Fourteen of Oxford, played on May 19, 20, and 21, 1874.

talk in which he expounded the nature of faith and pointed out the relationship between it and positive knowledge, at the bottom of which it lies. He said that people talked of philosophy as something different from and opposing faith and particularly Christianity, but that such people were in reality muddling up human experience with philosophy, whereas his idealistic system at any rate quite led one to expect a revelation such as Christianity. Altogether his philosophical speculations had led him to the belief that sciences in trying to explain beyond a certain point became unscientific and that a materialistic philosophy was the most unscientific of beliefs as it did not comprehend the problem before it. I proposed to him some difficulties that had come up in an analysis that I have been making lately of Causation in Willing, whereupon he got quite excited in pointing out how by faith philosophy raised itself above such difficulties in the freedom of the will and yet took the most scientific course. . . . I told him that philosophy was my *Herz-studium* but that I felt it to be very insufficient unless it culminated in faith. That he said rejoiced him to hear, for he felt himself convinced that without faith all fell to the ground. Then he told me of a book to read on Psychology. He has quite recovered of his rheumatism but his face tells of much suffering. I am afraid he will not live much longer and his body looks washed away and quite inadequate to the support of his gigantic head. When he goes, all scientific Germany will be materialistic with the exception of one or two second-rate men.'

A truly remarkable prophecy from a boy. After a short tour in Germany Richard came home to Cloanden in August 1874, a convinced disciple of Lötze's idealistic philosophy. The mental cure which Blackie had recommended had proved effective, but it could only have been effective in the case of a boy of very exceptional parts.

At Göttingen young Haldane had been friendly with most of his fellow students and had joined a students' *Verbindung*, but of those he had made one special friend in Hugo Conwentz, afterwards Professor Hugo Conwentz, and with him he maintained a regular correspondence for many years. Not long after his return home he wrote to Conwentz from Cloanden: 'I am again established in my native land and studying law and philosophy. I suppose that you are prosecuting your botanical researches in your home at Danzig, and, probably, you are a member of the botanical society of that city, whose proceedings I have read in *Nature*, where they are recorded weekly.... The weather is very cold here, about 13° Reaumur, but Scotland is always so. I study through the day here, but we are living in a lonely place among the hills, far away from any other house. We sometimes see no stranger for a long time, and have to ride or drive to the nearest village. I am sometimes out shooting amongst the hills before the sun rises, in order to get food for the pot, while others of us fish for trout in the streams.'

Scotland was going through at this time yet another religious revival, with which the visit of Moody and Sankey to Edinburgh had been connected. If in the summer at Göttingen, amidst the heat and dirt of his stuffy rooms, he had pined for the fresh air of the Perthshire hills, now, on returning to Edinburgh in readiness for the opening of the university session, he found himself intellectually stifled by the narrow religious controversies and materialistic philosophy of the city, and he pined for the inspiration of Lötze's teaching. He wrote to Conwentz towards the end of October 1874: 'As the University session has not yet begun, I am at present doing nothing but private reading in Philosophy and Law. We have come to town from the country where we always live for four months in the year as my father does not like the town in summer. Tyndal gave a most eloquent address to the British Association. His opinions on Science and Religion have aroused a great outcry in the religious world. I sympathise with Tyndal and am therefore an object of suspicion to many of our people in this town. Can you believe it? I actually dislike my own country now. The people seem to think of nothing but how to make money and never how to attain to a high culture. I dislike going into the streets because everybody is so dressed up. . . . One dare not here express one's religious opinions if one is not orthodox, and nobody studies anything but the *Brotwissenschaften*.'[1] One may balance this outburst against the obvious longing for home in his Göttingen letters, but it shows clearly the line on which his mind was developing. Actually he settled down happily enough on rejoining the university. He studied philosophy under Professor Campbell Fraser and found him stimulating. He rejoined the Philosophical Society and resumed work with Andrew Seth and others of that group. He introduced to the society and to his brothers and sister the principles of Lötze's philosophy.

In the spring of 1875 a great grief fell upon the family in the death of George, Richard's second brother, and a very charming bright lad, with a real musical talent and a keen sense of humour, who brought a touch of lightness into a family much given to religious questionings, while he had been quite satisfied to accept the faith of his father. The lad's untimely death was an especial blow to Richard in that it removed the one bright and lively companion of his boyhood.

In the next eighteen months Richard's career at the university prospered. A letter to Conwentz dated Christmas 1875 tells of his reading at that time: 'I am very busy just now with the study of the work of your great and too-little recognised countryman Hegel. The extreme difficulty of this study makes one get on very slowly even with the help of a great number of commentaries. I have also been busy with Wundt's *Physiologische Psychologie* and Fechner's *Elemente der Psychophysick,* books, the former of which at least, you have no doubt heard of. . . . Have the German apostles of *Naturwissenschaft* as great a horror of metaphysics as our English men of science?

[1]Getting and spending.

Haeckel, whose *Schöpfungsgeschichte* has just been translated into English, appears to have great repugnance to Philosophy in general, which, seeing that he knows nothing about it, is not to be wondered at. What reputation has Haeckel got in Germany generally? He is very much admired by us as being one of the foremost of living workers in science. Helmoltz has always seemed to me a man of scientific type, in fact I should say he was on the whole the greatest man of science living. I wish we could meet again and drink a few *Schoppen* in the Ratskeller. I have just been reading the scene in *Faust* at Auerbech's Keller and it reminded me very much of our old times.'

Richard obtained his degree with first-class honours, and won the Bruce of Grangehill medal for philosophy, the Gray scholarship, and the Ferguson scholarship in philosophy open to the four Scottish universities. He met with one check, he proposed to take the degree of Doctor of Science in Philosophy and prepared a thesis on the subject of Immortality, which was accepted by the Professor of Philosophy, but under the regulations of the university it had to be approved by the Dean of the Faculty of Science, a botanist, who was strictly orthodox, and he refused to approve of a thesis which he held to be heretical.

As soon as he had taken his degree Richard set himself seriously to the study of law. He worked in the offices of two well-known Edinburgh writers to the Signet, one for conveyancing and feudal law, the other for the mercantile side of legal business, and he began to eat his dinners at Lincoln's Inn. He was still so engaged when his father died in the summer of 1877. This threw upon him a heavy burden of responsibility. His elder half-brothers were all out in the world, and the settlement of his father's estate proved to be a somewhat complicated business. At first money was none too plentiful and matters were not made easier by the fact that Mr. Haldane had managed himself every item of family business, and at the time of her husband's death Mrs. Haldane had never had a banking account nor signed a cheque. However, the fact that the younger brothers had practically settled their careers themselves relieved Richard of one responsibility. His brother John had gone to Jena to study. He was deeply interested in Richard's philosophy, but physiology, of which he made himself a master, was even in those days his first love. The third of the brothers, William, had decided upon the law as career, and he became a successful writer to the Signet, and a little later relieved Richard of all the cares of family business. With the family affairs in some measure straightened, Richard set out for London, borrowing on his reversionary interest in his father's estate sufficient for his needs. He came to the Bar with an unusual equipment. He had in London none of the friends which the promising young barrister makes at his public school and university, indeed such friends as he at first made in London were usually men far older than himself, mostly professors of science and philosophy, the former of whom he met with his uncle, Professor John Burdon-Sanderson. He knew no solicitors, had a poor voice, and few of the social graces which make a young man known and popular. But he had a mind thoroughly exercised in wrestling with German metaphysics and a very remarkable memory, and from the first he found that problems in equity did not present to him much difficulty.

He had begun by reading in the chambers of Mr. William Barber, a junior with a large practice in the Chancery side, and as had been his habit from the days when he first began to study, he worked hard. He wrote to his sister not long after his arrival in town: 'Court begins to sit to-morrow and we expect to be very busy. Indeed, Mr. Barber's wig has been airing before the fire for the last two days and we expect a shoal of briefs. His chambers consist of five rooms, one for himself, where I sit and work with him, in the absence of the chief devil, and in the other two sit the barristers and uncalled members who work for him, and junior clerks of whom I am one. When Ingham, the chief junior barrister, returns he will sit beside Barber, and I shall move out into the next room beside Burnell, Lady Pine's nephew, who is a tall dark young man of seven and twenty. The clerk, who gives out opinions and drafts when Barber approves them, or burns them when he doesn't, which at times is the case, sits in a den at the door of the chambers to receive briefs and cases for opinion. He also makes tea for Mr. Barber and any one else who wants it, but as he is not skilful I get it elsewhere.'

In 1878 Richard's kinsman, Lord Camperdown, the head of the Haldane-Duncan family, began to take an interest in his clever cousin. Lord Camperdown was a very keen politician and he sensed in Richard a promising recruit. He put the young man's name down for Brooks's and for the New Club, Edinburgh, and on this Richard wrote to his mother: 'I am committed to Whig politics somewhat prematurely, but this would have been the case sooner or later.'

While he was still uncalled he took up, successfully, a family case. I have mentioned in chapter one that Richard's great-great-grandfather Lt.-Colonel James Haldane of the Life-Guards had married Margaret Pye. He had in fact eloped with her, and no proper record of the marriage had been traced. It was indeed hinted that there had been no marriage at all. This produced complications, and at the request of his uncle Alexander, Richard took the case up and successfully verified the marriage. His uncle offered him a fee of £70 for his work, but though he had barely sufficient for his needs he refused to accept anything for what he regarded as a family duty.

Mr. Robertson of the parliamentary and Scottish bar found that there was often difficulty in finding in London an expert in Scottish conveyancing questions, and he advised Richard to specialize in this, and he therefore returned to work for three months in an Edinburgh office. Mr. Farrer

Herschell, later Lord Herschell and Lord Chancellor, who was a brother of Mrs. Burdon-Sanderson, promised to get him into the chambers of a common law counsel on his return from Edinburgh, and so it came about that he moved from Lincoln's Inn to the Temple to the chambers of Mr. Lumley Smith, where he learned a good deal of common law and had occasional chances of making use of his special knowledge of Scottish law. He was called to the Bar in the autumn of 1879.

Chapter III

FROM STUFF GOWN TO SILK

1880 to 1890

The struggles of a briefless barrister are a commonplace and Haldane's early difficulties and disappointments were as great as those of any beginner at the Bar. In 1880 his correspondence with his mother was chiefly concerned with family business. He explained to her that his father had wisely delayed making certain payments and that these had, on his death, to be met by the estate, which would be consequently somewhat embarrassed for a few years. He urged her not to part with Cloanden, but agreed eventually that the Edinburgh house should be sold. All this made him the more eager to be earning himself in order that he might contribute to his mother's comfort. The waiting for briefs in what he described as his garret in Lincoln's Inn was therefore particularly trying, and the fees for his first year at the Bar only amounted to £31 10s. 0d. The General Election of 1880 and the urging of Lord Camperdown took him into active politics rather sooner than he intended. His cousin George Duncan brought him to tea at Lord Northbrook's and there he met Mr. Albert Grey, afterwards Earl Grey, and other Liberals; the talk turned chiefly on Afghanistan, Russia's advance towards India being then a burning question. This resulted in his joining 'the Albert Grey committee', an organization designed to collect and bring together promising young Liberal speakers. At Easter he went to stay with Lord Camperdown at Weston House, and from there wrote: 'I felt myself in want of a change of air rather badly as excepting

28

Sundays I have not had a holiday since the beginning of February. Lord Camperdown and I went to Cherrington and then to an election meeting. I have had a busy time of late. On Wednesday I was drawing drafts all day in Chambers and was going home at six in the evening rather tired when a summons came to address a couple of meetings at Westminster. I felt one quite enough and spoke along with Sir A. Hobhouse.'

During the election he went down to Liverpool and spoke for Lord Ramsay, afterwards Lord Dalhousie, a close friend of Lord Camperdown's. These first efforts on political platforms made him realize that he was handicapped by his weak voice and he consulted an elocutionist, but with little benefit.

The result of the General Election of 1880 was the return of Mr. Gladstone to power with a large majority. Haldane and a good many of his friends found that Albert Grey's political principles were somewhat vague and erratic, and the 'Albert Grey committee' broke up, but Haldane was of opinion that a group of the kind could render very useful service, and mainly by his personal efforts he got most of the friends with whose political views he was in accord to join together to form the '80 Club, so called after the Liberal victory, with Lord Richard Grosvenor as its first president and Haldane as its first honorary secretary. It was an exciting time politically, for a new portent had arrived in the form of Parnell, the Land League was in full activity in Ireland, boycotting was rife, and Mr. Forster as Chief Secretary was seeking to keep order with the aid of coercion. Reviewing, particularly in the *Westminster Review*, devilling in chambers, political work, and the study of law and philosophy kept the young man very busy, but little of this work was remunerative. 1881, the year of the Phoenix Park murders and of dynamite outrages by Land Leaguers in London, was a time of great perturbation in England over the Irish question, and of as great perturbation in Haldane's mind over his private affairs. Briefs did not appear, the earnings for this year were only £109. This was depressing and still more depressing was an attack of rheumatic fever. 'I seem', he wrote, 'to be passing through a valley of dark shadows, nor is the morning in sight.' While he was recovering from illness he wrote to his aunt, Miss Jane Burdon-Sanderson, who was herself an invalid: 'Ill health is the most terrible of all misfortunes, terrible because of its influence on our way of looking at things. When I last wrote to you I wrote in a strain which was not a little depressing and I hope you saw that the reason why the letter was so empty and hard in its tone was because I was myself out of spirits. One is often in the dilemma either of not writing at all when one is not feeling fit to write or of writing badly, and I have been quite conscious that at times of late I have written and spoken to you in a somewhat inconsiderate and apparently unsympathetic strain. Still, to those who can read between the lines it is better to write so than not to write at all, and you know what the feeling of illness and depression means. When I wrote to you last week I was in a fair way to have number two of an attack of acute rheumatism and was consequently in the bottomless pit of despair with things in general. Now I am all right again but feel as though I were beginning at the beginning again. Still, I can write to you with complete sympathy with what you have to undergo, still more often than I. The great difficulty about depression arising from physical sources is that, like all mental affections, it means for the time the whole of life, and we can rise above it only by the firm grasp of some principle to which we must blindly entrust ourselves. We have not at such times the support of the consciousness of a moral striving to rise, because there is a failure as a rule of moral and spiritual as well as physical force, and you have this additional trial that you are too prostrated to seek the last means of escape in action of some sort. Still, it does remain possible to say "I will strive towards the highest as far as my means of action admit and as for happiness or misery that is a consideration which is wholly irrelevant." This seems to me to be what is meant by the renunciation of self, and to the very weak extent to which I have sufficiently conquered myself to put it in practice, it has not failed me because it could not fail. The hard thing to accomplish is not the self renunciation but the abstracting from the hopeless consciousness of failure to do what one might have done. And yet I sometimes wonder whether we have anything to do with what might have been or with what may be. Should we not rather concern ourselves with the duties of the moment, their fulfilment, with the utmost of our strength, whether they are great or insignificant? Any other consideration seems to me to involve a personal element which should be inadmissable. Perhaps this was what Goethe, who was a very wise man, meant by saying that repentance was a waste of time. You and I must just struggle on. In some ways I am better off than you, for I have more possibilities in life before me and the chance of that most fascinating of temptations, a career. But there comes the counterbalancing consideration that a career and the struggle for it are after all purely personal matters and in absorbing the best energies of life make it more difficult than ever to attain the only end that is worth attaining. Therefore I think we are in difficulties which are after all not dissimilar. The lesson the year which was, and now is not, has taught me is that personal happiness, even the best individual well-being, must no longer be the end of my life, and bitter as the lesson has been and dark the days through which I am passing I would not for the whole world that these things should fail to bring to me the teaching they have brought.'

While he was still convalescent he sat at dinner next another briefless barrister a few years older than himself, H. H. Asquith, and an immediate friendship was formed.

Asquith asked Haldane to stay at his house in Hampstead that the more bracing air of the heath might help his recovery, and from that time the two men, who found that their philosophy and political views were in close accord, became increasingly intimate. As his health improved he was able to seek refuge from his troubles in more and more work. He had already become a member of the Council of the Workers' Education League, of which his friend Lord Dalhousie was a vice-president, and when his health recovered he remembered Betsey Ferguson's lessons and turned for relief of mind to the work of helping the poor who wanted education. The tradition of Frederick Denison Maurice was still fresh at Lincoln's Inn. He had founded the Working Men's College while Reader there, and had brought a number of young barristers to the college as voluntary teachers. Haldane went there in the autumn of 1881, while Tom Hughes, also a Lincoln's Inn man, was principal, and gave a course of public lectures on 'What is Philosophy?' These were a great success and he followed them by taking a class in philosophy. Of this he wrote: 'The lecture last night was a great success. I had three times the class I expected, the room not being large enough to hold my students.' So he was introduced to what became one of the great interests of his life, adult education.

He was planning to bring out with a group of friends a new philosophical review and a translation of Schopenhauer. He wrote to his aunt at the end of January 1882: 'I am now very well in body and fairly so in mind. The *Kampf ums Dasein* presses pretty heavily at times. Business at the Bar does not increase as it ought to increase and little things cause a good deal of worry. But these are, after all, matters mainly of chance and do not distress me unduly. It now rests with Trübner to say whether the translation of Schopenhauer is to be undertaken or not, and if so I shall associate John Kemp with myself in the business as he wants some definite literary work. The magazine is at last in a fair way of progress and I have come to excellent terms with Robertson,[1] who is to back us up with all the influence of *Mind*. This is to be a separate undertaking in a special direction, dealing chiefly with the application of philosophical criticism to the conceptions of modern science. My lectures are going on steadily; there remain only three more to be delivered. I have a good deal of speaking and lecturing on hand which I shall be glad to get past. I lectured at the St. James's and Soho Radical Club to about 80 working men on the socialist theories of Lassalle and Karl Marx in relation to Labour and Capital and their theory of value. The club is the centre of the "International" in London and of course, after my lecture, which lasted nearly an hour, some of the Republican and Communist members criticised it hotly. However I managed to persuade the bulk of the audience and I think I did some good.'

While he was lecturing at the Working Men's College a fellow lecturer there, Mr. Lehmann, sent him a pamphlet on 'Pessimism' which he had written and asked for his comments. Haldane's reply included an appreciation of Schopenhauer: 'No account of such a system as that of Schopenhauer could be, as regards an English public, other than misleading which did not in the first place give a detailed account of the idealistic standpoint of the system and in the second place show that "nothingness", to which the ethical side points as the goal of practical life, is merely the annihilation of the "phenomenal" world in which we live. This last point would have to be elaborated in great detail as it has been absolutely missed in England and cannot be understood without such a grasp of the system as is not to be found in any English writer. Correctly apprehended it at once alters the popular conception of the word "pessimism" and leaves Schopenhauer a religious writer of the highest order.'

He used to attend the dinners at the '80 Club regularly and became one of its advocates for the case against 'Fair Trade', as

[1]Professor Croom Robertson.

the protectionists called their policy, and this involved much study of blue books and trade returns. In 1882 he was elected a member of Brooks's and in that year at a dinner of Lord Dalhousie's he had twenty minutes talk with Mr. Gladstone. He was now recognized as a promising young Liberal and urged to stand for Parliament, but briefs had to come in before he could venture farther.

He, his brother John, and Andrew Seth, were at work upon a volume of 'Essays in Philosophical Criticism' by themselves and others of their friends. It expressed the idealistic philosophy associated with T. H. Green of Oxford, to whom it was dedicated. The book was published in 1883, as was the first volume of the translation of Schopenhauer.

Before the end of 1882 there had come a turn in his fortunes at the Bar. On Barber's advice and with his help he had gone into the chambers of Mr. Horace Davey, afterwards Lord Davey, who had an immense Chancery practice. The arrangement was begun as a temporary experiment, but the two at once suited each other and they became close friends. His first chance came in 1883. Davey had been briefed by Freshfield's, a famous firm of solicitors, on behalf of the Government of Quebec, which had sent its Solicitor-General over to get leave to appeal to the Privy Council against a judgement in the Canadian courts, but Davey on the day before this case was to be heard was summoned to conduct an appeal to the House of Lords at the same time as the Quebec case was to be heard by the Privy Council. Davey, unable to get another leader to take a complicated case at short notice, turned it over to Haldane. The brief reached him late in the evening, and he sat up the greater part of the night getting up the case. The next morning Davey and Haldane went to the Privy Council, when the former broke it to his clients that he was obliged to leave at once, and suggested that the Solicitor-General for Quebec should open the case. The latter replied that he was precluded by his orders from doing so, when, to the disgust of Freshfield's representative and the despair of the Solicitor-General, Davey announced that fortunately he had brought with him his friend Mr. Haldane, who was well acquainted with the case, and left in a hurry. Haldane suggested to his indignant clients that they had better get to business, and put on his wig and gown. A few minutes later he was opening the case before the Judicial Committee, not one member of that august body having any idea who he was, and he won for the Quebec Government the right to appeal. A few days later Mr. Wiseman, who conducted the Privy Council business for Freshfields, climbed the stairs to his garret in Lincoln's Inn with a brief for an important case for the Province of Ontario marked one hundred and fifty guineas.

From that chance beginning Haldane's work at the Bar went forward without a check; in his fourth year at the Bar his fees amounted to £1,100, and thereafter both business and income mounted rapidly. He had none of the gifts which make a great advocate or a brilliant cross examiner, but he had a remarkable capacity for getting at the salient facts of a case and for presenting them cogently to a bench of judges. He called in his knowledge of psychology to his aid and studied the idiosyncrasies of the judges before whom he appeared and presented his case accordingly. By the summer of 1885 he had already made a reputation as a skilful and reliable junior for Chancery business and he and Davey became firm allies. With an assured position at the Bar Haldane now turned his mind more seriously to politics. The period from 1885 to 1895 was a time of great political excitement, in which there were no fewer than seven governments. Ireland was the main issue, with Parnell as one of the dominant figures. Rumours were afloat in the spring of 1885 that Gladstone, whose second administration was drawing to a close, was preparing a measure for a separate parliament for Ireland, and the breach between the Whig Right wing and the main body of the

Liberal Party began to widen. Lord Hartington had already started his opposition to such a measure. This at once affected Haldane, who was from the first a convinced Home Ruler, for his cousins, the Duncans, and other of his Liberal friends were equally convinced Unionists.

Actually it was not the Irish question but the death of Gordon at Khartoum which brought about the fall of Mr. Gladstone's administration, and the Queen sent for Lord Salisbury, who in a brief session found his position in Parliament impossible, and he went to the country in the late autumn. During this time Haldane was constantly speaking at Liberal gatherings. His aunt Jane Burdon-Sanderson, who lived near Bournemouth, Davey's constituency, wrote an amusing description of a Liberal demonstration in that town, which Haldane went down to address in supporting his chief. The member appeared in a barouche drawn by four grey horses, with a mounted escort led by a doctor on a spirited steed. The ladies appeared dressed in Liberal colours, blue and white, there were four bands to help the long procession on its way, and numerous banners bore inscriptions, 'The House of Lords mend it or end it'; 'Why should the labourers wait?' The Liberal reform bill, with a programme of redistribution of seats and extension of the franchise, was then before the country. Political display was then much more prevalent, and a general election a much more protracted business than it has since become. Home Rule, parliamentary reform and the House of Lords were the main political issues of the time, but Haldane's most serious political work lay in discussions in the younger group of the '80 Club on social reform and in sustained effort to get into personal touch with the labouring classes and to understand their needs and aspirations. He had written to his mother: 'From what I have had an opportunity of seeing of the highest society amongst the younger generation in London it seems to me that they look far more to the intrinsic worth of life than they used to do, and have a growing dislike and contempt for worldliness, particularly religious worldliness. The new point of view seems to be of comparatively recent growth, but it is an invaluable one.'

God bless the squire and his relations
And keep us in our proper stations

was passing into the background as a social tenet and the thinking young men of Haldane's generation were giving themselves more and more to the problems of the working classes. Octavia Hill and Toynbee were busy with housing and social reform, Richard's sister Elizabeth, during a visit to London in 1884, joined the former, and Walter Besant's *All Sorts and Conditions of Men* was arousing West London to the condition of the East End. A great deal of Richard's spare time was spent in meetings with working men in east and south London. He had no taste for games, though he occasionally played tennis, which was becoming fashionable, and he wrote to his sister asking her to send him his tennis racket and Caird's Kant! He usually took his exercise walking, the love of which remained with him from his rambles with his brothers over the Perthshire hills, and when he felt the need to stretch his limbs and get some fresh air he not infrequently spent the week-end in walking to Brighton and back, or in tramping over the Surrey hills, combined with a call on George Meredith, who was one of the early friends he made in the south. He delighted in any social gathering where there was good talk, but had no taste for dancing. 'I have been', he wrote to his sister, 'to one dance but the reason was that it was given by a solicitor, whom I did not know, but whose wife pressed me to come. I spent the whole evening discussing with my host in recesses of the rooms the taxation of bills of costs and the operation of the new conveyancing Act, so I spent a very pleasant evening.'

He delighted in the opportunities London afforded for hearing good music and was an enthusiastic Wagnerite long before London society turned to Wagner. He attended the Richter concerts whenever he could spare the time and wrote to his sister, 'I have joined Mrs. Garett Anderson's "Quartette Association". We have a series of concerts in private houses with first-class artists. They don't however lean much to Wagner.'

When Lord Salisbury dissolved Parliament in November 1885 Haldane decided that the time had come for him to seek a seat. By the terms of the Liberal Reform Act Perthshire, which had been a single constituency, was divided, and he had hoped to stand for West Perthshire, in which stood Cloanden. As it happened Sir Donald Currie, the Liberal member for the old constituency, chose West Perthshire. Sir Donald had recently purchased a large estate in the constituency, and when Mrs. Haldane suggested that it would be appropriate that her son should represent a part of Scotland with which the Haldanes had been connected for centuries, he replied: 'But, Mrs. Haldane, your son has no landed interest in West Perthshire.' To which Mrs. Haldane replied promptly: 'Sir Donald, my son does not own a foot of land, but he has more than land—brains!' Baulked of West Perthshire Richard boldly transferred himself to East Lothian, which was regarded almost as a pocket borough of the Wemyss family and for which Lord Elcho was the sitting member. The invitation to stand came to him from Professor Calderwood, who accompanied it with a flattering reference to the *Essays in Philosophical Criticism*. In accepting Haldane wrote: 'I feel that Mr. Gladstone has made possible for the Liberal Party higher and purer principles than those of the past, and the belief that we are on the eve of a period in which we may set an example of unselfishness in Europe, both in domestic and foreign affairs, has for some time past increased my desire ultimately to take part in the work of the House of Commons.' The fight was a stiff one. Mr. Balfour came to the help of Lord Elcho, and Lord Tweeddale to support the Liberal candidate, while Lord Rosebery gave Haldane a great deal of valuable advice and help. East Lothian was then to a large extent a constituency of big properties and the lairds followed the general practice of the time in seeing to it that their tenants were of their political colour, but the new Reform Act enfranchised the hinds and the small artisans and no one knew which way they would go. Haldane introduced a new method of electioneering. He saw that few except those whose politics were well known would care to affront the lairds by coming to his political meetings, and he spent much of his time tramping up and down the constituency and talking to the farm labourers and working men. This method proved to be completely successful, and he was returned by a large majority. He never lost the confidence of his people, whom he continued to represent until he went to the House of Lords. His brother John sent him an account of the arrival of the news at his home:

'Mother asked me to write to you about last night's doings at Cloanden. I suppose she had already told you how the news was received at two yesterday morning. After leaving Cloanden the man who came up with the news seems to have gone to Aberuthven and set the bells ringing. They had apparently just made a bonfire in Auchterarder, mostly with wood taken from the closets in the back-gardens of Auchterarder houses.

'Last night there was a bonfire on the hill, a thousand people came up with torches and a band, and there were fireworks afterwards. The people were immensely enthusiastic.'

The election only gave Gladstone a majority of eighty-six, exclusive of the Irish Nationalists, and Parnell brought with him eighty-four of these to Westminster, so that the political situation was uncertain, and Haldane and a good many more Liberals, who were anxious to avoid splitting the party prematurely, thought that Lord Salisbury should be left in office. However, the Government was defeated on an amendment to the address and Mr. Gladstone formed his third administration, with Lord Herschell as his Lord Chancellor and Davey as his Solicitor-General. Haldane was now well aware of his qualities and defects. He knew that he had not in him the makings of an orator and he wisely decided to confine himself to speaking briefly and to the point on matters on which he had expert knowledge. He made no formal maiden speech and first spoke in February 1886 in committee on the Civil Service estimates on the vote for Courts of Law and Justice in Scotland. In this way he soon acquired a reputation as one who knew what he was talking about and whom it was worth while to consult in the lobby. His first Parliament had a short life. Gladstone introduced his Home Rule Bill and it was defeated on second reading by thirty votes, ninety-three Liberals voting with the majority. The split in the Liberal ranks was complete, and the Liberal Unionists had come into being as a party. In the General Election of the summer of 1886 Haldane was again returned for East Lothian, but with a much reduced majority. He had introduced his friend Herbert Asquith to the Liberals of East Fife, and was delighted when he was successful, but the result of the election was to send back only 191 Liberals to Parliament. Mr. Gladstone resigned and Lord Salisbury formed his second administration.

In the Parliament of 1886 there was formed a group of Liberals destined to become the future leaders of the party. It was composed of Haldane, Edward Grey, Sydney Buxton, Ronald Ferguson, Tom Ellis, and a few others. They chose as their leader A. H. D. Acland, whose interests in education made him particularly welcome to Haldane. Their prime interest was in social reform, and they went about their business systematically, each taking up some particular subject for detailed study. Asquith, whose ability as a speaker was at once recognized, was made the occasional voice of the group in the House and the rest did not often try to catch the Speaker's eye, to the disgust of Sir William Harcourt, who considered that they did not give enough time to Parliament.

Haldane's first speech of any length in the House was not made until March 1887, when he spoke on the Criminal Law Amendment Bill, Ireland, popularly known as the Crimes Bill. In this he declared his belief that the attempt to govern Ireland by coercion was bound to fail, and that the only statesmanlike solution was Home Rule. Gladstone was in the House when he made it and complimented him on it afterwards. In 1886 he and Asquith had gone to Ireland together. They were present at the eviction on the Kenmare estate of the chief local Land Leaguer, which took place under the protection of seventy police. The two spent much time cross-examining both landlords and tenants, southern loyalists and Land Leaguers, and came back more convinced Home Rulers than ever.

During the early months of 1887 *The Times* produced a series of articles upon Ireland, making grave charges against Parnell and the Irish members in general, and on the eve of the second reading of the Crimes Bill published a letter purporting to be signed by Parnell, in which he implied approval of the Phoenix Park murders. Parnell declared in the House that this letter was a forgery and demanded that the facts should be investigated by a Select Committee. The Government instead appointed a Statutory Commission to examine not only the authenticity of the letter, but also the charges made in *The Times*. The proceedings dragged on until 1889, with Asquith as junior to Sir Charles Russell for Parnell. In February of that year one Pigott, who had produced the letter to *The Times*, broke down under cross-examination, confessed to forgery, and committed suicide.

In celebration of this the '80 Club gave a dinner with Lord Rosebery in the chair, to which Parnell came as Sir Charles Russell's guest, and Russell got Haldane to sit next to him. Neither in his talk during dinner nor in his speech after dinner did he refer to the Pigott letter, which he seemed to regard as an incident beneath his notice. In his talk with

Haldane he said that the book which in his opinion threw more light than any other on the Irish question was Froude's *The English in Ireland*.

Haldane's group of friends as a whole took an independent political line, and of them all the most independent was Haldane, which did not make him popular with the whips. Though he was doing well at the Bar his position in his profession was not yet secure, and legal work naturally absorbed most of his energies. He found that the views of the bulk of the Liberal Party were too materialistic for his taste, and outside his own group of friends he found little sympathy for his ideas on education. So he went his own way, working for those things on which he had set his heart, and not paying much attention to what the whips told him was for the good of the Liberal Party. With legal and political work absorbing his time, philosophy had to be relegated to the background, though it was still his guide to life and conduct. The third volume of the translation of Schopenhauer's *World as Will and Idea*, on which he and his old friend John Kemp, who was now one of his 'devils', had been engaged for four years, appeared in 1886, and this was the last of his philosophical publications for a number of years.

Haldane sent his translation of Schopenhauer to George Meredith, who wrote from Box Hill in April:

'*Nunc ver egelidus refert tepores*. Now therefore we turn to those who love the spring and the fields, and I shall gladly tell you of my obligation to you for the fruitful perusal of Schopenhauer, whom I have recommended in your version, right and left. I hope you can come on Saturday for Sunday. I will get your quarters, and you can have a Leith Hill tramp.'

Of all the group of political allies, Grey, Asquith, and Haldane were the most closely associated. Grey and Asquith, with his wife, were visitors at Cloanden, and Haldane went to Fallodon and was often at the Asquiths' home at Hampstead. The whips regarded Haldane as the mischief-maker of the three, and he indeed often originated proposals, which they introduced to the party, and which were rarely welcome to the old stagers. Proposals for the payment of members, free education up to the university, were regarded by them as rank socialism, and they were not particularly enthusiastic about Free Trade. So that for a good many years Haldane was not popular with the party as a whole, though his own group freely recognized his ability and the value of his judgement.

Haldane's researches into social and economic problems brought him into touch with the Fabian Society, where he made the acquaintance of Bernard Shaw and the Sidney Webbs, and from the latter in particular he derived much help in formulating the ideas with which he sought to inoculate the party. His talks with Sidney Webb and his researches in economics led him to produce in 1887 a monograph on Adam Smith, which he used to expound the principles of Free Trade. The celebrations of Queen Victoria's first jubilee were somewhat marred both by the bitter feelings aroused by the Irish question and by economic depression which produced much unemployment. In November 1887 there were angry meetings in Trafalgar Square, accompanied by some rioting. The Chief Commissioner of the Metropolitan Police prohibited further meetings in Trafalgar Square on the ground that the square was crown property. This was to pour oil on the fire, and a huge meeting in the square was organized in defence of the rights of free meeting and free speech. There was great excitement, special constables were enrolled, and soldiers were called out to help the police. The meeting was addressed by Mr. Cunninghame Graham and John Burns, who were both arrested on the charge of incitement to disturbance. Haldane had got to know the former well during visits to south and east London. He thought that his friend had behaved foolishly and agreed with Gladstone, who wrote: 'Until a decision can be had, it is the duty of every citizen to refrain from all resistance to the Executive Government', but he would not leave him in the lurch, and he at once left a case on which he was engaged, and stood bail for him. At the trial at the Central Criminal Court Asquith appeared for the prisoners and Haldane gave evidence on their behalf. In cross-examination an attempt was made to make him commit himself to approval of incitement to violence. This he had no difficulty in turning aside, but his two friends were sent to prison for six weeks.

Haldane's legal business before the Privy Council was largely concerned with cases submitted by colonial governments, which naturally led him to study closely their constitutional and political problems. The visit of colonial statesmen to London for the jubilee and the plans for the foundation of the Imperial Institute were beginning to arouse public interest in the problems of the Empire and schemes for imperial federation were voiced. Haldane was not attracted by these proposals, which he regarded as unworkable, his knowledge of colonial sentiment convincing him that the colonies would never be willing to hamper their free development by putting themselves into harness with the mother country, but he was taken by Lord Rosebery's suggestion of an Imperial Union for Defence, a *Kriegsverein*, as Rosebery called it, and to further this aim both he and Asquith joined the Imperial League, which did not increase their popularity with their leader in the House, Sir William Harcourt, who was definitely a 'little Englander'.

Shortly after their entry into Parliament Haldane and Asquith began a custom, which they kept up for six years, of giving an annual dinner at an inn in Cork Street, 'The Blue Posts'. To this dinner were invited eight guests, four of them distinguished politicians, and the other men distinguished in the law or the arts. Balfour, Rosebery, Morley, Curzon, and Grey were amongst the political guests, and on one occasion Lord Randolph Churchill and Joseph Chamberlain proved to be uncomfortable neighbours; Burne-Jones, George Meredith, Russell Lowell, Lord Justice Bowen, and Sir Charles Russell were amongst the guests of the other categories, and the dinners generally produced a stimulating discussion. Haldane had for some time been engaged on a revision of Barber's edition of Dart's *Vendors and Purchasers*. He had begun to take pupils in chambers, and one of these, Mr. Sheldon, collaborated with him in this work, which was laborious. It was completed and published in 1888.

Towards the end of 1887 he had applied to the Lord Chancellor for a silk gown and was disappointed when nothing came of this. Lord Macnaughton, to whom he had sent a copy of Dart, wrote to him: 'I ought to have written to you before to thank you for the new edition of Dart. It must have meant a great deal of hard work. I dare say old Barber was not a very pleasant fellow to work with, but they do say that you tried him much at times by inserting the germs of revolutionary doctrines.

'Seriously I am sorry that the Lord Chancellor has not seen fit to comply with your application, that is, if you are disappointed. For your own good I think it better you should wait a little, it is a disadvantage, especially if you are thinking of "special" work, to be too young. What the grounds of the Lord Chancellor's action was I don't know. Youth or Cunninghame Graham or both combined.'

In 1888 Mrs. Humphrey Ward published *Robert Ellesmere*, which had an immediate success. Gladstone's warm appreciation of the book naturally commended it especially to Liberals, and Haldane was at once attracted by the writer's interest in and understanding of the philosophy of religion. He sought and made her acquaintance, which quickly developed into a friendship. When in the following year Mrs. Ward published an appreciation of the 'Spirit of German Criticism', he wrote to her:

'I have been reading your article with the greatest interest, I am sure that your account of the spirit of German Criticism has come as a revelation to the majority of people here. It fits into the subjective side of the question as present in Green's two sermons on "The Witness of God" and "Faith". What I personally have felt about the subject for a long time you have expressed and more than expressed, and all who have drawn spiritual sustenance from German thought must feel grateful to you.

'The more one thinks of these things the more clear does the conviction become that we must answer Strauss's question "Sind wir noch Christen?" differently from his answer. Schopenhauer teaches us the great doctrine of the necessity of suppressing the will to live. Hegel shows us that this doctrine, if we are to live by it, must be supplemented by the duty to live a life which suppresses the life of the individual in very truth just because and in so far as it is greater than that life. And in the teaching of Christ and St. Paul we have the perfect presentation, in a practical form, of the completed doctrine to which assent on the theoretical side has been won by the great philosophers. There is a passage somewhere in the small print of Hegel's *Logic* in which, when speaking of the mythical account of the Fall, he points out that child-like innocence must not be confounded with child-like ignorance, and describes the long and weary path by which the only child-like condition of mind which is worth having must be won back, but only after a long struggle with the difficulties of belief. It is surely worth while to call people back to read their Baur and their Pfleiderer and learn that Christianity is after all, when its history is translated, only that to which on the theoretical side they give their unreserved assent as soon as they understand it.

'I should like very much, if I may, to have some talk with you on these things when you come back. Too few people know what a deliverance from their difficulties is possible for them, and we ought all to do what we can to make the way known.'

To descend from high thinking to good living, Haldane made a name for himself amongst his friends as a host whose dinners were worthy of serious attention. He owed one of his first briefs to a proper appreciation of the favourite claret of a host, who was a prominent solicitor, and he cultivated a nice taste in wine and cigars. This he shared with George Meredith, who, having discovered a case of Burgundy which had been lying in his cellar for twenty years, sent Haldane half a dozen bottles. On getting an appreciative acknowledgement Meredith wrote in the summer of 1889:

'I am glad that the Côte Rôtie has reached you safely. When sipping it with a cogitative brother Scot do me the favour to count me beside you in spirit. Of course you know the nice conduct of Burgundy. Rhine wines throw an even greater roughness. Therefore they should be stood upright a day before the drinking, after lying in a warm room a day or two, or if this has been forgotten, a couple of hours in the kitchen, away from the fire, will serve your turn. I am working and not badly, but it seems the giving out of freightage from a cranky vessel that is coming to the end of its voyages.'

During 1889, after the excitement of Pigott's flight and suicide, the lengthy proceedings of the Parnell Commission were an anti-climax. Mr. Balfour was attempting to apply 'resolute government' in Ireland, and pending the report of the Commission there was a comparative lull in political controversy. Haldane was finding his work at the Bar as a prominent junior more and more exacting, and he was now making £2,500 a year. His appearances and speeches in the House became more and more intermittent, and such spare time as he had was given mainly to addressing meetings on educational and social questions. In January 1890, when he had completed ten years service at the Bar and was in his thirty-fourth year, he took silk.

Haldane did not find himself in sympathy with the radical wing of the party, which he thought had an undue influence

47

on the Liberal policy, and he was anxious that his group of political friends should make their weight more felt. He therefore tried to bring them together as a group under the leadership of Lord Rosebery, and after some preliminary soundings he went to Mentmore to secure the leader. Of this visit he wrote to Mr. Ronald Ferguson[1] in November: 'The plot thickens! After arranging everything as well as I could with John Morley and Asquith I went to Mentmore on Saturday. There I found Henry Fowler, to whom John Morley had spoken. I had a quiet talk with Rosebery in his dressing-room. On Sunday we gave a mixed crew of guests, consisting of Christopher Sykes, Sandhurst, Smalley, Oscar Browning, and Canon Macoll, the slip and went out for a walk in the rain with Fowler. Rosebery has been thinking over the plan almost continuously since it was broached to him, and he and Fowler began by cross-examining me closely as to what you, Asquith, Edward Grey, and I proposed. I said we aimed not at a new party—still less at a conspiracy—but simply at the formation of a group bound together by a common point of view, rather than any definite organisation. This group should aim at gaining the confidence of the public by its constructive propositions, and should be the means of gaining a position from which to criticise with the utmost frankness and firmness the people with whose ideas we were at present being associated, i.e. Labouchere and Company. We would at the same time be perfectly loyal to our front bench while stimulating it to give the party a lead.

'Rosebery said that it had occurred to him that a meeting of the party might be summoned by Mr. G. to strengthen his leadership. I pointed out that however useful this might be Laby and Co. would surely profess loyalty and then ask what Mr. G. proposed in home affairs. The answer would be that neither Mr. G. nor anyone else had an idea to broach.

[1]Later Lord Novar.

RONALD FERGUSON, LATER LORD NOVAR, AND
R. B. HALDANE, 1888

Our function would be to prevent Laby and Co. stepping in to fill the gap by applying ourselves to a constructive programme. Rosebery on reflection concurred in this, and finally he and Fowler agreed very warmly with our proposal. We are—this is the result—to look to John Morley and Fowler on the Front bench as those with whom we are informally, but in substance, in touch and we are to distribute amongst ourselves the work of thinking and working out an effective programme. This is provided that the proposal is ratified, as I think it will be, at a dinner which John Morley is to convene on the 13th at which Fowler, Asquith, Sidney Buxton, Grey and I are to be present. Everything is being kept quiet at present, Harcourt being rather the *bête noire* of the gathering. Rosebery made many very acute suggestions. He is really keen about the whole business, and will, I think, give us most astute guidance and help. Of course we are only at the beginning of wisdom but we must buckle to and put our backs into the business; our credit is at stake.

'I had, as far as I am concerned, much the most satisfactory two days with Rosebery I ever had. I know that you always wanted to promote a friendship between us and he has always been kindly to me. But there have been differences in point of view, which the dour Northumbrian nature, I have inherited from my mother, would never, hitherto, permit me to minimise. But on this occasion all this has been merged in common interests and I find myself at one with him on his Imperial policy. He is going in a few days to advocate a programme of regular Colonial Conferences and to this even a Morleyite like myself can wish God speed!

'What we have to do at home is to try to gain the confidence of the electors and to mould their opinions. To my dying day, I think, I shall maintain the proposition, based on the analogy of my own mind, that a democracy has not got, as is assumed in practice, a body of definite opinion, for the expression of which in Parliament it seeks delegates, but that it is an assembly of human beings earnestly seeking guidance from those of whose sympathies it is sure.'

Morley's dinner endorsed the proposal, which brought the Liberal Imperialist group into being and was the beginning of real intimacy between Haldane and Rosebery. The particular subjects which Haldane took up as his share of the group's work were the extension of university education, women's suffrage, and housing. Towards the end of 1889 he again applied to the Lord Chancellor for silk, and this time he was successful. In January 1890, when he had just completed ten years' service as a barrister and was in his thirty-fourth year, he was called within the Bar. On the eve of the occasion of the presentation of his patent he wrote in answer to his mother's congratulations: 'It is certainly a step. I am supposed to be the youngest Q.C. made for fifty years. It is clear that I am going to get a chance. I hear already of briefs coming to me. Soares [his clerk] is nearly off his head with excitement and pomposity as he has to arrange the ceremonies to-morrow. When we have been sworn in and the Lord Chancellor has delivered our patents to us, we are to go round all the Courts where we are formally called in in each to plead. We are attired in full court dress and the procession is a very tedious one. My youth as a Q.C. is the subject of much gossip in the press and about legal circles and is an advertisement in itself. A silk gown seems to be regarded as something very wonderful by the public. Perhaps from familiarity with its wearers I do not possess so much reverence for it. Anyhow it is quite curious to see what social importance even people like Lady Rosebery and the Spencers attach to it. I think it must be the lace ruffles, which by the way, I have declined to wear.'

Lord Halsbury, on handing him his patent, whispered, 'I think this will be a great success', and it was, for he had none of the anxieties which so often follow this change of status at the Bar. In March his happiness seemed to be completed by his engagement to Miss Valentine Munro Ferguson, a very charming lady, a few years younger than himself. Congratulations and wedding presents poured in, when, a few weeks later, Miss Munro Ferguson decided that she would never marry. This was a terrible blow, which for a time affected his health. He took his disappointment like the philosopher he had trained himself to be: 'I am convinced', he wrote to his mother, 'that there came a sudden break down of feeling due simply to some physical cause. . . . These things are not after all so very difficult to understand if you take them as external misfortunes like death or a severe illness.'

One result of this blow was to bring mother and son, who, whenever they were apart, exchanged letters daily, even closer together. He wrote to her in the summer of 1890: 'Your letters have always been a great pleasure to me, but never more than during these last months. I began to realise that we as a family feel things more than other people. This was so with yourself and my father and it has descended.'

Miss Munro Ferguson died, unmarried, a few years later.

Chapter IV

THE LIBERAL DECLINE

1890 to 1895

In the summer of 1890 Haldane went with his brother John to Germany to renew his contacts with German philosophers, and in the intervals of a holiday in the Black Forest to prepare a paper on Schopenhauer. From Freiburg he wrote to Mrs. Humphry Ward:

'You were concerned about me when I left and it has always been a pleasure to write and talk to you, so I do so now. I came here last week with my brother—partly for a holiday, and partly to do some work. There are several people in the University here whom we wanted to see, and we wished particularly to do what we could towards working out the next step in getting hold of a subject, on which we wrote a little book together several years ago,[1] and at which we have in our different ways been busy ever since—the relation of the organic world, in which life and God and psychical phenomena are the distinguishing conceptions, to the sphere of pure mechanism. Prof. Weissmann is the chief apostle of the reduction of the former to the latter, and we are spending a good deal of time with him. It is really the same problem as the one in which you are so much engrossed, that of the possibility of lifting up Christianity from the region of *Vorstellung* into that of *Begriff*. Weissmann is analogous to those who would make the whole truth depend on an historical "yes" or "no". So it is, too, with Hegelianism. We have long since thrown over the cast-iron deduction of the Universe which

[1] *Essays in Philosophical Criticism.*

52

Hegel presented to us. Yet the real point of view is there, and I, for one, who owe nearly everything of the little I know to him, cannot listen with patience to ignorant sneers at his memory. God will remain the supreme reality to us, though "we sweep the heavens with our glass and find Him not", and so, too, there is a life which is greater than that on earth, though we may not be able to figure to ourselves a personal continuance after death. Kant taught the world that Nature as we know it could not be adequately represented in relations and categories of time and space, and Hegel carried this still further. To what extent then have philosophy and biology not inflicted loss on themselves and distorted these very facts, by mere dogmatic assumption that the relations of life are reducible and must be so to those of mechanism. This is what my brother's book will seek to answer from the point of view of a biologist who has read his Kant and Hegel, and striven to escape from dogmatism, and it is the philosophical chapters I am working at with him.

'So I have begun this letter with a whole screed of philosophy. I do not apologise for it, for I know how much this point of view has meant to yourself in other regions. It seems to pervade everything. Even politics have become for me penetrated with it. It helps us like reading St. Paul—in examining the meaning of Socialism—and in asking whether the self-conserving power of a living organism can be expressed adequately or at all in terms of the doctrines of physicists.

'I am also writing a short review of Schopenhauer's *Aphorisms* and reading the *Ring and the Book*. What a power genius has of grasping and expressing situations and experiences which it probably never has or can have itself gone through. This seems to me to be one of its distinguishing characteristics. Robert Browning is very great in his short pieces, but I think one does not know how great a man was until one can get engrossed in one of his colossal efforts.

'I wonder whether you yourself suffer from any tendency

to become what the Germans call *zersplittert* when you get among a number of interesting subjects. It is an insidious temptation and you may well think I have yielded to it in this letter. We never know each other—but I do not think you let yourself get led away by it. You have always seemed to me to remain more easily in a condition of concentration on your work than most of us. And after all has been said and done when the highest call has been discharged and we have done our duty to our neighbour, and are free to turn to ourselves, there is no satisfaction so deep and so lasting as that which arises from a sense of concentration in real work. It gives us all our deliverance even when we are dissatisfied with what we have accomplished.

'I have been talking this morning with Prof. Rhiehl—one of the younger German thinkers. He is full of the cry, "Back to Kant." This is excellent but one cannot help believing it ought only to be the prelude to something better. It is satisfactory, however, to find how deeply Green has influenced every German like Rhiehl. Of the theologians I have seen nothing so far. But this is a Catholic state and Ultramontism is too strong to let freedom of thought find congenial company in the University here. To an English politician, one of the regrets of whose life is the difficulty of stirring the working classes in a free country into action, it would be amusing were it not pathetic to observe the terror of the educated classes at the Social-Democratic movement in Germany. The University has no notion, apparently, of throwing itself on to the forward movement with the hope of winning the confidence of the people and so guiding them aright. As far as I can judge by what is told me, there is a great whirl of popular sympathy in the educated classes here. The names of Marx and Lassalle occasioned a little torrent of feeling from a quiet going professor this morning. Yet after all, what is the good of our reading to us, who are in public life, if we cannot use it in the effort, with all the strength we possess, to guide the current of opinion among our constituents. The thought has come strongly upon me for the last six months that there is near at hand the greatest opportunity for trying to make our public position one of real and noble influence that ever has been. These great social questions which have exercised the minds of men for so long are at last before us practically or presently will be so. This is a long letter on one subject. But when a soul has missed the goal towards which it was striving, and is still staggering, it naturally, in recovering its balance, seeks to restore the prop which it knows of old and has never found to fail. It is more relief to me than I can express to find myself again engrossed in the old searchings, and to be able to believe that they will mean, even in a practical life where they are supposed to be remote, an amply sufficient future to me. And I have no fear that you will look on this letter as a mere phase of egoism, or on the spectacle as meaning something different from what it does. There is too much of a common nature in your work and mine.'

From speculative philosophy Haldane came home to the practical problems of establishing himself in his new position at the Bar and to a disturbed political situation.

As Queen's Counsel Haldane practised first in the court of Mr. Justice Kay, and when Kay went to the Court of Appeal, before Mr. Justice Romer. He did not feel that his special qualities were altogether adapted to a court of first instance, and was usually much happier in the Court of Appeal. He did not therefore yet feel confident that he had established his position at the Bar and there was a tug-of-war not unusual in the career of a rising barrister between the calls of his profession and those of the House of Commons.

An event which had political consequences of the first magnitude occurred in November 1890. While the Parnell Commission was still in session Parnell had been cited as a co-respondent in a petition of divorce, and when the case came into court and the facts were made public Parnell's political career came to an abrupt end. Roman Catholic Ireland was somewhat reluctantly compelled to follow a Protestant, who led the way to Home Rule with courage and ability, but it threw him over with little hesitation when he transgressed its moral code, while nonconformist England and Presbyterian Scotland were equally shocked, and, with the revived influence of the Roman Church in Irish affairs, more ready to listen to the assertion that Home Rule meant Rome rule. All this seriously affected the prospects of the Liberal Party, and with a general election drawing near Haldane had to give more time to his constituency.

He welcomed work as an anodyne, and, though during 1891 his business in the courts was growing rapidly, he rarely refused an invitation to speak and was constantly travelling with a bag of briefs to study as his companion. On the anniversary of the breach of his engagement he wrote to his mother:

'To-day a year ago I was left alone. I came back to you, and good has been the result. I can truly say that I would not be without what has passed. One gains wide knowledge in the sanctuary of sorrow and a strength and experience which cannot be gained in any other way. There is no royal road to all this. I am older, but this year has been the richest of my life and it has been well worth living. I am very grateful to you.'

Probably his deep affection and respect for his mother was an influence in making him one of the first advocates of women's suffrage, which this year he supported both in the House and in the country. 'Life', he wrote to his mother, 'is rather a racket, but it is good to be busy. I had a night of it last night. Left Court at 1 p.m., when I had spoken for two hours. Read a brief and prepared my speech and addressed 3,000 people at Bradford, 7.30 p.m. Caught the 9.45 train, read two briefs with the aid of a candle. Reached my chambers at 3.30 a.m. to find an earnest intimation that I must read a brief which had been sent down to meet me. Got up at

7.30, read the brief, and was in court at 9.45 a.m. and was on my feet at 10.30 to deliver an elaborate argument. Not a bit tired, only hustled a little!'

In the summer of 1891, before Lord Salisbury's administration drew to its close, Mrs. Asquith died. This meant to Haldane much more than the death of the wife of a dear friend, for Mrs. Asquith had nursed him at Hampstead during his illness and had been a visitor at Cloan, and he held her in very real esteem and affection.

Salisbury dissolved Parliament in June 1892, and the resulting general election was no triumph for the Liberals. Gladstone's majority in Midlothian, which had been numbered in thousands, fell to 700. Haldane and Asquith were both returned, but with much reduced majorities, and several of the Liberal leaders fell by the way.

Of his own contest Haldane wrote to his mother: 'My telegram will have told you that I am in but by the skin of my teeth. The Church question and a section of the miners did it but the main cause was the falling off of enthusiasm for Mr. G. We had no notion of the peril we were in and expected on our canvas a majority of 800 to 1,000 when we went into count. Prestonpans and Dunbar were solid against me and but for the personal affection for me of true friends, who came from all quarters to poll for me, I should be out.'

Soon after the election Haldane went south and spent a week-end with Meredith at Box Hill. Of this visit he wrote to his mother: 'I have just ended a very pleasant visit to George Meredith. He is extraordinarily good at summing up in a phrase, sometimes with barbed words, the value of a writer or of a piece of literature. While I was there Admiral Maxse brought over Alfred Austin, whom, to the amazement of the literary world, Salisbury has made Poet Laureate.[1] Austin was somewhat full of his promotion, and talking of this as a well deserved tribute to his poetry said, ". . . and it

[1]Lord Tennyson had died in June 1892.

gives me the sense that I can speak to the Prime Minister at last on the terms of an equal." Meredith suddenly burst out, "The cock sparrow can perch his claw on the head of Olympian Jove", which brought the conversation to a hasty end.'

Without the Irish Nationalists the Liberals could not count on a majority, and these, now under the leadership of John Redmond, came back to Westminster as strong as ever and were the masters of the situation.

In this situation neither Haldane nor Asquith were at all eager that their party should take office, but in the event the Government were defeated by forty votes on the Address, the Irish Party going into the lobby with the Liberals. Lord Salisbury thereupon resigned, and the Queen sent for Mr. Gladstone, who formed his fourth and last administration.

While this was in the making Haldane wrote to Sir A. West, Mr. Gladstone's Chief Whip, a letter which shows the way in which his political sympathies were tending:

'My desire in writing now, if I may do so without seeming to intrude, is to emphasise the importance of a step towards securing the confidence of the nascent body of opinion in the constituencies which cares little for any Irish policy and concentrates itself on social questions. As I said to you, I am convinced that the man in our ranks who possesses, beyond anyone else of his standing, the confidence of the labour party, using the term in its widest sense, is Arthur Acland. He has, as none of us younger men has, the personal respect of not only prominent leaders like Tom Mann and Burns, but of the great body of artisans of the northern and midland counties. He is looked on by them, and I think rightly, as having done more really good work in the House of Commons in the last five sessions than any other member of his standing. Besides this he is regarded by the Welsh members as one of themselves, because of the services he has rendered them in intermediate education and other matters. I believe that I am expressing the sentiments of the bulk of the rank and file in the House when I say that it will be a deep disappointment if he is not placed in a position under Mr. Gladstone where he may exercise real influence and attract to us still more of that confidence of the industrial classes on which we greatly depend to-day for our future. What occurs to me I venture to suggest for consideration in the light of your experience. Why should not the opportunity be taken of doing what would at once be useful and popular, making the labour department of the Board of Trade a reality by putting it under his charge and extending its functions? The Secretary of the Board of Trade is not a very important office at present. Might not a vice-presidency be created, with the announcement that the labour department was to be extended and annexed to it, and Acland be made the first vice-president? This may be a difficult step. I have not the knowledge to judge, but I am satisfied that both generally and in connection with Acland it would be very popular. The minister in charge of the labour department would have abundance to do and Acland's large experience in settling industrial disputes and getting at the minds of the working people would enable him to develop the functions of his office from the very first. He is in an unique position. Burt, for example, is regarded with an approach to hostility by the Labour Party, and there is probably no man within their ranks whom their jealousies would permit to fill the most prominent position in the Labour sphere, witness the defeat of Tom Mann by Burns and others for the secretaryship of the Amalgamated Engineers. But in Acland there is no sense of rivalry. They look on him as a highly educated outsider who has devoted his life to the study of the relations of capital and labour. I am aware that to talk of a Labour ministry is to suggest what is easy to speak of and difficult to do, but if some step towards it could now be taken I feel sure that it would strengthen Mr. Gladstone's position both in the Constituences and in the present House of Commons.'

Thirty years were to pass before the proposal for creating a ministry of labour was to mature. In this, as in other matters, Haldane was looking farther ahead than his leaders could see.

In the event most of the members of Haldane's group took office under Mr. Gladstone. Asquith became Home Secretary, Acland went to the Board of Education, and Grey to the Foreign Office as Under-Secretary. His friends were grieved that a place was not found for Haldane, but he was not himself eager to take office. He wanted to make his position at the Bar more secure and to have a free hand to promote the causes which he had most at heart, education and social reform, causes for which he did not find much enthusiasm amongst the Liberal leaders. Shortly after Mr. Gladstone's resignation he put his views on taking office in a letter to a friend which may well be quoted here:

'Do you remember my saying to you that I had a strain of insanity in me and your replying "Yes, but you ought not to tell it to anyone"? It is the best strain in me really, that insanity. The struggle over what was good and decent in the Liberal revolt brought out, and has lifted me away from, much that had become or was becoming familiar. I will tell you in a few words what I mean. Some one sent me a portrait of myself in a Scotch newspaper on Saturday which I believe to be partly a true one, and I enclose it to you to save repetition. It represents, so far as political work is concerned, what I wish to do and be thought to do. Political success is not to be an admired Minister surrounded by a devoted group of adherents. It is to have a belief that is true and leads others to follow it. I do not propose to leave the Bar. I must live by it. Besides I like it, and have never before done my work so efficiently as I am doing it now. But I cannot allow it to swallow me up. If I were to become like Lord Herschell or Lord Selborne I should look back on chances wasted of doing really good work in the world. Just at present I am exercising what I believe to be an useful influence in the direction indicated in the Scotch article. I mean to follow it out, going to meetings in large centres of industrial life where I can do most. Later I shall try to exercise influence, so gained, in office—not legal office, but one like the Local Government Board or the Scottish Office—if I can persuade them to appoint me. If they won't, the outside process must continue. That is the life which seems to me best, and it is no breach, so far as externals go, of the life I have been pursuing. I would rather be like Arthur Acland, with all his fanaticisms, than anyone I know just now. This is, I think, a plain statement. As for the Sidney Webbs, whatever be their failings socially, they are splendid workers, and I should be proud to feel I had given up so much for a cause as they have.'

His tour of the universities of south Germany had taken place when the industrial development of that country which followed on her victory over France in 1870-1 and her unification was in full blast. He was deeply impressed by the use which Germany was making of the scientific training provided by her universities in the development of her industries and was very conscious that in that England lagged far behind. He decided to devote himself to remedying this and to work for the establishment of universities in each of the great centres of England which should cover the country as the German universities covered Germany. He put his views on the development of university education in England in an address which he gave at Liverpool, and in this he outlined a programme which he was to live to see realized:

'He would be a pedant who thought that education alone could determine the commercial position of a nation. Yet more than ever, as science tends increasingly to reduce nature to subjection, education becomes important. In the United States a highly practical people are taking this view, and it is noticeable that the rapid increase there of universities and technical schools is largely due to the faith in their efficiency shown by practical men of business. The millionaire in

America seeks to save his soul by building, not churches, but colleges, and if he insists on embodying in their constitution ideas of his own which are not always the highest ideas, this shows his zeal. The British people are not yet a decaying race. The Anglo-Saxon, here as in America, is probably in energy, in courage and in doggedness of purpose superior to all his European rivals in commerce. If proof of this be wanted it will be found in the way in which the absolute volume of our trade continues at a high level. It is a remarkable tribute to our race that the assessments for income-tax purposes have, during the last ten years, shown an increase of about 20 per cent., while the population has increased only 10 per cent.

'But organization and instruction have been carried to a far higher pitch in Germany and Switzerland than with us, and if we are to hold our position we must furnish ourselves with the discipline and the weapons with which the foreigner has prepared himself for the contest. Now, in suggesting that reform of our education, and particularly of our tertiary education, is essential, I am far from desiring to suggest that we ought to wish to see it entirely subordinated to utilitarian considerations. Culture is an end in itself, and if it is to be won it must be sought for its own sake. But the Germans have shown us how the University can fulfil a double function without slackening the effort after culture. In a certain exquisiteness the flowers of scholarship which Oxford and Cambridge have produced are probably without examples to rival them, unless it be in France. But for breadth and understanding who will dare to place the record of the work done in Oxford or Cambridge in the department of classical literature above what has been turned out in Germany? Take the editing, and with it the criticism, of Greek philosophy, and compare the shallow formalities which did duty in the English Universities up to about thirty years ago, when German ideas began to penetrate, with the work of German scholars. The memories of Plato and Aristotle owe the influence they have to-day to Hegel, a Prantl, and a Zeller, and certainly not to the commentators who until about thirty years ago ruled the Universities of this country. But it is not right to try to exalt one phase of scholarship at the expense of another. And when we turn to the history of mathematics and of physical science we may well be proud of the series of great thinkers whose spiritual mother Cambridge has been. Only let no one imagine that in the record of the German Universities, in pure scholarship and pure science alike, in the pursuit of knowledge for the sake of knowledge alone, the work done at Berlin, at Leipzig, at Jena, at Göttingen, during the past hundred years, has not been of a quality as high as any that the world has seen. The conclusion of the whole matter seems to be that we could establish in Great Britain and Ireland a system of teaching of a university type, with the double aim of Germany, and that without injury to the quality of culture. We are proud of Oxford and Cambridge. They have taken centuries to grow up, they are rooted in splendid traditions which we seek not to disturb. But that does not make the educational reformer desire the less to see the expansion of another kind of teaching which they are not adapted to give, and which is none the less a national necessity. The Victoria University and the University of Wales have taken the way we want. Let us assist still further the magnificent private efforts which made them what they are to-day. Why should not Liverpool and Manchester, with their public spirit and rapidly increasing populations, possess, as in Germany they certainly would, their own Universities? How ridiculous it is to dread that such Universities would prove Liliputians! Why should Leeds not be the head-quarters of a Yorkshire University? Why should not Birmingham, where the energy and influence of Mr. Chamberlain have brought about a remarkable fresh development, be the centre for the Midlands; and why should not Bristol, where the soil so far has proved somewhat less fertile, be made by State cultivation the centre for the South-West of England?'

This address was designed to interest business men in the development of university education in the centres of industry, but Haldane was no less interested in the organization of a great teaching university in London, and with that end in view he in 1891 became a member of the Council of University College, London. That college, the foundation stone of which was laid in 1827, was intended by its founders to provide for London a university 'freed from those exclusions and religious distinctions which abridge the usefulness of Oxford and Cambridge'. This movement at once aroused controversy, and controversy in one form or another was for many years to clog the development of the university. As a counter-blast to University College King's College was in 1831 opened as 'a college in which instructions in the doctrines and duties of Christianity as taught by the Church of England should be forever combined with other branches of useful learning'. The solution of controversy was, as usual, compromise, and in 1836 the University of London was incorporated as an examining body, with the power of awarding degrees, but with no teaching functions. As a body offering university degrees, which soon acquired a high standard, without religious tests, the new university played a very valuable part, but as the years passed the colleges increased both in size and number and from them came a demand of increasing insistency for a teaching university in London. In response to this demand the Government in 1884 appointed a royal commission under the chairmanship of the Earl of Selborne to inquire and report on the matter. The commission found that the case for a teaching university had been established, but did not consider it possible to combine the existing university with a new teaching university, and proposed that, after a reasonable lapse of time the existing university should disappear and be replaced by a new one

constituted on the general lines of the old teaching universities. In the fifty years of its existence as an examining body
the university had created a great number of graduates, and
these had strenuously opposed the recommendations of the
Selborne Commission on the grounds that their rights and
privileges would be jeopardized, while the professors of the
colleges were as urgent as ever in demanding a university in
which the colleges should have an effective vote. This was
the position when Haldane joined the Council of University
College. He recognized the advantage to education which the
opportunity of obtaining external degrees had conferred, and
himself as a youngster had matriculated, not without difficulty,
as an external student, but he was also in entire sympathy
with the demand for a teaching university, and he set himself to devise an arrangement which would meet the conflicting views of the two parties. It was some years before a
solution on those lines became possible, and in the interval
much had happened in the political field.

Haldane was delighted with Asquith's immediate success
in office. One of the new Home Secretary's first acts had been
to find a solution of the problem, in which, as we have seen,
Haldane had been involved, of the use of Trafalgar Square
for public meetings. They were permitted, after due notice
to the police, on Saturday afternoons, Sundays, and Bank
Holidays, when they would not cause public inconvenience.
In 1893 Haldane became involved in another of his friend's
problems. A coal strike, prolonged and bitter, occurred in
the north of England. It was accompanied by much violence,
and at Fetherstone in West Yorkshire the civil authorities
called in the soldiers. Eventually the troops, some thirty in
number, were ordered to fire, and two men were killed.
This provoked an immediate outcry from the representatives
of Labour, and the Home Secretary promised an inquiry into
the action of the troops. He persuaded Haldane to be a member of the commission, which found that the military had

done no more than duty required. But it was Mr. Gladstone's second Home Rule Bill which dominated the political situation, and Haldane was kept busy in drafting and in defending it in the House until it went up to the Lords to meet its inevitable fate. The fact that there was no prospect of getting the Home Rule Bill passed during the session was one factor in causing his colleagues to agree that it was time for Mr. Gladstone to go. Another was the Prime Minister's almost isolated opposition to an increase of the Navy. There had been for some time an agitation for this. Naval manœuvres appeared to show that we were not strong enough at sea to conduct an effective blockade and to protect our coasts from raids, and agitation reached a dramatic climax when the *Victoria* was sunk in the Mediterranean in a collision with the *Camperdown*. Lord Spencer, then First Lord, had prepared a naval programme which was accepted by almost all the Cabinet save Mr. Gladstone. On this Haldane wrote to Grey:

'As you know, my work brings me into touch with a number of prominent men from the Colonies, particularly Canadians. I find them one and all perturbed about the naval situation. I believe myself that we have allowed the Navy to sink, relatively to that of France, below the margin of safety. Our three links with the Colonies are the Crown, the Law, and the Navy, and if we weaken the latter we risk weakening the others, while you know better than I do the importance of an adequate Navy if we are to make our voice heard in Europe. Parting with Mr. G. will be a painful business, but on this matter I feel that we cannot give way.'

So Morley was deputed to tell Gladstone that the time had come when he must go, and the Queen sent for Lord Rosebery, but there were some searchings of heart in the party before that decision was reached. Haldane wrote to his mother on 1 March:

'Mr. Gladstone will resign early next week as things stand. Meantime the struggle for the leadership is in full swing. I have been forced into the midst of it as negotiator, Labouchere being my opponent on the other side. I have practically abandoned Lincoln's Inn for a few days. To-day the *Chronicle* proposes that I should go into the Cabinet, and there has been some talk of the Scotch Secretaryship, but I shall stay where I am. It is all very interesting. Asquith, Acland, and I spent last night together talking it all over.'

Rosebery was the recognized chief of Haldane's group of Liberals, and during his short reign he consulted him regularly and put a good deal of extra work upon his willing shoulders. When Harcourt introduced his famous Death Duties Budget Haldane served on the committee which prepared the Bill and had much to do with the drafting, while he had to be in regular attendance in the House to see it through committee. So for a long time his legal work had to take second place.

He won the ear of the House, his interventions in debate were increasingly successful, and he thoroughly enjoyed his success. 'I had a great success in the House last night', he wrote to his mother in April, 'with a speech delivered in reply to Sir Michael Hicks Beach. It was chiefly concerned with a constitutional argument about Home Rule. It took an hour and ten minutes to deliver, and when it was done Davitt, Blake, O'Brien, and other Irish leaders came across the floor to thank and congratulate me. One of them said touchingly, "I would live and die for a man like you!" Even the Parnellites did the same. I had spoken of the debt Ireland owed to "the great Irishman who eighteen months ago was laid to sleep in Glasnevin cemetery" and old Colonel Nolan came with tears in his eyes to thank me. Mr. G. was not there but Morley thanked me personally and even the Tories poured in congratulations. The Speaker whispered, "A very great constitutional speech." John Burns declared he could hear the silence with which it was received.' Of another effort he wrote to his mother from his bench in the House: 'I have

just finished a speech on the spur of the moment in reply to
Sir H. James. Arthur Balfour rose late and declared it to be the
ablest in the debate and Mr. G. cheered loudly.' With his
reputation established in the House it was not surprising that
approaches were made to him to join the Government, and
during the summer there was talk of making him Solicitor-
General, but the proposal was for technical reasons abandoned
and he was approached again with an offer of the Board of
Trade, but he held to his decision that he was not yet ready
to take office, and indeed he was preparing at the time for a
bold professional venture. Finding himself to be of real use in
the House he wanted some relief from the work of a busy
leader in a Court of First Instance, and as I have said he was
never quite at home in Romer's court. He therefore decided
to go 'special'. 'I like the higher courts', he told his mother,
'much better than my own. There is much more room in the
Court of Appeal for the qualities in which I am really strong
than before Romer—a shrewd rough-minded man, who does
his work excellently, but whose whole purpose is to avoid
points of law and get through the list as fast as possible. I have
therefore decided to go "special", which means that I do not
appear in a Court of First Instance without a special fee of
fifty guineas in addition to that marked on my brief. Of
course it is a bold move for I am only 37 and no special has
ever been anything like so young. But I have always done
apparently rash things and this seems a good opportunity to
make the start.'

As a Queen's Counsel and Member of Parliament known
to be in the confidence of the Prime Minister Haldane had become a man whom people were eager to know. Up till now
he had made, outside his immediate political circle, few
friends of his own age, and the philosophers with whom he
associated were mostly much older than himself. His illness
and his unhappy love-affair had tended to increase a natural
reserve, and he had not attempted to go about in London

society. Now, with his health and his confidence in himself restored, he was more ready to respond to invitations, and his circle of friends widened quickly. Mr. and Mrs. Horner[1] of Mells were amongst the first of those whose friendship became a joy to him, and Mells Park became to him a southern home to which he delighted to go for rest when he could spare a week-end. Through Mrs. Horner he met the 'Souls'. Though never a member of the group, which he first met about 1892, in which year he became a bencher of Lincoln's Inn, he was always welcome among them and delighted in their company, particularly because he found in Balfour, Curzon, George Wyndham, and Alfred Lyttelton, all of them Conservatives, more sympathy with his own particular interests, philosophy, and education than he found in his Liberal colleagues. With Balfour in particular he formed a friendship with which political differences and a divergent philosophical outlook never interfered. The Tweedmouths were others whose friendship was dear to him, and for Lady Tweedmouth he had very real affection. There was always a room for him at Guisachan, which became known as 'Mr. Haldane's room'.

In the society of witty women he took great pleasure, and amongst those whom he met in the circle of the Souls who became his close friends were Lady Ribblesdale and her sister Margot Tennant, Lady Elcho, Lady Desborough, and Lady Tweedmouth's sister Lady Howe, and with these as hostesses he became a regular week-ender. In the autumn of 1892 he gave his sister an account of a dinner which he and Asquith gave to some of their lady friends: 'The dinner last night was a great success. There was no spikiness. The ladies were very brilliant. Mrs. John Richard Green bore off the palm. I think she inspired Margot and Mrs. Horner with a wholesome respect for her powers. She came late and gave a most amusing account of how, having lost the address and

[1]Afterwards Sir John and Lady Horner.

remembering that she was to meet the Home Secretary, she applied to the Police, who advised her to call at a house in Green Street, where lived a lady a great friend of the Home Secretary. This she did, and found that the lady was the friend of the late Home Secretary, but the idea occurred to her to go by analogy to 40 Grosvenor Square[1] (one for Margot). Then after raising hopes and explaining how at dinner the night before she had failed to make an impression on Burne-Jones, a great friend of Mrs. Horner, she went on to say that Burne-Jones told her that after 35 all women ceased to interest him. (One for Mrs. Horner.) Asquith and I agreed that Mrs. G. was a dangerous person to fight with. However all went smoothly. Margot made herself charming.' One of the excitements of the season of 1894 was the engagement of Asquith to Margot Tennant. Haldane was one of the first to hear the news. Asquith wrote to him in January:

'You will I know be glad to hear that the uncertainties that have so long clouded my private prospects are at an end, and that we became engaged last week—two days before the catastrophe in the hunting field. I should have told you last night but that we are both agreed to keep the state of things to ourselves for the present in order to shorten, as much as possible, the period of publicity with its attendant horrors. Practically the only two persons who know the actual situation are Lady Ribblesdale and Lady Manners (and doubtless their respective husbands).

'As however I have a message from her this morning asking me to tell you I hasten to do what, under any other circumstances, I should have done at first. For the time being please keep it strictly and entirely to yourself.'

The marriage took place in May, Haldane being Asquith's best man. 'You will see', he wrote to his mother, 'the description of the wedding in the papers. All went well. She was very pale and nervous but got through it. I stood with him

[1]The Tennants' town house.

for quarter of an hour waiting for the bride, rather an ordeal. Mr. Gladstone looked magnificent but very infirm. Smallpage had made me a very smart coat and I looked quite presentable. Asquith had been dressed for the occasion by Poole and it made him quite young.' In a letter to his mother written in February 1894 he gave an amusing instance of the varied company into which his very various interests brought him. 'On Sunday the 17th I had two odd engagements, one to spend the evening with the Battersea Labour League, the other to meet the Prince of Wales at a small luncheon, to which he had asked Lady Dorothy Nevill to invite him and me, in order that he might make my acquaintance. I had a good deal of talk with him and learned that he wanted to know me as he expected that I would be his Chancellor one day.'

As early as November 1894 Haldane felt strongly that energetic measures were needed if the Government was to survive, and on this he had a talk with Rosebery, who asked him to put his ideas in a letter. He therefore wrote:

'What I ventured to say to you this morning represented things that have been in my mind for some time past. Summarised they amount on a review of the situation to this:

'(1). Your Government leaves but little to be desired in point of firmness and range in its administration and in its foreign policy.

'(2). It is probably stronger in the country than in the House of Commons.

'(3). What is lacking appears to be any general interest or enthusiasm about its future.

'For this deficiency there are proximate reasons. Apart from the difficulty about the House of Lords, the majority in the House of Commons is too small and uncertain to let the Government be felt to be effective.

'Another and cognate reason is that the country is sick of political platitudes like the Newcastle Programme. It feels that society is in a transition stage, and that section of it which has faith longs for new watchwords for its idealism, for some one to express for it what it cannot express itself and yet earnestly desires. How, then, is this feeling to be satisfied and this enthusiasm which is latent to be aroused from political into active energy? Not, I think, by any further legislative programme while the machinery to give effect to it remains inadequate. What the people look for from their leader, in such a transition period as that through which we are passing, is a guidance which will move them and mould them. If you doubt this turn back to the torrent of gratitude which followed your Bradford speech.[1]

'Two more such speeches and a dissolution upon them would I believe return you to power with a doubled majority. The difficulty of to-day seems to me to lie not in personal relations within the Cabinet nor on the weak majority in the House of Commons. There is latent in the electors an energy which would sweep these difficulties from your path if it is possible to repeat on wider lines what you did last month.'

But Rosebery's health was failing and he had neither the will nor the energy to conduct such a campaign as Haldane suggested, with a dissolution and a general election as its goal. He was in fact looking forward to retirement to his books and his race-horses, when he could withdraw with honour. So the Liberal ship drifted on to the rocks.

In December 1894 Haldane sent Balfour an article he had written on Hegel and received in reply a note which ran: 'I am going to denounce you on Friday at Haddington if I am well enough to denounce anyone. At present I am unfortunately laid up with a cold, which brings home very clearly to my mind the insoluble character of the problem of evil.'

[1]Rosebery had made a stirring speech at Bradford in which he said that while he was a second-chamber man the present second chamber was nothing but a permanent party organization. The House of Lords as at present constituted was a great national danger from a constitutional point of view. 'We fling down the gauntlet, it is for you to pick it up.'

To this Haldane answered from Mells, where he was staying with the Horners: 'I was glad to see from *The Times* that you were well enough to take the field at Haddington. I am not sure that I do not agree with a good deal of what you concluded on the subject of Liberalism (I hate the name, and call myself "Progressive") in Scotland—but this, not because I disbelieve in what *ought* to be the cause of my party, but because I have not a high opinion of my Scot as a social reformer. There will be a different geographical distribution of political opinion five years after this. Meantime I shall do all I can to prevent your giving me more leisure for the study of Hegel. My hope is that the farm servants still love an abstract disposition in politics. If you have time to look at the article on Hegel you will see in the latter part of it why I sent it to you. It is the confession of faith of a believer in existing institutions —theological and of other kinds—as developing features of the whole. I think that Hegel, when redeemed from the load of rubbish that has been laid on him, really says this. Seth and I are now quite at one about these things, although I have not yet got him to regard your own criticisms as profoundly sceptical. I am watching for your book and I wonder whether I shall find myself farther off after reading it. My feeling is that our period is one in which the melting-pot is predominant and that it cannot be made otherwise, and that the gold is not lost. But I will not come to this book with a part taken.'

In March 1895 he wrote to his mother: 'Yesterday I received an unexpected approach from Lord Rosebery and the Cabinet that I should take the Speakership, I refused quietly but firmly. I think I was right, though the position of first commoner is a great one. But I felt that the life would be artificial and a complete break with my work, while I do not think you would appreciate the social entanglement it would have plunged you into. It appears that the Tories do not like Courtney, Campbell-Bannerman could not be spared, and it was thought that all sections would take me. To have been considered is a thing to be proud of. Before finally deciding I had a long talk with Asquith. He was strongly of opinion that it would be a cleaving of my life and a dereliction of duty. I am quite sure I did right though it looks as though my candidature would have solved some difficulties.'

He wrote to Rosebery: 'It is very kind of you to have written as you have done. The high honour you have proposed for me has naturally flattered and pleased me, and I have given it very careful thought. The one fear that I have had in declining it is that I should seem to you to belittle your kindness. Indeed, indeed, the response to your words came from my heart. It is true that I should have liked this office had the course of events made it right that it should come to me. But it was as something external, not of the essence of things, and appeared to me—perhaps more vividly than to some of my friends—that there were difficulties in the way when that was looked at which alone ought to be looked at, the common interest of a great party, hard to hold together, but one to which we are all of us, in whatever station we hold, most deeply attached. Believe me when I say that it is my sense of duty to you and to our party, which has influenced me in refusing this prize. That you have given me the confidence you have makes life seem a larger thing and I need not add that my attachment to yourself is and will remain of the deepest.'

To this Rosebery answered:

'MY DEAR JUSTINIAN [his pet name for Haldane]

A thousand thanks for what you have written. I think that when in the years to come you review what can hardly fail to be a brilliant career, that letter will not be the least gratifying and honourable incident that will occur to you. At anyrate in my arid experience of the allocation of office it stands alone, and a pleasant oasis it is.'

Mr. Courtney also declined the speakership, which was offered to and accepted by Mr. Gully.

Rosebery succeeded to an uneasy throne. Many of his colleagues and a considerable portion of the Liberal Party
thought that the Queen should have sent for Sir William Harcourt, while both Harcourt himself and the Radical wing of
the party were suspicious of Rosebery's imperialism. With a
divided Cabinet and the mission for which they had been
returned, Home Rule, outside the field of practical politics,
the Government steadily lost hold both on the House and
the party. Majorities diminished through the session of 1895,
and on June 21 the Government was defeated in a snap division on a motion to reduce the salary of the Secretary of
State for War on grounds that the reserves of small arms
munition were inadequate. On June 27 the Government resigned, and Lord Salisbury, whom the Queen sent for, decided to go to the country.

If the fall of the Government was inevitable the circumstances which brought it about were curious and dramatic
and had an effect on Haldane's future work. Campbell-
Bannerman had been a popular Secretary of State for War
and had just completed the first of what was to be a long
succession of plans for the reorganization of the War Office.
He had adopted a part of the recommendations of the report
of a commission over which Lord Hartington had presided,
and proposed to limit the powers of the Commander-in-
Chief and introduce what was in fact the embryo of an army
council. Both Liberals and Conservatives were agreed to seek
ways and means of obtaining greater governmental control
of the Army, but the position of the Duke of Cambridge,
backed by the Queen, had stood in the way of this. Campbell-
Bannermann had tactfully induced the duke to retire, and
had gained the Queen's consent. He was just about to put
in Sir Redvers Buller as Commander-in-Chief when the
Government fell, and the Conservatives on coming into
office appointed Lord Wolseley. Haldane apparently had no
doubt as to the result of the election, for on July 24 he wrote to

Balfour, who was designated to lead the Commons in the new Parliament, to secure a chair for the younger brother of his old friend Andrew Seth:

'My mind is distracted from the necessary business of preparing the defence of my fortress against your speech by the fear that in the turmoil the Aberdeen Chair of Logic may get filled up with someone not so good as James Seth. I can bear to see the Established Church Ministers continue for a time in the pulpits under the auspices of the State, but, if under those auspices, they should seat themselves in the Chair of Bain and teach his philosophy, my light would become very low.

'But it is probably unnecessary for me to write about a thing you will not forget. Only I gather that wires may be pulled in more high places than one.

'I wish this election were over—It leaves one not a moment's peace. I have even been made to attend a cattle show.'

The result of the election was disastrous to the Liberal Party. Haldane, after a hard fight, was returned with an increased majority, but both Harcourt and Morley lost their seats, and the party came back to the House with its ranks reduced by nearly one hundred, to remain in opposition for ten years.

Chapter V

UNIVERSITY REFORM

1898

With the Liberals in opposition Haldane took less and less interest in the routine of party politics. After the Jameson raid the split in the party widened as the crisis in South Africa developed. Haldane thought that the Government handled the business of the disastrous raid badly, but he did not share the belief of some of his Radical colleagues that Chamberlain was in any way implicated in it. He had much sympathy with Milner, whom he knew well and with whom he corresponded, and none with Kruger. Rosebery, his political chief, was at loggerheads with Harcourt, and Haldane saw little prospect of the party taking any useful part in those social reforms in which he was specially interested; therefore, while he was regular in attendance at the House and often intervened in debate in such matters as the Conservative Education Bill, the Women's Suffrage Bill, and measures affecting the condition of labour, he devoted the greater part of such spare time as his increasing business in the courts left him to work on the questions which he had at heart outside the House. The first of them was the reform of the University of London.

In 1892 the Government had set up yet another royal commission, under the chairmanship of Earl Cowper, to report upon a scheme for the establishment of a teaching university in London. Haldane's uncle, Professor Burdon-Sanderson, who had been head of the oldest research institution in the university, the Brown Animal Sanitary Institution, was a member of the commission, and through him Haldane was able to get his views considered. The commission reported in 1894 that there should be one university and not two, and that the constitution of the new university, combining in one whole teaching and examining functions, should be settled by legislation. As soon as the report was issued Haldane, with the assistance of Sidney Webb, set to work to draft a Bill which would have some chance of acceptance. This involved long and protracted negotiations, for differences between the professors of the colleges, who wanted a teaching university, and the holders of external degrees, who feared that under the proposed amalgamation their rights would be extinguished, or at best seriously diminished, were acute. At length arrangements were embodied in the Bill which were accepted by a majority of the Senate of the Examining University and of the professors of the universities. But this was only half the battle. It was necessary to remove possible opposition in the House, and in the summer of 1896 Haldane was hard at work at this. 'All day long', he wrote to his mother, 'I have been working at the London University Bill trying to get cantankerous people to agree. I think we are now in sight of a settlement, but it has been a tough job.' Three days later he wrote: 'Alas, the University Bill is dead. The Bishops have killed it.' However, he stuck to his task, had the Bill modified to meet the views of its opponents, and was ready again in 1897, only to have it killed by another group of obstructionists. He then came to the conclusion that as a private Bill it would have no chance and that he must get the Government to sponsor it. In this Haldane enlisted the help of Balfour, whose interest in his projects for the extension of university education he had roused. Balfour promised to get the Board of Education to take up the Bill if he were assured that there was a reasonable measure of agreement. So the Bill went to the Lords, and eventually, at the end of the session of 1897, was ready for the Commons.

On the eve of the new session Haldane wrote to Balfour: 'You will soon be considering the business of next session, and the bores will be writing you letters. Here is a specimen! However, my purpose is no worse than to let you have information as to how things stand as to London University. From letters I have seen I gather that the Senate stands in its approval of the Bill as arranged, and that the majority of Convocation take the same view. There are one or two trifling changes that may be made with advantage in the clauses, one especially which would please Wace of King's College, and which other people would concede. However, I have no reason to think that King's College is otherwise than friendly. Now as to the Opposition. Dilke told me that he should probably not oppose the Bill if brought in fairly early next session. However, I never believe a word he says. The real opposition comes from Dr. Collins and Fletcher Moulton. I do not think they can get any substantial support in the House, for the Bill is strongly supported by Herschell, Bryce, Acland, Stuart, Cozens-Hardy, and all are leading people, now that the Church difficulty has been satisfactorily settled. Lubbock[1] is of course in two minds, and he will have to make some show of opposition but I believe he would be heartily glad to have the matter disposed of. The attitude of Collins and Moulton is that they do not want any change at all—a position which the Cowper Commission negatived with the approval of every learned body in London.

'I have rather discouraged suggestions of deputations to the Government this autumn, as I know they are a great nuisance.

'As regards time two hours ought to do for the second reading, and a night for the Committee. The grounds on which substantial opposition can be made are few. Dillon says his Irish will not oppose and I think I can do something

[1]Sir John Lubbock, afterwards Lord Avebury, then member for the university.

with Healy—whom I saw before the House rose. As for Redmond he hates the Irish priests and is probably unconcerned—but I have not sounded him.'

While he was waiting for the Bill to make its third appearance Gladstone died. 'We are in a strange state of feeling,' he wrote to his mother. 'Tory and Liberal alike think only of the great one who has passed away and left England the poorer. We all realise vividly how great Mr. Gladstone's hold on us has been. Rosebery and I went at midnight to stand for a little alone by the coffin in Westminster Hall. The earlier part of the evening I spent with John Morley. He really minds most, and understands him best.'

The Bill did not come up for second reading in the Commons till June 1898, and it became clear at once that Haldane had somewhat overestimated the effects of his efforts at conciliation. It was introduced by Sir John Gorst, President of the Board of Education, with a somewhat lukewarm commendation from the Government. Fletcher Moulton and Sir John Lubbock, the member for the university, whose constituents were to a man graduates of the existing examining university, had been busy in the lobbies, and, after a succession of speeches, all of them against the Bill, Haldane sprang to his feet and for the first time made a speech of some length in the House without a note. He said:

'Mr. Speaker, what is the proposition of this Bill? what does it propose to do? If any Honourable Member will take the pains to turn up the useful little map published by the Technical Education Board in London, showing the distribution of all sorts of teaching centres throughout the metropolis, he will see that the map shows the distribution of education which is of a university type. He will find that all through and round and about London there are scattered a number of bodies, some of which he may not have heard of, but others which are very well known to him. He will find such well-known institutions as King's College and University College, the Royal School of Mines, South Kensington; he will find institutions such as Bedford College, and various other bodies where science is specially taught, and he will find a large number of minor schools and colleges in which education, sometimes of a special kind and sometimes of a general character, is given in almost all cases of a type approaching to the university kind of teaching. There are laboratories, and there are places like the Royal Institution, where scientific investigations and research and lecturing take place, but over and above these he will find a number of institutions which are rapidly springing into life, and increasing their number, such as polytechnics, in which there is beginning to be given teaching quite of a university kind, attended by men who are earning daily wages, such as clerks, who are unable to attend except in the evening, and the object of which institutions is to introduce amongst the poorer classes the beginning of a university teaching, with the opportunity added, where possible, of obtaining yet more systematic teaching. He will find that in these polytechnic institutions there is some teaching—which is rapidly growing—of a very high type, which a university might be ready to recognize. I know one case in south London where a polytechnic is teaching the application of mathematics to electricity in a way that would be worthy of the higher teaching of the university; in fact, it is given by a very distinguished graduate of Cambridge. Now, that is a movement which is coming into operation more and more widely. The Technical Education Board is spending £170,000 a year in technical education, and that board is deeply interested in this university. If this university is placed upon a satisfactory basis that board will come to its aid, and assist it in the development of its work. Now, Mr. Speaker, that being so, what is the object at which a Bill of this kind ought to aim? The object must be this: the teaching of which I speak is scattered, is heterogeneous, and is combined in no common whole. There are, for example, lectures on law given at University College by distinguished professors on the same topics and the same subjects as the lectures given close at hand in the Inns of Court. These compete, overlap, do the same work, and involve a large waste of educational force simply because there is no centre round which they can cluster and no co-ordination round which they can close. The London School of Economics—where there is some of the finest teaching of applied economics to be found in this country and probably in the world—in its variety overlaps the work of King's College and University College, and other institutions, and there is no common centre through which that work can be focused and regulated to the best advantage. Well, obviously, the first and primary function of this teaching university must be to do what it can to focus that kind of work and harmonize and distribute it so that it may be made to reach the largest number of students. Well, Sir, how is that to be done? There I think a certain amount of confusion enters the mind of my honourable friend who moved the rejection of this Bill, and he supposes that our object is probably the same as it was in Manchester and Liverpool. Why, Sir, if we were starting colleges in London, if we were introducing education of a university type for the first time, it would be perfectly true that you would require a great expenditure of money to start erecting buildings and employing professors and so on. When he asks "Where are the buildings and the money, and where are your professors to come from?" I venture to answer, "We have got the buildings, the professors, and the money, and all we want now is to organize and co-ordinate."

'My honourable friend has spoken somewhat doubtfully of the kind of teaching. Well, the intention is to have men like Professor Ramsay, the discoverer of argon, men, too, like the late Professor Huxley, who was a distinguished advocate of this Bill, and who gave evidence before the Royal Commission, in which he laid down a scheme for a university which is now practically embodied in the Bill. In it we propose that you shall have all the best teaching elements in London. Not only this but the students will have access to the great research establishments, and every inducement would be used to get their teaching such as to fit in with the hall-marking degrees of the university. The university will be in close relation with the polytechnics and the university extension movement, and you will be able to extend to the children of the working classes step by step the opportunity of receiving that cheap and efficient university education which is enjoyed in Scotland and Germany, but which we know too little of in this England of ours. You will have a chance of dealing with the problem of technical education, and of giving to workmen that class of knowledge which it is absolutely necessary we should give to them if we are to keep pace with the artisans of Germany and France. Those interested in the passing of this Bill hope to see it applied, not only in the direction of stimulating lectures during the day but also a system of evening lectures of a high university type, and in the nature of systematic training. At the other end you will have equal inducements of a different kind. Under the Bill power is taken to pick out and select the most famous teachers and mark them as professors of the university. I know of no greater distinction that could be given to a man who has reached eminence in the profession of university teaching than to be marked as a professor of the great University of London, of that great metropolis, which has the largest number of students to draw upon, which has a scope and ambition such as is given to no other university, and which may be, and I believe will be, the greatest institution of its kind, if this Bill passes, in the whole world. These are the reasons upon which those of us who are interested in the Bill appeal to the House to pass it. We feel that it is a Bill which is required, and which is absolutely necessary, and a Bill without which university education in London can make no progress. We feel that it is a stigma upon this metropolis that it should, in this respect, be behind all the other great capitals of the world. We feel that we have no chance of reaching the vast public which is available for university teaching and training unless you put this instrument into our hands. Without it we feel that we can take no step forward. We feel that we have produced a well-considered and well-thought-out measure, the result of much consideration and negotiation by some of the most distinguished men who have ever taken part in an attempt to solve this problem. We feel that we have got here a measure which in itself embodies the best tradition of the past and which completes the work of Bentham and Austin, of Mill and Grote, of the men who were the pioneers of university education in London; and that it is a measure which, if it is allowed to bear fruition, will place us in a position at least as good as that of any metropolis in the world.'

This speech completely changed the atmosphere in the House, and when Balfour, who had come in to help his friend, rose and appealed to the opponents to withdraw their opposition the motion against the second reading was withdrawn. Both Asquith and Chamberlain told Haldane afterwards that this was almost the only case within their recollection in which a single speech had turned opinion in the House. This did not end the matter, for when the Bill went upstairs to a grand committee it was found that the Irish members led by Mr. Healy were making trouble. Balfour then told Haldane that unless the Irish opposition could be reduced he would not be able to find time for the Bill. Interviewed by Haldane Healy said that he had no objection to the scheme for a London University but that Ireland had a more pressing university problem. He promised that if that problem were taken up he would support the London Bill. Balfour then asked Haldane to take up the problem of the Irish universities and to go to Ireland and get a solution of a difficulty which for years had confronted successive British govern-

ments. After making inquiries Haldane came to the conclusion that his negotiations must, if they were to be
successful, be conducted in strict privacy. He had in the summer accepted the chairmanship of a committee on the administration of death duties, and he persuaded his committee
that it would be advisable for him to investigate the application of the Act to Ireland on the spot. Haldane had naturally
consulted Morley, both as an old friend and old Chief Secretary, and Morley wrote to him in August: 'I hope that your
notion of an Irish visit ripens. I am sure that your trip will
interest and profit you and will advance the question as far
as the tortuous nature of certain gentry will permit.

'How often have I heard Mr. G. describe the mysterious
doings of the same gentry over the same question in 1873.
Let me repeat what I said the other day that no co-operation
with the politicians is worth a straw, until you know the
mind of Archbishop Walsh and of one or two of the other
prelates. It is their question, for the demand for a Roman
Catholic College or University is exclusively episcopal and
not a popular demand.

'Let me warn you that even the bishops are not all of them
keen, as I have been told. They suspect that their foe the
Jesuit means to get hold of the thing when it is set up, and I
expect he does.

'To your argument "that we should get the question out of
the way", I submit that there is no certainty that, if our party
were to come in, the question would be in the way. Irish
questions have a curious trick of bursting up and then sinking
down. It will depend on other things, on the general relations
between us and the Irish when the time comes. I must say for
my own part, I doubt if those relations would be improved
by any active demonstration of party interest in a Roman
Catholic College, but this would be sure to stir up the non-
cons both in the House of Commons and the constituencies
and I can see no counterbalancing gain to stirring up this dog.

'Of course there is no reason why you as a private member should not master the question, and for you to see some of the bishops, Redington, Dr. Delaney and Hamilton, could do nothing but good, only remember that there are deep and troubled waters unlike the limpid pool of the University of London!

'By the way, you recollect Edward Grey's declamation in your room against taking office, if we were dependent on the Irish vote. This involves and implies positions of some gravity.

'(1) It is equivalent to saying that the Irish vote is not to count in Parliament; it disenfranchises Ireland and she might as well be excluded.

'(2) It means a return to the old way of governing Ireland by a tacit or open understanding between the two English parties united against the Irish party.

'This understanding it is Mr. G.'s glory to have banished and broken.

'Grey and all Home Rulers who use his language about taking office, ought to realise these considerations.

'I hope that in writing to you the other day I gave you no impression that I am not alive to the signal merits of your performance in passing the London University Bill. May your new effort be a like success, but you have a far more formidable task.'

With this warning in his ears Haldane left for Dublin in October, ostensibly to deal with the question of death duties.

The position of higher education in Ireland was that there were two universities in existence. Dublin University, associated exclusively with Trinity College, and mainly episcopalian in character, and the Royal University. Trinity College Haldane likened to the Ark of the Covenant. 'Any Government which sets its hand upon it will perish.' The Royal University was, like the old London University, a purely examining body. There were a number of colleges distributed over Ireland, such as the Queen's Colleges of Belfast, Cork,

and Galway, University College, Dublin, Catholic in atmosphere and government, Maynooth, which trained Catholic
priests; the Magee College in Londonderry and the Presbyterian College in Belfast, which trained ministers for the
Irish Presbyterian Church. Neither the Catholics of southern
Ireland nor the Protestants of the north were content with the
existing arrangement, which both felt was overweighted in
favour of Dublin. Both wanted a university with control of
both internal and external teaching. The problem was the old
one, of how to get Protestants and Catholics, north and south,
to agree on a scheme. Haldane's plan was to apply to Ireland
such a system as had proved acceptable to London and to
constitute two universities, one with its seat in the south, the
other in the north, the first being designed mainly to attract
Catholics, the second Protestants. Having ascertained from
the Chancellor of the Exchequer that there was a sum of
£50,000 a year, available for an agreed scheme of higher
education in Ireland, from the funds remaining after the
disestablishment of the Irish Church, he foreshadowed a
scheme on these general lines:

1. Leaving Dublin University and Trinity College un-
touched, to persuade the Royal University to consent to the
substitution for itself of two new universities—one to have
its seat in Dublin, the other to have its seat in Belfast.

2. These universities to have each a teaching (internal) and
an examining (external) side. In this way those Catholics and
Protestants, in whatever part of Ireland, who were not able to
attend the lectures of recognized teachers, would be able to
present themselves for external degrees.

3. These universities to have open constitutions, i.e. not to
be stamped denominational in the face of their constitutions,
but to be *de facto*, though not *de jure*, the one Catholic and the
other Protestant.

With this scheme in his pocket Haldane started on a long
series of negotiations, first with the heads of the University of

Dublin and of the Royal University, then with Archbishop Walsh and with the Catholic hierarchy, and found both to be ready to accept his plan with modifications which would not affect the general scheme. He then went to Belfast, where he held a similar series of meetings with those concerned with higher education in the north, and there he obtained a similar measure of agreement. He then came back to Dublin and again saw Archbishop Walsh, who told him that all turned now on the agreement of Cardinal Logue, the Papal Legate. The archbishop told him that he had arranged for him to make a secret visit to the cardinal by night. Haldane kept a detailed diary of his negotiations, which he sent to Balfour, and this concludes:

'I left Dublin for Armagh by the evening train, and was received by the Cardinal in private. I presented letters from Mr. John Morley and Mr. Healy. The Cardinal examined the scheme in detail, and after doing so expressed, somewhat to my surprise, exactly the same views as Archbishop Walsh. He spoke quite as cordially, and, as far as I can judge, as genuinely. I inferred that he must have had a conversation with the other Bishops, after parting from Archbishop Walsh at Maynooth, and was possibly influenced by the strong appeal made by Mr. Healy's letter. At all events he took the same line as the Archbishop of Dublin. He had evidently devoted some study to the matter. He said that the formal approval of the hierarchy would be required to such a scheme, but that this would be a formality which he could obtain by convening a meeting, and that I might take it that, if such a scheme could be successfully brought forward in England, "matters would be made easy in Ireland, so far as the Catholic Church was concerned."

'After supping with his Eminence, I left in his carriage for the station, and took the train for Kingston.

'I entertain little doubt that the various individuals whom I saw are sincerely desirous for reform, and, being sceptical of the willingness of the British Government to deal with a question of rapidly-growing importance, are anxious to seize any chance there is at present of getting it speedily settled on such lines as those above indicated. I do not think there should be any difficulty in framing a detailed scheme on this basis.'

Haldane was particularly delighted with his success with Cardinal Logue, of which he wrote to his mother: 'Last night I cleared my last hurdle, and return having accomplished what no Irish Secretary has ever succeeded in doing, and what even Mr. Gladstone failed in. The Irish Hierarchy, the Nationalist Party, and the Irish Presbyterians, have been brought to agree on a scheme of Irish University Education.

'I left Dublin in great secrecy with a warning from Archbishop Walsh in my ears that I should probably fail with Cardinal Logue. I descended on him at night at Armagh and lo! in half an hour we had settled everything in accordance with my scheme and were sitting down, he in his Cardinal's red hat and I in a suit of dittos, over two dozen oysters (it is Friday) and a bottle of champagne. If the Government have any pluck, of which I am doubtful, we ought to succeed now in solving this great problem. Healy and Dillon are much moved over my mission and I foresee a statue in Phoenix Park.'

As soon as Balfour had digested this memorandum he asked Haldane to put its recommendation into the form of a Bill, and this he did with the help of Sir Courtney Ilbert, but when the Bill came before the Cabinet the majority, fearful of arousing religious discord, refused to sponsor it, and the draft remained in a pigeon-hole until ten years later, when the Liberals, again in power, proposed to take up the problem of the Irish universities. Haldane then produced his Bill and Mr. Birrell, then Chief Secretary, took it up and it was passed through both Houses with little alteration.

Meantime the University of London Bill had become an Act, and under the Act a commission had been set up under Haldane's friend, Lord Davey, to draft statutes and regulations for the reconstituted university. These were approved, not without rumblings of discontent between the rival parties which lasted for a good many years. Haldane recognized that the new scheme was a compromise, which he did not think ideal, in that in his opinion the Senate was too large to be an effective governing body, and he thought also that the external side had more than its due representation, but he believed that the importance of the teaching side would before long become manifest and would assert itself in the government of the university. He soon found that several of his professional colleagues on the Council of University College considered that he had sold the pass and refused to accept his compromise as the best solution attainable. He therefore resigned from that body in 1899.

With the University of London Act in being and the statutes in force it was necessary to provide a home for the increased administrative staff which the new constitution and functions of the university made necessary. At the time the university was uncomfortably housed at the back of Burlington House, and while a search was being made in London for suitable quarters the Prince of Wales sent for Haldane and asked him to use his offices to get the university to take over a portion of the Imperial Institute, which had been founded as part of the celebrations of Queen Victoria's first jubilee, with the object of fostering intercourse and trade between the colonies and the mother country. But South Kensington was not a business quarter and the high commissioners and agents of the colonies preferred to have their offices nearer the City. The Imperial Institute was in financial difficulties and the Prince of Wales, who was its president, was anxious to have those mitigated and the institute put to greater use. He was delighted when Haldane conducted the negotiations with the university successfully and so began an association which continued until the King's death. Thus ended the first piece of constructive work to which Haldane had put his hand.

While the protracted negotiations which resulted in these two Bills were going on he had been invited in 1896 to stand as a Liberal for the Lord Rectorship of Edinburgh University. He accepted with no expectation of being able to break the succession of Conservative Lord Rectors. That was to come later, and in the event Lord Balfour of Burleigh was returned with 990 votes to Haldane's 771. Two years later the university conferred on him the honorary degree of Doctor of Laws, the first of many honorary degrees, and that which gave him the greatest pleasure.

Despite all this work, which would have occupied fully the time of most men, his lessened preoccupation with the business of Parliament gave him more leisure than he had enjoyed since he came to London, and he became addicted to week-ending in the houses of his growing circle of friends, and was more often at Cloanden, where he delighted in playing the host, and most of all in his association with his mother and sister. He was a good and keen shot and always enjoyed the autumn shooting in Perthshire. His professional income was mounting up and it gave him real pleasure to be able to assist in the development of the family property. He was pleased when his brother William purchased the adjoining property of Foswell and took an active interest in consequential improvements at Cloan.

Appreciation of his mother and of his home by his friends always delighted him, and his pride in the latter was sometimes the subject of mild chaff. Curzon wrote in reply to a letter congratulating him on his appointment as Viceroy of India: 'In Château Haldane, if you are there entertaining sportsmen, socialists, and society beauties, I must intrude with a line of thanks for your kindly message. I am glad you think I chose well. My heart has for years been in the work and the subject, and public life teaches one lesson more than other, that sincerity is that which helps to success. We look to seeing you on an elephant and beguiling you with the *nautch* girls.'

In the summer of 1898 a development in international affairs still further widened the breach between the two wings of the Liberal Party. Kitchener had, by his victory at Omdurman, completed the re-conquest of the Soudan, when he found that a small French expedition under Marchand, coming from Central Africa, had reached the White Nile at Fashoda, and hoisted the French flag. Kitchener had gone down to Fashoda by steamer and told Marchand that he was in Anglo-Egyptian territory and must withdraw. This produced an explosion in France and relations with that country were for a time dangerously strained. It happened that during Lord Rosebery's administration Sir Edward Grey, as Under-Secretary at the Foreign Office, had had reason to declare that an advance of France to the Nile would be regarded by England and Egypt as 'an unfriendly act'. That statement had horrified the Left wing of the Cabinet, but as at the time when it was made there was no indication of preparations by France for such an advance it had been allowed to pass. Now the situation envisaged by Grey had arisen and had created an international crisis. Rosebery and his followers at once decided to support the Government. Both he and Asquith took early opportunities of expressing their agreement with the Government's demand that Marchand's little force must be withdrawn.

Before making his first public statement Rosebery sent for Haldane and together they went through the draft of the speech. One part of this speech Rosebery delivered exactly as Haldane had drafted it: 'If the nations of the world are under the impression that the ancient spirit of Great Britain is dead or that her resources are weakened, or her population less determined than ever it was to maintain the rights and honour of its flag, they make a mistake which can only end in a disastrous conflagration. The strength of Ministers in this country with regard to Foreign affairs does not lie in the votes they command in either House of Parliament, it lies in the intrepid spirit of a united people.'

Harcourt, while refraining from open condemnation of the Government policy, classed this passage as pure jingoism. France was at the time riven by the Dreyfus case and was not prepared to go to extremes, so that after some weeks of excited feeling on both sides of the Channel the French Government agreed to order Marchand to withdraw. But the rift in the Liberal Party remained and was to become patent on the outbreak of the South African War.

Chapter VI

THE SOUTH AFRICAN WAR—THE GIFFORD
LECTURES

1899 to 1902

In the second week of December 1898 the political world was stirred by the publication of correspondence between Sir William Harcourt and Mr. John Morley, in which the former announced that his position in the House of Commons had become impossible, and his resignation from the leadership of the party in the House. Mr. Morley expressed his concurrence with his leader, and a little later he announced that he had concurred because he saw that the Liberal Party was being infected by dangerous doctrines in foreign policy. This was a direct challenge to the Liberal Imperialists and Haldane was at first disposed to take up the glove. He used his best efforts to get Lord Rosebery to return and lead the party, with Asquith as his lieutenant in the Commons. He wrote to his mother: 'I went down to Durdans to-day and had a long walk and talk on the downs with Lord R. He is not at all clear as to his future, unless he can, which he is trying to do, but is not at all sure that he can succeed in doing, remodel the Liberal Party. It certainly needs it. I tried to persuade him that he could give the party and the country the guidance it wants to-day and that, with Asquith to lead the party in the House, he and we should soon be in a strong position, but I had no success.' He therefore agreed with the proposal that the leadership should be offered to Sir Henry Campbell-Bannerman, but without much enthusiasm. He wrote to Mr. Spender, the editor of the *Westminster Gazette*, on Christmas Day, 1898: 'For your own ear. C.B. is likely to accept with full knowledge of what is expected of him provided Dr. Montague advises him that he may. This is not quite certain but it will be decided in the first week of January when C.B. comes up. It is not the best, but it may do.'

Dr. Montague gave Sir Henry a clean bill of health and on February 6, 1899, he was elected at a party meeting at the Reform Club to the leadership. But the harmony in the party thus obtained was short-lived. As the relations with the Boer republics became more and more critical the old differences between the Liberal Imperialists and the remainder of the party became more and more evident. Haldane was always of opinion that the negotiations had in their early stages been clumsily handled by Chamberlain, but he was in regular correspondence with Sir Alfred Milner and was well acquainted with his side of the story, and gradually he became convinced that to give way to Kruger would be disastrous. The number of cases which he had to handle before the Privy Council on behalf of colonial governments was now more numerous than ever and this brought him into touch with their representatives. He became convinced that the general trend of opinion in the colonies was Liberal in outlook and he saw in unity of the Empire a great power behind the causes he had most at heart. He also became convinced that to allow Kruger to throw over the Sand River Convention and finance his government by taxes levied on British settlers who were allowed no political rights, would raise in the colonies the cry 'To your tents, O Israel; now see to thine own house, David'. He therefore regarded war with the Boer republics as the lesser of two evils. When on October 9, 1899, President Kruger's ultimatum was published and this was accompanied by the news that the Boers had forces assembled on the frontier for the invasion both of Cape Colony and Natal, Haldane made up his mind that the time had come when he must openly support the Government and on October 11, on the eve of the Boer invasion, he went down to his constituency and there explained his attitude:

'Let us', he said, 'realise in the first place what is the true issue which is dividing people upon the question of the present moment. There is one party which says that the war, which threatens, is a wicked war, a war which ought never to have been contemplated and should even now be averted. There is another set of people who maintain equally strongly that not only is this not such a war, but one which, if it were necessary in the last resort, it would be a moral duty to wage. It is between these two views that we have to choose. It is a situation in which people stand at the parting of the ways, and the ways lead in very different directions.'

He went on to make his choice clear. Kruger, he said, in accepting the Sand River Convention, under which he obtained independence for the Transvaal, had promised rights and privileges to British subjects in the Transvaal equal to those enjoyed by the Boers. That promise had been broken. 'This was not', he said, 'a question of depriving a country of self-government which it has enjoyed for years. It is not a question of "Civis Romanus sum", of swaggering down the High Street of the world with arms akimbo, looking out for grievances. I hate that as much as anyone. It is a question of obtaining equal rights between the Uitlanders and Boers, who are in the position of having the monopoly of political power. If this country does not interfere to redress the growing oppression and abuses that are being committed at the present time, we shall have the whole of South Africa in danger, and the race question upon us with an intensity which you cannot realise at present.'

Three days later he explained his position more intimately in a letter from Cloanden to Mr. Spender. 'I must tell you that nothing for a long time has caused me such deep anxiety and emotion as this question. Two months ago I should have pronounced against this war, a month since, while doubtful,

I held the issue to be one that diplomacy could solve. It was not until after the dispatch of September 8[1] that I felt that we were being impelled along a path which must branch into two that were widely divergent, with no middle way. I then shut myself up here to scan and weigh the two alternatives and to study, with the materials which I could obtain, the story of the last few years. I saw no one till about ten days ago when I got Asquith to come here to talk it all out. The result of this period of seclusion has been to convince me that the question is one of *fact* pure and simple. My reading of the story is that since the days of President Burgers there has been no desire or intention on the part of the Boers to redress grievances, much less to give the franchise that Kruger promised in 1881. The situation seems to me to have been one in which the determination to assert ascendancy grows with the growth of the Uitlander population in wealth and numbers, and I see no sign that this determination has ceased to grow.

'I agree that the Government miscalculated the force with which they had to deal and the risk they were undertaking. I think they had to face both the force and the risks and that events have shown that there was no way out. I think Chamberlain's dispatches have allowed a false issue to be raised and have put us in a worse position than we should have been in. All the Unionists I have met agree that he is a hopeless diplomatist where delicacy is requisite. The business of the Opposition was to keep a free hand, while showing that it was in earnest about the grievances and had its own mode of procuring their redress. To ask, like Campbell-Bannerman, what we were going to war about was ridiculous

[1]C9521. 1899, o. 64. A telegraphic dispatch from Mr. J. Chamberlain conveying the unanimous decision of the Cabinet. It offered to accept limited political rights for the Uitlanders provided that an inquiry, either joint or unilateral, showed that their rights would not be encumbered by conditions nullifying them.

with the country in its present temper. We could never get people to acquiesce in 100,000 of the British nation, owning three-quarters of the property in the Transvaal, being kept and treated in the fashion Kruger is insisting on doing.

'I agree that Kruger was face to face with the loss of Boer ascendancy, but we should not be fighting against that ascendancy if he had not made it an engine of oppression. It is a question of sentiment, as much as of material hardship, which he has raised by his impossible statesmanship. Had he treated the Uitlanders properly we should not now be asking for the franchise with the result of threatening his ascendancy. The Transvaal has never of recent years been a decent place for foreigners to live in. You cannot ignore the feeling which systematic ill treatment produces on people like ours. Why do they go there? Because the Transvaal was in the midst of British territory and open to them by the invitation of the Boer Government who were willing to have the Uitlanders come and make money. They came there originally when things were comparatively easy for them and the conditions have been made more and more galling almost every year. It is the 100,000 British Uitlanders, who do not and never will live in Park Lane, and the hardship of whose case is testified to not only by men like Wessels but by Hofmeyer and Schreiner and by Joubert himself, who stir me. I admit that Boer independence is threatened. I do not wonder at their ultimatum, I do not blame the Orange Free State for joining. Blood is thick. But what I do say is that the whole responsibility for a situation which need never have arisen rests with Kruger and his obstinate Burghers. They brought about what I deplore and hate, and they, when they finally refuse redress, drive moderate people to the other and only way. For sit down in the face of this we cannot. It is the refusal to meet us in any way which has made me now hopeless and convinced me that the situation of to-day could have been postponed only and not avoided.

'Of course we shall now have an unjust attitude in the country. The Boers will be traduced, no credit will be given to the Free State, for what seems to me to be not conspiracy but heroism, and there will be great difficulty in averting demands for such an ending as will revolt people like you and myself alike, by its injustice and its inexpediency. But for this avalanche I blame Kruger. A little kindness and forethought would have averted it all, but there was no kindness and no forethought. Now you see why C.B. drove me to plunge. I have preserved the right of criticism but I cannot honestly say that the faults of the diplomacy of the Government have made any great difference. I did not know until I had spoken to my constituents, whom in August I did my best to keep quiet, what a strong deep feeling there was—not jingoism but the sense of wrong done to them in the person of some brother or nephew or son who had been ill used in the Transvaal. It is this which has made Scotland practically solid in condemnation of C.B.'s speeches, for which I blame not so much him as the silly decision of the ex-cabinet not to commit themselves. There is nothing now to be done but to take one of two diverging ways, to condemn the Government for waging a wicked and unnecessary war or to support them in a position into which events much more than their own want of foresight have driven them.'

This attitude Haldane preserved consistently throughout the war. It meant for him a definite breach with his leader and with a large section of his party, and, as he remained a Liberal and had no intention of joining the Conservatives, he took the risk of destroying any chance he had of obtaining office in a future Liberal Government. Fifteen years later the men whom he then supported were either to make, or acquiesce in the making of, the charge that he was a traitor. Having, as he described it, 'burnt his little boat' by his speech to his constituents on October 11 he supported the Government both in the House and in many speeches up and down the country. Rosebery and Grey both took the same line and Asquith approved, with rather less emphasis in public, but of all the Liberal Imperialists he was the one who most clearly and cogently maintained that it was the true function of Liberalism to protect the rights of an oppressed minority.

In spite of the additional calls all this made upon his time and his growing practice he was able to return to a piece of work which he had long had in mind, a more serious presentation of his philosophy than he had yet attempted. The first draft of this, which later formed the basis of his Gifford Lectures, he sent to Balfour, who returned it with the following: 'I hope the manuscript came in time—I read it with the greatest interest, though with less care than I should have liked to give it. But you can guess under what pressure I have recently been working.

'I think the style excellent, and the success with which you have avoided technicalities in a discussion so inevitably technical is really admirable. You know I have never been able, in spite of much temptation, heartily to acquiesce in the idealist standpoint, but I do not think a more lucid defence of it has ever been put forward. The sort of difficulties I feel are of this kind:

'(i) Have you any right to describe thought as the *prius* of the universe? Such a phrase seems to me to involve the categories of "Time" and "Causation", and therefore to be wholly unfitted to describe the inseparable elements of Reality.

'In the same way is it proper to talk of the *activity* of Reason or of Will, or to discuss whether this fundamental activity is Reason rather than Will, or Will rather than Reason? This seems to me mere psychology.

'(ii) You talk in several places of different "planes of intelligence"—e.g. of a worm, of an elephant, of a man, of an angel, and so forth. Any such distinction may be relevant to the natural history of Mind and to various theories of development. But surely it has no meaning when applied to the "Subject", involving, as it does, among other difficulties the existence of subjects of many different kinds, and all numerically distinct.

'(iii) As it seems to me, the idealist theory in your version of it, as in others, is consistent only with the "solipsism" which you repudiate. There is only one subject known to each of us *as* subject, namely ourselves, and not only is there no evidence of the existence of other subjects, but such existence appears on the idealistic hypothesis intrinsically absurd.

'(iv) You avoid the charge brought against Idealism of being a "ballet of bloodless categories" by assuming an ἄπειρον but is an ἄπειρον anything more than Kant's "Thing in itself" under a new name? I thought that the idealists had hounded it out of Philosophy. Frankly, I do not see how this is to be worked into a system: nor do I see how, if it be worked in, any philosophical theology is possible except a kind of refined Manichaeism.

'(v) I say nothing in detail about the theory of "categories"—waiting till I see this worked out with regard to the special sciences in later parts of your book. You will probably be grateful to me, as I should think these rather hasty and crude criticisms are already as much as the most long-suffering patience could endure!'

To this Haldane replied in January 1900: 'Thank you much for having written about the proofs of the book with such pressure upon you. Things look better, but I shall not be happy until, and it has got to be done somehow, the Tugela battle has been fought and won. I fear we cannot hope for this excepting at a very heavy loss of life.

'The town of Auchterarder is a strange place. The Hopetown station-master, who was shot as a Boer spy by Methuen, is the son of an Auchterarder citizen, and the son of another is fighting against us with the Orange Free Staters.

'I am glad you have not found the style of the book very obscure. I intend, if and when I manage to get the whole finished, to recast it, and so gain distinctness in thread of argument.

'(i) Ought I to talk of thought as the *prius* of the Universe? It is not a good expression. It means and can only mean logical *prius*. All it expresses is that reality resolves itself into being Object for the Subject—to use Schopenhauer's phrase —which is perhaps your own criticism, made in both your books and in an old article of Green in *Mind*, that there is no clear meaning to be got of the phrase "activity of thought" excepting a psychological one. But, with Seth in his article on Munsterburg's Psychology in "Man's place in the Cosmos", I doubt whether psychology gives anything but an artificial picture. The source of the difficulty seems to me to be an inherent one. There can be no presentation of thought excepting a pictorial one, and this can give only the object, never the subject. The latter is the asymptotic limit. The relationship is the *conditio sine qua non* of objectivity, but it is only abstractedly transformed that it can be made object for intelligence at the plane of self-conscious intelligence. Now as to (ii) the expression *plane* I think is a legitimate one. Self-consciousness such as ours is the closed circle out of which we cannot escape. But we can determine the reasons of its limits although we cannot *pictorially* present a condition of things in which the subject should be directly conscious of itself as subject. Planes of thought are not *things* numerically distinct, they are rather standpoints which, logically speaking, are potentially possible concurrently. In the world of reality self-consciousness is at the plane we pictorially present to ourselves. There is neither one subject nor many subjects. It is only in the objective and external world that we get the distinction of individuals and species, and these at a late stage and as a derivative of the abstract processes of intelligence.

'(iii) And therefore solipsism, the essence of which is that it identifies a single objective self with the subject, falls to the ground when it is realised that the subject cannot be and is not pictorially presented.

'(iv) The ἄπειρον is only the limit which the plane at which we are in intelligence discloses. Logically, though not pictorially, that is in objective psychology, we can conceive intelligence at a plane at which it would be conscious of itself as wholly constructive of its object.

'No one of these replies can be made distinct without more expansion than I am willing to inflict upon you just now, and even so, I am fully conscious of the difficulties which arise. But these difficulties notwithstanding I feel that it is so, and so only that an intelligible theory of the universe can be worked out, and I hope some day to get not the whole way (for the language and capacities of *my* plane of intelligence are not adequate) but some further way towards establishing them.'

But the book had to be put aside for a time, for early in 1900 he became involved in two matters of great public importance. His close association with the representatives of colonial governments had long convinced him that two of the chief factors in keeping the Empire together were the Crown and the Law. He conceived the idea of strengthening the latter link by a reorganization of the Supreme Court of Appeal so as to include in it permanent representation of the colonies. His scheme was brought within the region of practical politics by the proposal to federalize Australia, from which an important delegation had come to England to support the Australian Commonwealth. This delegation was entertained at the Colonial Institute and Haldane propounded his views in an address entitled 'Federal Australia within the Empire', and followed this a little later by another address delivered in Edinburgh on the 'Appellate Courts of the Empire'. Both of these were included in a collection of addesses published in 1902 under the title *Education and Empire*. Ere this he had succeeded in interesting Balfour in his proposal and through him Mr. Joseph Chamberlain, who took the matter up with enthusiasm, and the Colonial Office formally announced that it was proposed to amalgamate the Judicial Committee of the Privy Council with the House of Lords and provide for some representation of the colonies.

Difficulties, however, arose in the negotiations with the Australian representatives, and the proposal did not become fully operative until Haldane himself became Lord Chancellor. The other public service to which he was called arose out of two great cases in which he appeared before the Court of Appeal. Of his professional work at the Bar I have said little, for Haldane has given us in his autobiography a full summary of his most interesting cases, and this a layman could not hope to better.

These two cases were both concerned with high-explosives. In the first he had appeared for Sir Andrew Noble against the Crown, and in the second for the Crown against Maxim. In these cases he had shown such mastery of the technicalities of explosives that when, in May 1900, the War Office, as the result of the experiences of the war, decided to appoint a committee to advise on the best smokeless propellant for the Army he was invited by Lord Lansdowne to become a member, under the chairmanship of Lord Rayleigh. So Haldane entered the War Office for the first time, and obtained an insight into one side of its work.

The work of the Explosives Committee interested him greatly and his enthusiasm for education made him wish to share his interest. It was indeed his general practice to use his power of mastering and explaining technical detail to try to arouse public interest in the particular problem with which he was at the time concerned. So when he felt himself ready to expound the technicalities of explosives he took advantage of a visit of his brother John to announce 'A Public Lecture on

Explosives by Mr. R. B. Haldane, M.P., illustrated by experiments conducted by Professor J. Haldane', to be given at
Auchterarder. When he and his brother arrived at the hall he
found that the police, alarmed by the title of the lecture, had
cleared the first three rows of seats and put a constable in
charge of them.

He was naturally much concerned at this time by the fate of
his cousin Aylmer, afterwards General Sir Aylmer Haldane,
who early in the war had been taken prisoner in Natal, and he
importuned the Government to obtain facilities to send
money and food to him in his prison in Pretoria. In July he
went to the Royal Garden Party at Buckingham Palace and
had his last sight of Queen Victoria. Of this he wrote to his
mother: 'I had several close views of the Queen at the Garden
Party. She drove in a low carriage round and round with the
Princess of Wales. She looked old but very well, was most
gracious and very queenly. It is hardly yet realised what she
has done for the Crown merely by being a real Queen during
her long reign.'

Towards the end of July the so-called pro-Boer section of
the Liberal Party openly challenged the Government in the
House. Of this Haldane wrote to Rosebery:

'Grey arranged with me that I should write fully to let you
know what has happened in the House this afternoon. As
you will see from the newspapers Wilfred Lawson and Reid
made stiff speeches in support of the reduction of the Colonial
Office vote moved by the former. The old split of October
reappeared. C.B., despite pressure by H. Gladstone to vote
against Lawson's reduction, insisted on a general abstention.
The party refused to acquiesce. In a small House 37 Liberals
followed Grey in support of the Government. About the
same number voted with Channing and Lawson and Reid,
and some but not, I think, very many walked out. Asquith,
who was with us but did not vote, and Grey think that C.B.
was riding for a fall. He may change his mind in the morning

but our impression is that he means to resign and set off for Marienbad on the advice of Maclagan, his good physician. If so what has happened has merely anticipated what, later on, would have happened and it is now necessary to see what should be done.

'(1) The party is not likely to agree on any leader in the House. Grey and I think there will be two sections now. Asquith is pretty sure to be the *de facto* leader. He took me aside to-night and from what he said I think he is ready to act as chief of our group in the House, should C.B. not go on.

'Now what he and Grey and I are all keen about is your own position. I do not know whether you will consider that what has happened makes a difference to you. But if you choose to emerge and lead those Liberals who may be called "Lord R.'s friends", with Asquith and Grey as lieutenants in the House, I think things will work out. Of course a mere section cannot hope to win at the next election. But it would probably be, from the first, not only a large but a growing section. The others would form some sort of organisation like a Radical Committee. This would probably steadily dwindle. *We* have the machinery and the Whips and the future, and this means that we grow and become the party. What we want is a policy of criticism for the Election which will now probably be in October. And this seems a good chance for the purgation of the party.

'Grey and I think it would be unwise to try to rope it all in. The attempt would simply fail. It is best to say that we are going to take our own way and leave who likes to follow.

'I shall be going to stay with Asquith over Sunday and should like a sign from you. We will come up to see you if you would like it. Of course C.B. may change his mind to-night, but I do not think so. He tried to do the impossible. It now remains to consider another way.'

In fact if Campbell-Bannerman ever contemplated resignation at this time he changed his mind, while Rosebery kept to his resolution not to resume an active part in politics. So one more attempt by Haldane to consolidate his political friends into a group under Rosebery's leadership failed.

A few days later he received a surprising offer: 'Last night', he wrote to his mother, 'I was sent for by the Government. Sir Alfred Milner had telegraphed to them earnestly requesting that I should come out to South Africa as British Commissioner to settle certain important questions, which are about to arise relative to the settlement with the Boer Republics and the organisation of some form of interim government. I should have to set out for Cape Town and Pretoria, starting at once. Important as is the duty to respond, if possible, to an appeal from the Government on a matter of this importance, I felt bound to decline in the present state of politics, and after taking six hours to decide I told Mr. Chamberlain so. He said that the Government would give me almost anything to go and that Milner thought me peculiarly fitted for the work which was delicate and required decision. But the adverse considerations were too heavy. I have taken risks with my political career and this might well finish it, for I cannot be beholden to the Conservatives for advancement.'

He had in fact, as his letter to Rosebery shows, already an inkling that Chamberlain was proposing an early appeal to the country on the grounds that the war was over. When on September 18 the Government announced the dissolution of Parliament he wrote to Spender: 'Chamberlain will disgust and split the Unionist majority before two years are over. He is dragging them into dirty paths.' The 'khaki' election of 1900 was fought with unusual bitterness, and the Conservatives went to the country with the cry, 'Every vote given to a Liberal is a vote given to the Boers', and not even Liberal Imperialists, who had consistently supported the Government, were exempted from this attack. In Haddingtonshire this had little effect upon electors, who had been kept informed of their member's views from the very beginning of the war, and Haldane was returned with an adequate majority. Indeed, the election only increased the Conservative majority at the dissolution by four.

In this election Haldane was deprived of the support of his old friend and chief political ally in Haddington, Mr. J. D. Lawrie of Monkrigg, who had helped him from the days of his first appeal to the constituency and became one of his closest and most intimate friends. Monkrigg was his campaigning centre in each of his elections. After a long illness borne with great courage Mr. Lawrie passed away, to Haldane's great grief, in July 1901.

Soon after Haldane returned to London for the opening of Parliament he wrote to his mother: 'Yesterday I was at Tring, where I met Mr. Adrian Hofmeyr, a cousin of the Boer leader, but himself an Afrikander supporter of British policy. I had much talk with him. He was in prison in Pretoria with Aylmer, for whom he has great admiration. He says very definitely that the Boers meant war and that its coming was only a matter of time. They meant to choose their own moment for invading Natal, and the dispatch of our reinforcements settled the choice of the moment. He says he is quite certain of this from talks which he had with Boer officials while a prisoner in Pretoria. It is a lamentable miserable business, but the least of two terrible evils, and that is my conclusion of the matter.'

With his opinion thus confirmed he refused to support Sir Henry Campbell-Bannerman's attack upon Sir Alfred Milner, and in that he was consistently supported by Sir Edward Grey.

He wrote to Milner in December: 'It may be of interest to you to hear the result of the short session from someone, who, while doubtful how far the Government has energetically supported it, supports your own policy in South African affairs. Anyhow, this letter needs no acknowledgement. You have more than enough on hand apart from answering letters. The result of the Election has been, I think, to deepen the sense of the gravity of the situation in the House of Commons. You must not judge the Opposition by the speeches of Harcourt and Bryce. They do not represent the bulk or anything like the bulk of Opposition opinion. That bulk was represented by the refusal to divide on the amendment moved (most mild in character) after hearing Chamberlain's speech. A minority would have divided and would, if they dared, have moved for your recall. But they turned out to be a very small minority indeed. Grey may be taken as an exponent of the views of the majority of Liberals about South Africa, and representing as he does the opinion of Rosebery this means that we have won in the Election. On the Government side there is unrest. Dissatisfied aspirants to office, people who represent a genuine dislike of the Government attitude on the question of Ministers and their private business entanglements, and critics of the general slackness, represent an element of support that sits very loose. But of a change there is no chance. There is so far no alternative Government ready or, for the time being, practically possible. What I most fear is that it seems to me that above all things you need money, and lots of it, to establish good government in the two late republics. Beach plus Harcourt plus the heterogeneous malcontents may give trouble over this. Those who are prepared to trust you far must see what they can do. The only thing I wish to say in this connection is that if, the white heat which things are in in South Africa notwithstanding, it is possible for you to make a friendly utterance to the Boers, it will lighten our task here. But our task here is a light burden in comparison with the difficulties you have to cope with . . . that I know. You are not the ruler while the soldiers are in command. I only wish to assure you that, if things continue as they are, you need not be afraid of the adverse majority in the Opposition. We argued that issue out and won in it at the Election. Our attitude to the Government is very different from that towards yourself. If you ask for money for the good of the two annexed territories I believe that you will get it easily. What hinders, and the only thing that really hinders, is that the Government have gone down 30 per cent. in popularity since the Election. People are beginning to long to turn to someone else. Were it not that they dread the influence of Harcourt (really very small) and the feebleness of Campbell-Bannerman, there would be a great reaction. The point is that, so far as I can judge, it would not be against yourself or what you have done. But of all this and the assistance which a deliverance of friendliness to the Boers, if such a deliverance be, or it may well not be practicable, I feel you probably know. *Our* confidence is not abated by a hair's breadth.'

The breach in the Liberal ranks very soon widened. Early in 1901 it became clear that the war was far from over. In an endeavour to circumscribe the guerrilla warfare, which spread from the frontier of Portuguese East Africa into Cape Colony, Boer farms which had been used as bases for attacks upon our communications were burned and Boer women and children were collected into concentration camps in which their disregard of ordinary sanitary precautions and the difficulty of providing adequate medical control produced a very high rate of mortality. This procedure Sir Henry Campbell-Bannerman described in a speech in June as 'methods of barbarism'. Mr. Lloyd George followed by moving the adjournment of the House to call attention to the methods by which the war was being carried on, and in his speech made a bitter attack on Sir Alfred Milner. Haldane rose and dissociated himself with the criticisms both of Milner and of the generals in the field. War, he said, was of necessity a brutal business, but he regretted the use by his leader of the word 'barbarous' of methods which were militarily necessary if the war was to be brought to a successful conclusion. Nor was this the only cause of difference. Haldane's work in the War Office brought him into touch with many of our lead-

ing soldiers and he was coming more and more to the conclusion that one of the main causes of our failures in South
Africa was defective organization. Sir Henry Campbell-
Bannerman, as an old War Minister had an affection for the
War Office, and great confidence in his friend Sir Ralph
Knox, its permanent Under-Secretary, and would not have it
that the War Office was to blame. This difference acted as a
spur to Haldane, who began to examine carefully constructive proposals for the improvement of our military organization. In a speech delivered to his constituents in October 1901
he advocated a generous settlement with the Boers, but insisted that there must be a reasonable interval of time in
which matters might settle down. He roundly refused to
support the demand of the Left wing of his party for Sir
Alfred Milner's recall and advocated Milner's policy of South
African federation as the object at which we should aim. He
then turned to the subject of imperial defence and for the
first time gave an outline in public of the proposals to which
he was later himself to give effect. A strong navy, he said, was
the greatest guarantee of peace that we could have. The
tradition of our country was that our strength lay not in military but in naval supremacy. Given that, we wanted also to
see that the intellectual equipment of our naval commanders
was up to the level of the times. We required a small army
which was extremely efficient, mobile, and capable of
foreign service, and a clear policy of defence elaborated by
the Imperial Defence Committee.

The public was now much concerned with the defects in
our military organization which the South African War had
exposed, and there was keen discussion, which was to continue for many years, as to how these defects could best be
remedied. The country was interested and surprised to find a
Liberal making serious contributions to this discussion. Haldane's attitude and speeches throughout the South African
War had made him a public figure. He had long been known

in his profession as one of the ablest and most successful barristers of his day, he had for many years been listened to with attention and respect in the House of Commons, he was freely consulted by those responsible for government, and was well known both to philosophers and educationalists. Now the cumulative effect of the reputation he had made for himself in these various and varied circles, combined with the courage and good sense of his public utterances during the war, began to bring his name before the man in the street.

Asquith wrote of him at this time to a friend: 'My only amusing visit was in Perthshire to the Haldanes. Richard Haldane is the greatest philosopher and the greatest politician now alive, though he is only now beginning to come before the public, being very modest by nature. He has written excellent books on Adam Smith and Schopenhauer and is now engaged on a crushing refutation of A. J. Balfour's *Foundations of Belief*, which should be worth reading. He also does all the brain-work of the Liberal Party and, though never in the Cabinet, thinks for those who are. In the domestic circle he is the most amusing creature I know, he is a real humourist and a thorough-going epicurean, with the finest cellar and the best table in Scotland.'

Balfour had in September sent him a new edition of his *Foundations of Belief*. In acknowledging the book Haldane wrote:

'I have now had a chance of reading carefully the Introduction to the new edition of *The Foundations of Belief*, of which you gave me a copy.

'It is so plainly written that none can have any excuse for mistaking the argument. The standard is adequacy of the supposed origins of belief to their results and value. The outcome of the examination of scientific method is to shew how Science, taken as a system of thought, ethics and last but not least aesthetics, cannot as the world accepts them be accounted for on the principles or under the conceptions to which naturalism is limited, and that it is reasonable to look for another foundation for them.

'With all this I most cordially agree, and my recollection of the detailed treatment in the book (it is three years since I read it last through) is that it does the critical part of the work with great power. So far the metaphysicians will follow you to a man. Indeed the whole of this new introduction I think they will accept. It is over the book itself that controversy has arisen and will arise. In accepting the conclusion that the explanation is to be looked for elsewhere than in naturalism and its methods is it not to proceed *per saltum* to speak of a theological setting for the truth? I am not yet convinced that the history of philosophy cannot be so read as to shew that the half-dozen great systems that the world has seen are more or less inadequate presentations of a view that is as old as Plato, if not as Heraclitus. Once let analysis do its work in breaking up the hardness of the world as it seems, by disclosing the abstractions on which it depends and it appears to me that a single great thought has been in course of evolution. The first step towards interpreting the object-world as mind is to get rid of the notion of it as Mechanism. With this you would probably say you concurred, and that you were content to take the road as far in common with the philosophers. And ought you not, if you say so, either to go further with them or pause! Whether one turns to Plato or Schopenhauer, or Hegel, or even Kant (who knew but little how to read Greek philosophy) they seem to go in common along the same path further than you do. And their advantage is that they give a definite meaning to such expressions as God, the Soul, and Immortality and Freedom which your method will not admit of.

'But this letter was not written in criticism but in appreciation. For taking this Introduction as it stands it seems to state a point of view on which all may agree—and to state it with a lucidity which has rarely been rivalled and never excelled. And for that, as a believer in the further lesson which it seems to me the History of Philosophy has to teach, I am grateful.'

As Asquith says, the philosophical work on which Haldane was engaged, whenever he could find time to give to it, was to be mainly a reply to Balfour's philosophy. One of the links which united him to Balfour was, as we have seen, their common interest in the development of the higher education. Haldane had already gained Balfour's support over the problems of the universities in London and in Ireland, and he now turned to him again for support of his scheme for the establishment of provincial universities. Another ally and wise adviser he found in Sir William McCormick, later to be chairman of the University Grants Committee; and he got enthusiastic support from Joseph Chamberlain, with whom he rarely found himself in agreement, but who was eager to establish a university in his native Birmingham. Assured of this backing, which was very necessary, for there was powerful opposition to the proposal, Haldane went down to Liverpool and there in October gave the address from which I have already given an extract.[1] Both the corporation and the business men of Liverpool backed the proposal and decided to petition the Privy Council for the grant of a royal charter of incorporation for its university. Balfour, then, at Haldane's instance, agreed that the Government should support the grant of the charter, if recommended by the Privy Council, and appointed a committee of the council, under the chairmanship of the Duke of Devonshire, to hear evidence and report. Haldane persuaded Lord Rosebery and Lord Balfour of Burleigh, who had been his opponent for the Lord Rectorship of Edinburgh University, to be members of the committee with Lord James of Hereford and Sir Edward Fry.

While this ball was rolling towards its goal Haldane turned to yet another educational development. The new

[1]Cf. p. 64.

teaching university of London was in being, but it was not yet equipped as he thought it ought to be, to apply science to the uses and developments of industry. He conceived the idea of providing the university with a college specially designed for this purpose on a scale such as had never existed in this country. He interested Mr. Wernher and Mr. Beit of Wernher, Beit & Co., and the firm provided £100,000 for the scheme, and he also obtained noble contributions from his friends Sir Ernest Cassel and Lord Rothschild. The funds and property of the 1851 exhibition were administered by a body of commissioners in whose work King Edward took an active interest. The King saw at once that Haldane's scheme followed the lines of the development of the property of the commissioners in South Kensington, designed by his father, Prince Albert, and through his influence the commissioners contributed a valuable site for the new college. Out of that exhibition had grown the Royal College of Science and the Royal School of Mines. These were protégées of the Government and were administered under the direction of the Treasury, and Haldane persuaded Sir Francis Mowatt, then head of the Treasury, to agree that they should be incorporated in his plan. The City and Guilds of London College, which had been founded by the corporation and livery companies of the City of London in 1878, was also brought in. In an endeavour to get more financial help from the Government he wrote to Mr. Joseph Chamberlain telling him how far the scheme had progressed, and got this reply:

'I believe we are in entire agreement as to the object to be aimed at and I am certainly ready to work with you for the attainment in any way that is most likely to be useful. It may be that I am unable to take an altogether impartial view, but I certainly had thought that there was hardly energy enough to go round all the Universities at once, and my hope and expectation was that we might make a beginning and show an example in Birmingham, in which case it is quite certain that all the others will quickly follow suit. I imagine that your chief interest is in London, and you have already been working a mine which I had hoped some day to open up. As long as I am in office I cannot have any dealing with South African millionaires, or I should certainly be told by Mr. Lloyd George, or some other gentleman of equally delicate morality, that I had sold myself to them. I have, however, felt that fortunes of such size, and made so quickly as are those of many of the South African financiers, were the proper subjects for an appeal for large benefactions to a Technical University. If I could get half a million more, or still better a million, I could start Birmingham University complete, and I then should fully expect that Manchester, Liverpool, Leeds and London would benefit by our experience both in their work and in their finances. I am convinced that ultimately the Government must come more largely to our assistance. Any contribution from them would be a mere drop in the bucket in comparison with the whole expenditure on Education, but I have not pressed this part of my policy, as I have thought it most desirable to give proof of local energy before asking for additional Imperial assistance.'

It was several years before the needed financial help from the Government was secured and the whole scheme, which involved not only the erection and equipment of new premises, but the amalgamation of a number of existing institutions, with separate and sometimes conflicting interests, was completed, and it was not until 1907 that the Imperial College of Science and Technology, one of the great monuments of Haldane's vision and skill as a negotiator, received its Royal Charter of Incorporation. One of the results of this enterprise was that Haldane was again brought into close relations with the King, and this had a consequence which took him completely by surprise. In August 1902 he received a letter from Lord Salisbury, the Prime Minister, announcing that he was to be made a Privy Councillor, and he learned on inquiry that the suggestion had originated with the King. As he had never been a minister of the Crown this was an exceptional honour, and one which he felt he could not refuse, though it had an immediate reaction on another of his activities. The application to the Privy Council for a royal charter for the University of Liverpool was pending. Haldane had offered the promoters to appear as their counsel without fee, but as a Privy Councillor himself he was not able to do this. Instead he gave evidence on behalf of the application, which was granted, and Haldane received the formal thanks of the Corporation of Liverpool. Birmingham, with like help from Joseph Chamberlain, had shortly before obtained its charter and so began the great extension of university education in England and Wales which was one of the features of the life of this country in the early years of the twentieth century.

Another result of Haldane's negotiations for the establishment of the Imperial College was that he became intimate with both Mr. Wernher and with Sir E. Cassel, whose firm gave £100,000 to the College, and these friendships had two very different sequels. Mr. Wernher, who had a great admiration for Haldane, wished to improve his friend's financial position, and advised him to buy two blocks of shares in different concerns which he said were below their real value and were sure to rise. Haldane replied that he had never indulged in that kind of speculation and preferred to keep clear of it. In the event both shares fell heavily, a result which confirmed him in his decision to keep clear of the Stock Exchange. When he became a member of the Government many friends in the business world who admired him and wished to help him offered him tips, but he refused to profit by any of their suggestions and usually got out of them by referring the tips to his brother William, whom he told them looked after his business affairs. He had no desire for great wealth and the Bar had provided him with more than enough for his needs, while he was always of opinion that the outlook of the City upon affairs was narrow and short-sighted and apt to be falsified by events, and for that reason it was dangerous for any one, who could not give a day to day attention to the buying and selling of shares, to venture upon speculation. Sir E. Cassel, when his health began to fail, asked Haldane's advice as to how he could dispose of his fortune to the best advantage, and it was on Haldane's advice that the Cassel Trust, which has proved of such benefit to needy and deserving students, was founded.

The amount of work which Haldane did at this time is amazing. He had one of the largest practices at the Chancery Bar and was earning £15,000 a year in fees. He was, in such spare time as he had, carrying on his negotiations for the foundation of Liverpool University and the Imperial College, and, in the midst of this, events suddenly called him back to active participation in politics. In July 1902 Lord Salisbury resigned and Mr. Balfour became Prime Minister, an event which was followed closely by Mr. Joseph Chamberlain's campaign for tariff reform. This had the double effect of splitting the Conservative and uniting the Liberal parties, and was followed by the usual crop of gossip and speculation in political circles. Of these Haldane wrote to Rosebery in August:

'The courts are rising and the House is waiting to rise, and generally everyone desires to get out of this pleasant city. Asquith and I spent Sunday together in the country and exchanged the gossip we had brought down. That gossip is, and I think it is true, that strenuous efforts are being made to patch up the divergences of view in the Cabinet. The Duke [of Devonshire] is said to have intimated that if the Cabinet was broken up he was prepared to form a Ministry, with an offer to you of the Foreign Office, to defend Free Trade. Mowatt says that Nathaniel Rothschild at Tring pledged himself to go with the Duke even if Arthur Balfour went the other way. But all this goes for very little. The relevancy of it is that the story is growing that the situation is easier and that an autumn crisis will be averted. Meantime there is a good deal of friction in the Unionist constituencies and threatening of opposition by the Protectionists to Free Traders even where they are strong Tories. But the Tory Whips are telling their own men that there will be no dissolution before March. I had a walk the other day, for the first time for years, with John Morley. He was very friendly and spoke of the inevitable advent of a Liberal Government and of the necessity, which he was not sure that C.B. and Spencer appreciated as much as he did, of continuity of policy in South Africa. I shall continue this after dining at Grillion's.

'Later. Grillion's was not very lively to-night except that Asquith and Birrell were there, so there was plenty of good talk. Ministers are quite cheerful for the end of their present troubles is in sight with the rising of the House on Friday. They have not many such comforts, though the state of the opposition is a great stand by. Chamberlain is not, according to all the latest accounts, diminishing the number of his engagements to speak for the autumn, which does not look much like a satisfactory compromise.'

Within a month of this letter Chamberlain sent his resignation to Balfour that he might be free to advocate his policy in the country, and the Conservative free-traders, Lord George Hamilton, Mr. Ritchie, and Lord Balfour of Burleigh, left the Cabinet, followed shortly by the Duke of Devonshire. The Right and Left wings of the Liberals forgot the differences which the South African War had made patent and joined forces enthusiastically in support of free trade, and in this Haldane was as active as any, and spoke frequently and with effect both at by-elections and at free-trade meetings north and south of the border. In addition to all this he had received and accepted an invitation to deliver the Gifford Lectures at the University of St. Andrews. These lectures had been founded by Lord Gifford 'to promote a *thinking* consideration of the Nature of God and of His relation to the actual world.'[1] For these Haldane used the material for the book expounding his philosophy, on which he had been at work for some years. In 1902 he had published his addresses on 'University Education' and 'The Constitutional Development of the Empire' under the title *Education and Empire*, and he sent a copy to his friend Seth, now Professor Pringle Pattison. In reply to the latter's thanks and congratulations on his Privy Councillorship he wrote in August:

'Best thanks for a very kind letter. At first I rather shrank from this P.C.ship. So did E. Grey—my colleague—but we found we had no choice. H.M. did it with his own hand and consequently we were not even asked whether we would agree. On reflection this seems a pleasant way, and I feel I may get some sort of platform from it for Education. I have a big business on hand just now which needs all the strength one has—the creation of a school for the Empire for the application of Science to Industry—which is to have its seat in the Metropolis. The King himself is keen, and it shows how these things touch the national life that one great firm has—as the result of a single interview—given me £100,000 for it. So the first address in the book, about which you write so kindly, has not been launched wholly in vain.

'I think the tendency of events is strongly to work out Imperial Federations on the lines of the 3rd and 4th Addresses. Indeed, Chamberlain is virtually pursuing a similar policy with great energy. The last address is, as you surmise, a first Sketch of the lines of the Gifford Lectures. Over these I am groaning. In 10 days I hope to sit down and begin to piece together the first seven of them.'

The lectures were delivered between 1902 and 1904 under the title *The Pathway to Reality*. He delivered them extempore

[1]The Gifford Lectures for 1902–3, R. B. Haldane, *The Pathway to Reality*, vol. I, p. 4.

from carefully prepared but relatively few notes, a remarkable feat. Haldane's memory was a curious one. He never forgot the most intricate details of a case or subject which he had mastered, and could present either in a logical sequence with but occasional reference to brief or notes, but he had no memory for quotations and found learning by heart heavy labour. The Gifford Lectures were Haldane's first formal presentation of his philosophy and I cannot do better than quote here Professor Pringle Patterson's appreciation of them: '*The Pathway to Reality* is not intended to suggest that the real world is like a distant realm to which we can only penetrate by turning our back on the familiar world of ordinary experience. The author takes early occasion to disabuse us of such an idea by referring to the incident in *Wilhelm Meister* in which Wilhelm learns that "here or nowhere is his America". The problem of philosophy is simply to account for the actual world of the plain man—to get the most adequate and complete conception of it; and no conception can be adequate which does not take account of all its phases. If we do include all the phases we end by seeing them, higher or lower, in their due proportion or value; and by interpretation through the highest we come nearest to a true account of the ultimately real. "We ought to be prepared to believe in the different aspects of the world as it seems—life, for example, as much as mechanism; morality as much as life; religion as much as morality—for these belong to different aspects of the world as it seems, aspects which emerge at different standpoints, and are the results of different purposes and different categories in the organization of knowledge. And if philosophy gives us back what science threatens to take away, and restores to plain people their faith in the reality of each of these phases of the world as it seems, then philosophy will have gone a long way to justify her existence."[1]

[1] *The Pathway to Reality*, vol. I, p. 119.

'Such a passage, and the recurring use throughout the lectures of the expression, "the world as it seems", suggest that the title of the lectures was probably intended to convey an allusion to Bradley's *Appearance and Reality*, published some ten years previously. For Bradley also makes prominent use of the conception of "degrees of Truth and Reality"; but whereas, under his sceptical analysis, all degrees of "appearance" are exhibited as alike riddled by contradictions—the conclusion eventually arrived at being that to reach Reality or the Absolute we must discard relational thought altogether—Haldane declares that "if the standpoint of these lectures be a true one, we are free to believe in the world as it seems, and not driven to sacrifice any aspect of it on one altar or another."[1]

'It is in these Gifford volumes, it should be noted, that we find, on Haldane's part, the strongest and most unqualified statements of his Hegelian discipleship. "All that is in these lectures", he says at the conclusion of the first year's course, "I have either taken or adapted from Hegel, and in Hegel there is twice as much again of equal importance which these lectures cannot even touch." Aristotle and Hegel are mentioned together throughout as the two supreme thinkers of the world; and Hegel, it is said, "first taught the world how to read Aristotelian philosophy". Hence, "it seems as if the best preparation for the would-be philosopher must still be to find out what Hegel really meant and to learn to read him." The last few words are an accurate description of his own practice. He once told Professor J. H. Morgan that he had read the *Phaenomenologie des Geistes* nineteen times. I cannot speak to any definite number of times, but whenever we met I was sure to find that he had just been re-reading one or other of the master's works, perhaps the *Phaenomenologie* most frequently of all. It is hardly out of place to speak of them as his bedside companions; they were certainly the books to which he most frequently turned for relaxation, if

[1] *The Pathway to Reality*, vol. I, p. 169.

one may so speak, at the close of many a busy day. This constant communion with the master, though in Haldane's case, with his enormous capacity for work, it was far from excluding attention to anything of importance that appeared in contemporary thought, was, I think, not without certain disadvantages to himself as a writer. In the first place, the excessive abstractness of Hegel's usual style tended to infect that of his expositor; and secondly, the very familiarity with the formulas in which Hegel stereotyped his doctrines perhaps obscured for Haldane the difficulties which phrases that meant so much to himself might present to other minds, and the ambiguities, real or possible, which they might cover. He himself remarks upon the disadvantage which philosophy suffers from the nature of its subject-matter. It moves professedly in the region of abstract thought, whereas religion and poetry—art generally—express themselves in images and appeal to the emotions. He was himself very accessible to the poetic appeal, as is shown by the quotations he makes in the course of his lectures. "Something of direct insight", he says, "would seem to have come to great men, to great artists, to great poets. . . . In the poets, when at their best, we have the discernment of what has been the last and perhaps the highest result of the greatest speculative thinking in the history of philosophy." But when he sits down to write as a philosopher he seems resolved, as a matter of conscience, to eschew all use of image or symbol and to talk only the language of the *Begriff*. This seems to me to be especially true of his later writing, and it is perhaps particularly the case when he is avowedly striving to be as simple and direct as possible. The result makes very difficult reading. The spoken word of the Gifford Lectures, with its more vivid personal appeal and more natural flow of language, is easy in comparison, and the two volumes of *The Pathway to Reality* are likely, in my opinion, to remain the most attractive and representative of his philosophical writings.

'The second volume of the Gifford Lectures contains his exposition of Hegel's doctrine of God and man, as he understood it and was prepared to accept it. If we start from the position reached in the first volume that Mind or Self-consciousness is the highest category known to us, then it is to our experience as knowers or thinkers that we must turn for the most adequate conception of God. The universe in its ultimate reality must in fact be conceived as an Absolute Mind, that is to say, a Mind in its fundamental structure resembling our own, but freed from those features of our experience which we can see to be due to our limitations and imperfection.

'Now the fundamental structure of Mind—of Knowledge or of Thought as such—consists in the subject-object relation. This relation is all-comprehensive, for existence is meaningless out of relation to knowledge. When we speak of anything as existing, we mean its existence as an object of actual or possible knowledge. It is in this sense that Haldane so often uses the expression, "Knowledge is foundational". Knowledge does not supervene upon a world of self-existent things; it is itself the supreme and all-embracing Fact within which all our distinctions fall. It is, accordingly, as the universal and all-inclusive Subject or Self that we may, at the outset, best conceive of God. The term Self is habitually used in a double sense. We men, whose experience is mediated by our organic equipment, exist, each of us with our individual history, in a world which contains innumerable other selves. In that sense our individual self is for us an object correlated with other objects within the total world of knowledge. Yet we are more than that object-self. We are also the subject for which this individual self is the object, for, as knowers, we each of us place ourselves at a super-individual standpoint, as spectators of all time and all existence. And in this latter sense Hegel says there is only one Mind, one Thinker, the single subject which has the universe for object, and sees in it all nothing but its own manifestation. Hence Haldane, summing up the result of his second volume, defines God as "Mind that comprehends itself completely".[1] "Its comprehension is complete because its object can only be itself."[2] "Mind as it is in man is this same self-comprehension, but a plane or stage which is imperfect." And it is the imperfection of our finite comprehension which gives to the world of nature its "hard-and-fastness", as if it were something external to mind, with an element of contingency irresoluble by intelligence.[3]

'Some interpreters of Hegel have taken his doctrine of Absolute Mind as meaning no more than a formal unity of knowledge wherever knowing comes to pass, and have sought accordingly the ultimate reality of the universe in the abstract universals or categories which Hegel analyzes in his *Logic*, and which they suppose somehow to focus themselves in the human organism into concrete persons that think and act. The Absolute, on this view, first comes to consciousness of itself in men, and the process of its life is identified with the course of human history. Nothing, however, could be farther from Haldane's conception of the master's meaning. He brushes aside the idea of impersonal self-subsisting thoughts as a contradiction in terms. The abstract universal has no subsistence. Reality, he argues constantly, is throughout singular or individual—the concrete unity of universal and particular, which are both but abstractions from it. And this is preeminently true of Absolute Mind, the ultimate Real; it is "individual, unique, and singular",[4] "living, concrete, self-conscious mind".[5] God is therefore certainly "in some sense a Person",[6] though the limitations associated with finite personality suggest that super-personal (in the sense of imper-

[1] *The Pathway to Reality*, vol. II, p. 170.
[2] *Ibid.*, p. 156.   [3] *Ibid.*, p. 133.
[4] *Ibid.*, p. xvii.   [5] *Ibid.*, p. 70.
[6] *Ibid.*, p. xx.

sonal, but of personality and much more than what we know as such) would be the more appropriate term. Emily Brontë's *Last Lines*, which he quoted so often in life, to his friends as well as in his books, do in fact best express his own intimate sense of this Supreme Reality:

> *O God within my breast,*
> *Almighty, ever-present Deity!*
> *Life—that in me has rest,*
> *As I—undying Life—have power in Thee!*

'Philosophy, in short, is necessarily abstract, and although "for the intellect of God the conceptions of philosophy can be no abstractions, for us they will always be such". Hence, he says in his concluding pages, "we turn quite naturally to Art and Religion for the direct sense of the presence of what is truly closer to us than breathing and nearer than hands and feet". The language we meet there may be only symbolical but it is none the less practically true. "Abstract reason", he says elsewhere, "has no monopoly of the means of access to reality, although I hold it to be the only competent guardian of the pathway."[1] "It is for Philosophy to pursue the narrow path to the summit, and there to join hands with Art, Morality, and Religion. The accomplishment of this is for her the test of success. It is only when he finds that the world as it seems to the artist, to the good man, to the godly man, seems real to him also that the philosopher has done his work. Hence the characteristic tenderness with which he habitually treats the 'faith of simple minds'."[2]

'There is no such thing as "the undue exaltation of the abstract mind", which, if persisted in, is no better than "pedantry". Those who are supposed to regard highly the faith of simple minds would do well, he says, to bear this in remembrance. "For that faith is in itself a correction of ab-

[1] *The Pathway to Reality*, vol. II, p. xiv.
[2] *Ibid.*, p. 32.

stractions: it is the sense of the fuller significance of experience."[1] "Art and Religion", he says, in the concluding chapter of the *Autobiography*, "are never superseded by metaphysics."'

As I hope I have already made clear, the two realities in Haldane's life were his philosophy and his affection for his mother. He hoped that he could make philosophy a reality in government, but unfortunately few of those who understood his philosophy had any influence in government and few of those concerned in government believed that there was any relation between philosophy and reality.

He was delighted with the reception of the Gifford Lectures by those for whose opinion he cared. Caird, Bradley, Campbell Fraser, Scott Holland, Bishop Gore, and Edmund Gosse were amongst those who sent him letters of gratitude and appreciation. In answer to Pringle Patterson Haldane wrote:

'MY DEAR PRINGLE PATTERSON

Your letter gave me very great pleasure—for there is no one whose judgment I set alongside yours, and we have worked side by side, so to speak, at these problems, and are now near the same result. Like you, I would not foreclose the personal Continuance, simply because to do so is to set up the other side of the Antinomy. Despite his faulty scheme Kant was not far from the root of the matter when he sought to call in an Intelligible world to redress the balance of this empirical world. But as you say there are "substantial interests which yield a present satisfaction", and so give us the same thing in another form.

'I think there is a large region, pretty well untrodden, to be investigated. It has to be shewn *in detail* how the ends which shape the models of thinking in spirit, which though free is finite, determine the aspects of its world. Something towards

[1]*Reign of Relativity*, p. 413.

this has been contributed in the sphere of Logic by Bradley and Bosanquet. But I feel that they have only got to the verge of the ground. I know no one else who could do the hard thinking the work requires, as you could, and hope you will. I doubt whether there is much more to be extracted from Hegel. We want more systematic treatment of detail. However, I think I shall read over again the *Phaenomenologie*, starting from this basis: "Taking myself as just the realisation of this particular purpose, a meaning of Absolute Mind, how do I work out beyond it?"

'I hope we may manage to have a long talk before a great interval has passed.'

Chapter VII

THE LIBERAL REVIVAL

1902 to 1908

The fact that the Right Honourable R. B. Haldane, K.C., M.P., was now a public figure was signalized by his election in the summer of 1902 to 'The Club', that curiously English coterie of men of all parties and callings recognized as distinguished in public life. He was, as we have seen already, a member of Grillion's, and between the two he came in touch with most persons of importance. A good dinner with good company was one of the pleasures of his life, and he was regular in his attendance at both dining clubs. Edmund Gosse was secretary of Grillion's and the two soon became friends. When in 1904 Gosse became librarian of the House of Lords friendship passed into intimacy, for Haldane, whose pleadings before the Lords were frequent, used the library a good deal, partly for work and partly for the recreation of a literary talk with the librarian.

Haldane was now a very different person from the shy, reserved young man who had come to London to eat his dinners at Lincoln's Inn and had associated chiefly with the elderly friends of his uncle. He had a habit of taking stock of himself, and when he found a defect in his equipment he set about remedying it with that delight in meeting and overcoming difficulties which he had inherited from his forebears. I have mentioned that he was far from satisfied with his delivery as a speaker, and was at pains to improve it. Nor was he satisfied with his memory, and he tackled that defect with even more determination. He used his study of case law to

this end, and by sheer hard work acquired the faculty of re-
calling not merely the principles of law laid down in a particular case but also its actual place in the series of opinions.
Later, when he became Lord Chancellor, it was his particular
pride, when presiding over an important appeal, to be able to
refer counsel to a decision with an important bearing on the
issue which had been overlooked. By this vigorous training
his memory became encyclopedic. He was a voracious reader
and could tuck away what he read on a shelf of his mind and
could draw the matter out at any time. He took pride in his
ability to discuss any topic which arose at any time, however
abstract, and this his friends were sometimes disposed to
condemn as 'showing off', but it was in reality a part of his
method of training himself.

He had not been very long in London before he discovered
that dinners and receptions were the occasions for meeting
interesting people, and that it was an advantage to have the
reputation of having something interesting to say. He took
particular pains to be a good host, and not only his talk but
his wine, food, and cigars acquired a reputation in his circle.
He developed a pawky humour and nothing gave him
greater pleasure than to set his table laughing. He was a very
generous man, and from the time when he had money to
spare he was at pains to give his friends the best, while he
was continually helping lame dogs. He usually spent Xmas
at Mills and arrived there with a load of presents. For
hogmanay he always went to Cloan, and from the time
when his nephew and nieces began to grow up he brought
up with him every year a bundle of new five-pound notes
for distribution.

He never had any ambition for great wealth, and entrusted
his business affairs to his younger brother, William, with instructions to invest in gilt-edged securities. He was punctilious
in paying his way and always had an annual audit of his
affairs with his brother. The Haldanes were a united family,

and few things gave him more pleasure than to find his brothers and sister appreciated by others as he appreciated them, but the real centre of his family life was his devotion to his mother.

His recreations, when he had time for them, were walking in the south, and walking and shooting in Scotland. He was quite a good shot, and enjoyed a day on the moors with his beloved dogs. In the south he used to astonish his friends, who knew that for days on end he had never taken any exercise, with his powers on a tramp, but he was not always the easiest of companions on a walk, for when he had some problem on his mind he had the habit of speeding ahead, rubbing his hands, and leaving his friends far behind.

Such were the ways of the man who was now coming to the front rank in politics.

As the split in the Conservative Party on tariff reform became more and more patent and the followers of Chamberlain grumbled more and more openly at what they held to be Balfour's irresolute leadership on the, to them, vital question of the day, the Government's hold on the country obviously weakened. They lost by-election after by-election, and the quidnuncs of politics began to prophesy an early dissolution and to forecast a Liberal victory at the polls and the composition of the next government. In this Haldane was freely tipped as the next Lord Chancellor. With a political issue before the country in which he could join with his party wholeheartedly, a new and refreshing experience for him, and the prospect of high office before him, Haldane gave himself more seriously to party politics and party organization than he had done for years. To help him in this he for the first time engaged a personal assistant, and took as his private secretary Mr., now Sir, Percy Ashley. Few men could have achieved as much as he had without this kind of help. He used Ashley chiefly to devil for him in the case for free trade and found his help invaluable.

As to the future of the party he had definite plans. It has, I think, been made quite clear that he had no confidence in Campbell-Bannerman's leadership. He regarded Home Rule as for the time outside the field of practical politics, and he saw that the Liberals could not exist merely on their opposition to protection, and he was therefore looking for a leader with an inspiring policy of educational and social reform and an imperial policy of defence, and he had satisfied himself that on these matters Campbell-Bannerman had no constructive ideas. He had Grey to stay with him and the two sat up into the small hours discussing the problem of the composition and policy of the next Liberal government. Eventually the two tackled Rosebery in the autumn of 1903 and endeavoured to get him to come back as leader. This he declined absolutely, but he promised to work for an Asquith ministry, a solution which Grey and Haldane accepted with joy. Haldane wrote to Asquith to tell him what had passed, but Asquith, who saw more clearly than his two friends that the majority of the Liberal Party was of the Left wing, advised caution.

Balfour sent him in September a pamphlet setting out his views on protection, and to this Haldane replied with a summary of his case for free trade:

'What is this "World of Protectionists"? Turning to the statistics I find that nearly every nation is increasing its absolute imports—and evidently means to continue to do so, as the indispensable condition of increasing its foreign trade. This means that larger and larger neutral markets—larger not because they are neutrally protected—are opening to us. In France, e.g., we compete for the supply of an increasing demand against Germany, and in Germany as against France. As we have cheaper food and raw materials we ought to compete under a Free Trade system at an advantage, and when we do not it seems to me that the cause is defective organisation and method on the part of our business men.

Such examination of cases as I have been able to make seems to me to bear this out, e.g. the increase in export of machinery. It seems to me—from a good deal of recent reading— that the German students of economics are beginning to realize this. I have translated the conclusion of an article by Schacht which I have been reading this morning, and also Professor Schmoller's comment on it. Schmoller—as you know—is generally the prop of the German Government, and his comment seems to me significant. The Brentano school speak much more strongly in the same direction, and even Wagner, in the book to which you referred, says that tariffs will not help Germany for much longer.

'Again, take "dumping". Even if this could not be met by organisations under which our steel producers would buy cheap and so be able to lower their prices for what they make themselves, the field seems to me too dangerous and uncertain a field for the Government to venture into. Our Manufacturers are often foolish when they are not tricky, and who could check their statements? Again I cannot see how any sustained inpouring of foreign goods on a large scale can continue unless it creates new industries here to pay in exports. For if it drains bullion, prices here will fall, and our people will again be able to compete because they have an extra and new advantage in cost of production. I cannot therefore satisfy myself that your hypothetical picture in the latter part of the pamphlet is either now defensible or likely to become defensible. But I agree that the whole matter is very obscure, and has to be worked out *de novo*. It is one of the advantages of the present movement that one gets new lights almost weekly.'

Next to tariff reform public interest was attracted to the problem of army reform. The South African War had made it clear that something was wrong, and a number of commissions had made prolonged inquiries and issued voluminous reports. It fell to Mr. Brodrick to produce the first post-

South African War scheme of army reform. This scheme was an attempt to combine the Regular Army, the Yeomanry, and Militia into a whole which bore some resemblance to the military organizations of the great military Powers of the Continent. It proposed to create a home army of six army corps, but when it was examined it was found that the greater part of this army had no existence. Neither the Yeomanry nor the Militia had any artillery, engineers or supply services, with the result that there were huge gaps in the army corps, while no organization, beyond an inchoate mass of Volunteers who were enlisted for home defence, was provided either for making good the losses of the army in the field or for its expansion. The six army corps scheme was laughed out of court. Mr. Churchill directed against it the shafts of his wit. 'The first three army corps', said he, 'are incomplete, the fourth consists of Sir Archibald Hunter, the fifth is in the War Office file, and the sixth Mr. Brodrick has taken with him in his pocket on his trip to the Mediterranean.' In the autumn of 1903 Mr. Brodrick gave way to Mr. Arnold Forster.

The new Secretary of State for War had for a number of years devoted his considerable powers as a publicist to the cause of army reform, and much was expected of him, but in fact the first great change which took place was due to the initiative of the Prime Minister, Mr. Balfour. It was he who appointed the Esher Commission to examine the state of the War Office and to make recommendations for its reform, and it was he who acted upon its recommendation. On February 6, 1904, the office of Commander-in-Chief was abolished, Lord Roberts was hustled unceremoniously out of the War Office, and the control of the Army placed in the hands of an Army Council, of which the chief military member was the Chief of the General Staff. The General Staff was thus recognized in principle, but during Mr. Arnold Forster's regime it hardly existed outside the War Office.

A few months later the Secretary of State for War explained his proposals in the House of Commons. They were drastic. He threw over the Cardwell system, which had served us well for more than thirty years, and offered instead two armies. There was to be a long-service army, in which enlistment was to be for nine years with the colours and three in reserve. The prime function of this army was to provide our overseas garrisons. There was to be a short-service home defence army, in which the pick of the Militia was to be incorporated, while the number of the Volunteers was to be drastically curtailed. This scheme was opposed by the military experts at the War Office, who had grave doubts as to the supply of drafts to the British garrison in India, and it was opposed by those interested in the Militia, who comprised many of the stalwarts of Mr. Arnold Forster's party. These foresaw the gradual extinction of the 'old constitutional force' by absorption into the home defence army. It was opposed by the friends of the Volunteers, who were looking for a plan which would give the citizen army a definite organization and place in the scheme of national defence.

The debates on Army reform dragged on and the public was becoming more and more impatient of talk and proposals and was demanding results. Haldane followed these discussions with the keenest interest. He cordially approved of Balfour's creation of the Committee of Imperial Defence and also the report of the Esher Commission and the creation of a general staff. These measures he regarded as the right approach to the problems, by setting general principles of organization, but he became more and more conscious that the outlook of neither Mr. Brodrick nor of Mr. Arnold Forster was broad enough, and that neither had any real comprehensive programme of imperial defence, and he became more and more convinced that one of the first problems of the new Liberal Government would be to translate into practical politics Rosebery's conception of an imperial *Kriegsverein*.

He found that professional sailors and soldiers, as well as members of Parliament interested in imperial defence, were looking to him as the one prominent Liberal whose views on the question were worthy of consideration, and whom it was worth while briefing. Sir Evelyn Wood, who was in command of one of Mr. Brodrick's army corps at Salisbury, invited Haldane down to stay with him, and he heard from that astute and experienced soldier some plain speaking on the defects of our military organization.

Sir John Fisher asked him to come and stay with him at Portsmouth. Of this visit he wrote to his mother: 'I had lovely walks and a most interesting time. A long talk with my host, who is a remarkable character, very original and very outspoken. He doesn't suffer fools gladly, and has plenty of enemies, but a devoted band of followers in the Navy. He took me to see one of the new submarines. Sir John Fisher was proceeding to tell me with pride about the white mice they had in the boat to indicate the presence of bad air when the commander said: "Ah! Sir, you needn't tell Mr. Haldane about bad air and mice. His brother at Oxford has taught the British Navy all it knows on the subject." I found Johnny to be greatly esteemed by the experts. Just what these new boats are going to mean nobody really knows. The young enthusiasts talk about eliminating the battleship, the old men wag their heads and say that the battleship has survived the torpedo discharged from a boat on the surface and there is no reason to suppose that a torpedo discharged under water will make any difference. Clearly this new invention is only at its beginning, and as the French are hard at work developing them we must do the same, and I am proud that Johnny has had a hand in making this possible for us.'

Sir George Clarke, afterwards Lord Sydenham, and then Secretary of the Committee of Defence, wrote to him in February 1905: 'I am venturing to send you some rough notes on the situation. You will, I know, forgive me for saying that in matters bearing on national defence a Liberal government would not, on taking office, command great confidence. The number of people who would welcome an immediate change if they felt assured on this point is very large. Of course, this feeling is unjust, but it constitutes a factor to be taken into account. You said you would give £50,000 a year to any one who would do for the Army what Fisher has done for the Navy. I am ready to do this and much more, for much more is required, and I don't want £50,000 a year. As you well know, it is an easy thing to strike 125 ships off the Navy List. Ships do not write to the newspapers to air their grievances. What is needed by our military forces is infinitely larger in scope and enormously more difficult in execution than anything Fisher has done or will have to do at the Admiralty. Am I not right in thinking that success at the War Office may very probably be the crux of the next government? At least success there would be a supreme advantage to the party.'

Undeterred by this statement of the difficulties of the problem from one who could speak with real knowledge and authority, Haldane replied the same evening:

'From the national point of view, it is vital that, if called upon to take office, the Opposition should be able to form a strong and conspicuously capable Government. Mr. Chamberlain has propounded a theory that an early dissolution is desirable because it would lead to the formation of a weak Cabinet, which, after serving as a target for the fire of the Opposition during a brief period, would be replaced by the Unionist Party purged of Free Traders and able to proceed to destroy the basis of our economic system.

'Apart from the extravagance of this theory, it is one no patriotic person can contemplate without dismay.

'The times are critical, much more so than is generally realised. The existence even for a year of such a Government as Mr. Chamberlain assumes might involve disastrous consequences. From every point of view, putting aside all question of party, it is essential to the national welfare that the next Government should be successful in all departments of State.

'The difficulties to be feared are altogether exceptional. The Liberal Party has been out of Office for 10 years, and had held office only for disconnected periods totalling less than 3½ years in the last 20 years. It has lost touch with practical administration, by which it will certainly be judged.

'A Liberal Government must evidently address itself to domestic affairs; but Imperial questions of first class importance and of great complexity will be forced upon it. Among such are questions relating to the Indian frontier, to the Far East, to South Africa, and to the organisation of the Army.

'It must devote itself in grim earnest to retrenchment and reform of the public finance, since the results of reckless expenditure are now being felt throughout the community and are visibly affecting the national prosperity.

'The surest way to benefit the country and to command success lies in the assertion of effective control over expenditure. Domestic reforms will cost money, and it is doubtful whether any considerable reduction of civil expenditure is possible.

'A Liberal Government will, therefore, be compelled to review the expenditure of the Admiralty and War Office, which according to Mr. Gibson Bowles has increased in 10 years from £36,500,000 to £83,000,000. Army estimates, as presented to Parliament, have increased from £20,000,000 before the South African War to £29,500,000 now, and this, as Gibson Bowles shows, is far below the present actual expenditure.

'The conclusion is inevitable that the success of a Liberal Government must depend mainly upon its handling of the general policy of national defence, by which alone can large economies be effected. For reasons capable of explanation it is precisely in respect to matters of this nature that a Liberal Government would, on taking office, inspire the least confidence. There are numbers of earnest men who fear a change of Government solely on this ground. The Admiralty is going to show considerably reduced estimates. The War Office will make reductions which will not prove permanent, and if a dissolution occurs at an early date, nothing will have been done to reorganise the Army.

'In these circumstances, it is possible that the War Office may form the gauge of the success of the Liberal Government. Substantial economies in our present enormous expenditure on national defence are perfectly possible on the following conditions:

'(a) A pacific foreign policy, and more especially the maintenance of good relations with France and the United States. (The geographical position of France is so extraordinarily well suited for attacks upon our commerce that her neutrality would be, to us, the equivalent of a powerful fleet in war. It will have to be recognized frankly that the United States will shortly be in such a position that we shall be quite unable to hold our own against them in the Western Atlantic and the Caribbean Sea.)

'(b) The assumption of no additional territorial responsibilities, such as have vastly increased in recent years.

'(c) Full recognition of all that the possibilities of a superior fleet confers. In other words, the practical acceptance of "blue-water" principles, in accordance with the teaching of all history.

'(d) Complete harmony between the Admiralty and the War Office. Want of such harmony in the past has led to great waste.

'(e) Recognition of the advantage of efficiency as compared with mere numbers. (This idea has become hopelessly submerged in military affairs.)

'(f) A drastic reduction of the Regular Army, which could enable a far higher standard of efficiency to be attained than at present.

'(g) The regeneration of the Militia with liability to serve abroad, when Parliament proclaims a national emergency. (This is perfectly practicable and it would have the great advantage of checking the jingo spirit effectually. It is ruinous to attempt to maintain in peace-time a *regular* force adequate to meet a national emergency, which is not likely to arise more than twice in a century.)

'(h) The utilisation of the Volunteers in reduced numbers as a second line of expansion of the army and for local defence, garrisoning fortified posts (etc.).

'(i) The preparation of a comprehensive scheme on Imperial Defence in which the Colonial Governments should be invited and encouraged to participate.

'(j) The abolition of superfluities and shams of various kinds.

'On the above conditions a substantial reduction of expenditure can be made. They can be fulfilled only by a strong administration equipped with the necessary knowledge, which must be complete, and the results of practical experience and long study. As I have not got the practical experience and have not made long study these are for your own ear to show you the way my mind is working. I shall not make any public statement save on broad principles till I have more knowledge of the facts and have had more time to study them.'

But I must go back a little. In 1900 Scotland was stirred, as only Scotland can be stirred, by a religious controversy. When the Disruption of 1843 occurred two bodies, the Free Church and the United Presbyterian Church, had broken away from the Established Presbyterian Church of Scotland. After protracted negotiations the great majority of the Free Church had agreed to join with the United Presbyterians under the title of the United Free Church of Scotland. A small part of the Free Church refused to follow their fellows into this union on the grounds that this would involve a sacrifice of principle, and in particular a departure from the doctrine of predestination as set forth in the Confession of the Free Church. The dissident body, which became known as the Wee Frees, maintained that the trust deeds executed at the time of the Disruption of 1843 created a trust for those of the Free Church who adhered to the doctrines set forth at that time, and that no general assembly had power and authority to alter those doctrines, as, in fact they had been altered by successive general assemblies of those who formed the new United Free Church. This was, in effect, a claim by the minority to funds amounting to more than £2,000,000, by far the greater part of which had been subscribed by members of the majority.

The Wee Frees, with Scottish determination, refused to compromise on what they held to be a matter of principle, and took the case into court. The Court of Session found unanimously in favour of the majority, but the minority appealed and took the case to the House of Lords, where it came on in the summer of 1904. Haldane, who led for the United Free Church, in what was to be one of his last great cases as a member of the Bar, was in his element. His familiarity with the history of Scottish theology and with metaphysics made it easy for him to present the kind of closely reasoned argument in which he delighted, but the English Law Lords were, for the most part, at sea. One of the points at issue was whether the doctrines of predestination and free will as formulated and accepted by the new United Free Church were in harmony with the doctrines of the old Church. In the preparation of his arguments on this point Haldane enlisted the help of his mother, whose knowledge of the Bible was remarkable, and he got her to make out for him a list of the texts in the Gospels and Epistles showing that the same statement of the two doctrines occurred side by side in many passages in the New Testament. With this equipment Haldane won his point. But on the consequential point, that the general assembly of a church had the right to mould its own doctrines and constitution and was not rightly bound to maintain the doctrine which had prevailed sixty years before, he failed, and the Law Lords by a majority of five to two found in favour of the Wee Frees. The decision deprived the United Free Church of the whole of its funds and condemned them to pay the costs of the litigation personally.

Principal Rainy, the leader of the United Free Church, an old man of eighty, as he listened to the judgement solemnly and slowly read out by the Lord James of Hereford, felt that the bottom had dropped out of his world, and broke down. Haldane, who was furious with the decision, took him to his rooms in Whitehall Court, and put new hope into him by declaring that this was an injustice which could and would be remedied by Parliament, and proposed that a fund should at once be raised to meet the costs of litigation and of preparing a case for Parliament. He on the spot headed the list with a subscription of £1,000, which meant returning his fees, and in a surprisingly short time £150,000 was subscribed. He then set about getting the machinery of Parliament to work. He secured the help of Mr. Balfour, Lord Dunedin, the Scottish Secretary, Lord Balfour of Burleigh, and the Archbishop of Canterbury, all of them Scots who understood the issue. The necessary statute passed through both Houses and a commission under Lord Elgin was appointed to make a fair distribution of the property between the Churches. So the United Free Church was saved to go forward from strength to strength.

Just as this case ended Haldane was shocked by the news of the death of his dear friend Lady Tweedmouth. Of this he wrote to his mother: 'We laid Lady Fanny to rest in the little church-yard at Chernside yesterday. I cannot get over her death, she was so splendidly alive and was always there to help others. If ever there was a noble character hers was noble. I have been very fortunate in my friends. She and Mrs.

Horner have in different ways meant very much to me. Her death is the severing of a tie that has lasted for years, but her influence is undying for those who knew her.'

In the summer Haldane was invited to stand again for the Lord Rectorship of Edinburgh University and agreed to do so. The election took place in November and he was returned by a majority of thirty, in a poll of 1,700, over Lord Dunedin. The success of a Liberal in this contest for the first time for many years was a feather which showed the change in the political breezes. Haldane was particularly pleased to have a very warm letter of congratulation from Lord Balfour of Burleigh, who had defeated him when he last stood for the Lord Rectorship.

Haldane had never had a busier year in the courts than that of 1904. Just before his Scottish Churches case came on he wrote to his mother, whom he had promised to visit to inspect an enlargement of his home which was in progress: 'I have returned briefs in both the House of Lords and the Privy Council for to-morrow and yet have my hands so full with cases that I dare not in honour desert the courts, so that it is doubtful whether I can get away before the afternoon of Saturday. No one since Lord Palmer's time has had so much work in the Privy Council. I am far ahead of Sir Horace Davey's busiest time in the Tribunal. My letters are lying in a heap waiting to be answered, and there is a pile of opinions asking for my attention.' In spite of all this he never forgot his daily letter to his mother, when he was not with her, and he was following with keen interest plans for the enlargement of Cloanden and the installation of electric light there. He persuaded his mother to revert to the original name Cloan. She, a Northumbrian, had not appreciated the fact that 'Cloan' had a Celtic, 'den' a Saxon, origin. The two did not fit. In November he was invited to Liverpool for the inauguration of the university of which he was the parent, and from there he wrote to his mother: 'I am having a great day

here. Last night I spoke at Ealing—a fine meeting. I then
caught the midnight train to Liverpool, slept in a sleeping-car
soundly and got in early. I addressed the boys of the New
Corporation School in the forenoon, went to an inspection of
the University building followed by a big luncheon. There
we robed in scarlet and went to St. George's Hall where the
Chancellor, Lord Derby, presided over 25,000 people. Lord
Kilburn spoke and then the degree of LL.D. was conferred
on me as the real founder of the University. It was the only
degree given. I spoke for twenty minutes, but I don't believe
that I could have made more than two-thirds of the people
hear, so packed was the Hall. There are more functions to-
night. I have to speak at a banquet, and to-morrow we go to
a state service at the Cathedral. I am not a bit tired, which
speaks well for my health.'

Soon after his return from Liverpool he for the first time
put on his Privy Councillor's uniform. The occasion was a
state banquet at Windsor to the King of Portugal, and he
wrote to his mother of his first experience of Royal splen-
dour: 'The invitation to Windsor was an unusual honour to
one who has never been a Minister of the Crown. I wish I
could find time to describe the gorgeous scene at Windsor
last night. Two million pounds' worth of gold plate was on
the table and sideboards. After dinner we went in procession
to the Saloon, where the Royalties stood apart, and we were
called out in turn. The King sent for me and spoke to me
about my College of Science in South Kensington in which
he is keenly interested and he presented me to the King of
Portugal. The Queen, who looked magnificent in the Crown
Jewels, then singled me out so I was made much of. The
Princess of Wales spoke to me of my memoir of Lady Tweedmouth in the *Westminster* which she had read and recognised,
and I also had a talk with the Prince. The Lord Chancellor
took me apart and said that I was probably to be his successor
and could do things which he had not been able to get

through, and he indicated the reforms in which he would support me. You will see in the *Westminster* some comment on the fact that Edward Grey and I were included amongst the six invited to represent the Opposition. The enemy will grumble. The whole thing was magnificently staged. Of all the unlikely people to do so Lord Rosebery made a mistake and came in evening clothes. He had to keep in the background. He had not noticed "full dress" on his card.'

In the preparations of his party for the General Election, which, as all agreed, could not long be delayed, Haldane found himself on one question in a minority of one. Balfour's Government had agreed to the introduction of Chinese indented labour into the South African mines. A great deal of money had gone to native labour during the war, and the inducement which had brought natives to work on the Rand in the past no longer prevailed. An economic crisis in the gold industry, on which the finances of the Transvaal were dependent, was threatened by shortage of labour, and to prevent this the importation of Chinese labour was permitted. This could be readily represented to be a form of slavery, and there were abuses in the conditions of employment of the Chinese. The managers of the Liberal Party saw in this a first-class electioneering cry and pictures of Chinese in chains made very effective posters. The party was therefore full of indignation when, on the question being raised in the House on February 19, Haldane abstained from voting against Chinese labour. 'There have', he wrote, 'been abuses in the compounds of the Rand, which can and must be remedied, but these abuses are being grossly exaggerated by our people for party ends. Our real aim must be to restore effective self-government to the Transvaal as speedily as possible and you can't have effective self-government on a deficit. I am not going to destroy the greater good for the sake of a temporary party gain.' The effect of that was to make him more unpopular than ever with the Radical wing of the party, which now declared openly that he must be excluded from office when the victory, which it expected, was won.

In January 1905 he received his first invitation to dine and sleep at Windsor. 'I arrived', he wrote to his mother, 'at 6.30 p.m. and was met by a carriage with postilions, which drove me in solitary state to the Castle. Then an hour with Lord Knollys on politics. Dressed in knee breeches and silk stockings and dined at 8.45. I sat next Miss Knollys, the Queen's lady-in-waiting. The party is mainly family, Princess Louise, the Battenbergs, some minor foreign royalties, Lord Mountstephen, the Archbishop of Canterbury, and two Ambassadors. We dined in the State dining-room. After dinner the King took me away and asked me many questions about the Imperial College, in which he is deeply interested. He is even more interested in the Liberal Party, about which we had much talk. He is most affectionate to me. He made me sit beside him on a sofa, on which he told me the old Duke of Cambridge used to sit. He said he counted on seeing me again at Mentmore on Monday. The whole arrangements here are extraordinarily comfortable; they could not be more so.' Of the visit to Mentmore he wrote: 'I have been spending another Kingly Sunday. Yesterday I went to church with the King and sat next him. It was odd to see how nervous the Rector of the little parish church was, when he prayed for the King in his presence. I saw much of His Majesty in private again. He is very interested in the future of the Liberal Party, which he evidently expects to be in office soon. He is like an old friend now and wanted to know how many cigars I smoked and how I arranged my work.

'He was happy in escaping ceremony and walked up and down the Terrace before breakfast in a tweed jacket and a not very smart tweed cap talking German to Mensdorff and me.

'He brought two valets, one private detective, two chauffeurs, and a telegraphist besides his equerry. So it is no joke to entertain the King as Lord Rosebery found!'

As the year 1905 wore on the position of Mr. Balfour's Government became weaker and weaker. The Chamberlainite whole-hoggers were in open revolt against his leadership and in the summer he told Haldane of his intention to resign at a favourable opportunity. On this Asquith, Grey, and Haldane then decided to meet and discuss future Liberal policy, and, as none of them had any doubt of the result of the inevitable election, the composition of the next Liberal Government. While recognizing Campbell-Bannerman's popularity with the party the three agreed that his age, health, and opinions did not fit him to be the energetic leader of a progressive Liberal policy. It was agreed between them that if Campbell-Bannerman became Prime Minister he should take a peerage and that Asquith should lead in the Commons as Chancellor of the Exchequer, and that failing this none of the three would take office under Campbell-Bannerman. The meeting took place at a fishing Sir E. Grey had taken at Relugas, and this agreement became known as the 'Relugas Compact'. It was agreed that it was very important not to embarrass the King, and that His Majesty should be informed. In view of Haldane's many contacts with the King over London University this task was deputed to him. So he wrote to Lord Knollys from Cloan:

'Dear Lord Knollys,

'When I had some confidential conversation with you in the end of July you asked me to let you know if any new development took place in the situation of the Opposition. As some things are happening which seem to come within this description I think it best to tell you of them early. Before I begin I wish to say that I have no knowledge of the attitude towards what is taking place of Sir Henry Campbell-Bannerman. He is reticent and shrewd and I doubt whether he has uttered a word to those who think they know his mind. All I have learned is that he was greatly gratified by the kindly notice taken of him at Marienbad by the King. He may well hold a sensible view of the position. But it has not always been so. During the South African War he took the line that the group represented by Rosebery outside the House of Commons and by Asquith and Grey inside did not represent the mind of his party, and that he must look to his majority as thinking differently. Now we have never admitted that this was a sound judgement. The majority of his Liberals in the House of Commons are sensible enough though they have often been weak and acquiescent. And, as far as we can estimate the situation, if, as it seems probable, the Liberal Party has a majority in the next election a very large part of that majority will in its heart be with us, though it may be timid in the presence of Liberal leaders. For instance, I believe that Sutherland, who has just been returned by a large vote for the Elgin Burghs, took the Liberal Imperialist position during the war in the most decided fashion. Anyhow, it seems more than doubtful whether a very large number of those who will sit as Liberals in the House after the next election will really be of the mind of the *Daily News*, and whether a Government which is undecided in its views on the external policy of the Nation and the necessity for continuity in it can hold their confidence for long. In my view what is above all desirable is to make a resolute attempt to build up a sane and sensible Opposition.

'But though Sir H. C. B. might, if left alone, be disposed to acquiesce in this policy there are unfortunately those who will not let him alone. Of this fact we have recently been reminded. I have just returned here from a private consultation with Asquith and Grey. We had, as you know, formed the view strongly that Sir H. C. B. might, if on a change of Government the King thought fit to send for him to form an administration, go to the Upper House leaving Asquith to lead the Commons with Grey by his side. But we have within the last few days been made aware that this course will not be acceptable to a certain section of the party. They are not, for the most part, men whose names carry weight with the public. But they are vocal and energetic and have access to Sir H. C. B. We have therefore come to the conclusion that we are driven to take a definite step in defence of our policy, if it is to have a chance of success. Pressure will doubtless be put on Sir H. C. B. to retain his lead in the Commons and to give his Cabinet the complexion which I have indicated. Asquith, Grey, and I feel that were this to happen we could in office render no real service in public affairs, and we have decided, in such a case, that it would be best for us to intimate early to Sir H. C. B. that we should stand aside and leave him with his hands free to follow another lure than ours. We believe that the Opposition cannot emerge from its present position unless we can, with our friends and followers, to some extent shape policy. To do this implies that our group should form a sufficiently strong and important minority in the Cabinet.

'What is proposed is that Asquith should, in as friendly and tactful a way as possible, and without assuming that Sir H. C. B. is adverse, tell him of the resolution we have come to. We are none of us wedded to the prospects of office. To Asquith and me they mean pecuniary sacrifice. This we do not shrink from in the least, but we ought not to make sacrifices uselessly. Grey delights in his new work, as Chairman of the North-Eastern Railway. But we are all ready to do our best cheerfully under Sir H. C. B. provided we have sufficient safeguards. What we would try to bring about is that, if the situation arises and Sir H. C. B. is sent for, he should propose to the King the leadership of the House of Commons with the Exchequer for Asquith, either the Foreign or Colonial Office for Grey, and the Woolsack for myself. As to this last I am merely recording for you the wish of the others. I will gladly stand aside. I do not desire to add to the difficulty by putting myself forward. But they attach weight to our group not being broken up, and there are besides reasons connected with the precarious state of the Supreme Court of the Empire, which make the point more important than at another time it would be. It is not from any desire for personal success that any of us wish to propose to Sir H. C. B. the tenure of these offices as a condition of our joining hands with him. But we have a strong feeling that without them we should have no sufficient basis from which to exercise real influence in the work of the reform of the Liberal Party. On our plan he would be left with thirteen places in the Cabinet of which to arrange the disposition. One longs for Rosebery. Had he been coming to his right place at the head of affairs we could have gone anywhere with the confidence that they would be set. But it seems now as if this were not to be, and we have to do the only thing we can do, which is to think out and follow resolutely a plan of concerted action.

'I write to you thus early to let you know of our difficulties and how we propose to meet them. The only thing that could affect the decision, which our conference of this week brought us to, is the thought that it could in any way embarrass the King. But it has not struck me that this would do so. We should take care to act with the utmost gentleness and consideration in making any ultimatum to Sir H. C. B.

'We ought to move soon, say within the next three weeks. The autumn speeches begin then, and Sir H. C. B. will be pressed by others on his return to make up his mind on a line of policy, and it would be unfair to leave him in ignorance of our position. To let things drift is to let them crystallise adversely. Of that we are clear. There may of course be reasons for delay which we have not seen. That is why I write confidentially and privately to you at the earliest moment. And anyhow the situation has seemed to me of sufficient importance to make it right that I should follow up the frank private conversation of last July by telling you what is passing. I hope you will not consider that I have done wrong in this. It is only under a strong sense of necessity that we are acting thus early. In a disorganised party things will gravitate one way or the other in accordance with our action, and that is why we feel we dare not remain still.

'I shall be at home for some time, and am of course at your service.'

To this Lord Knollys replied:

'CRAIG GOWAN,
16th September 1905.

'MY DEAR MR. HALDANE,

'Many thanks for your important and interesting letter of the 12th inst. which I presume you will not object to my showing confidentially to the King when he comes to Balmoral on the 25th. I do not know what his views will be on the subject in question, and perhaps therefore you will remember that I am only expressing my own ideas in what I now say. In the event of his sending for Sir H. C.-Bannerman my belief is that he will strongly urge him to go to the House of Lords as Prime Minister, partly because he would think that Asquith would be the best man to lead the H. of Commons, and partly because he would fear that Sir H. C. B., being a weak or at all events not a strong man like Asquith, would be inclined to give way to pressure from the extreme left, whereas were he in the House of Lords he would not be liable to this pressure to the same extent. If Sir H. C. B. declined to act on the King's suggestion and you and your friends refused to join the Government, H.M. would be placed in an awkward position. A Cabinet of which Sir H. C. B. was the head, without the moderates, would, it appears to me, be disastrous both for the Country and the Party. The Government would be a weak one, which would probably lead it to adopt very radical measures, possibly to interrupt the continuity of the Foreign policy of the present and former Governments, and, in order to enable them to carry out their legislation, they might be induced to bid for the support of the Irish Party.

'Of course what the King would desire would be the presence of a restraining influence in the Cabinet, being aware that many members of it would be men holding extreme views, and this could only be effected by the presence in it of men like yourself, Asquith and Sir E. Grey.

'I venture to ask you, and those whose names I have just mentioned, would not you be better able to advance the interests of those questions, to which you rightly attach so much importance, as well as the welfare of the Country and the Liberal Party, by joining Sir H. C. B.'s Government, even if he remained in the House of Commons, than by holding aloof and making yourselves powerless to moderate the dangerous influence which might be brought to bear upon him? At his age it is not probable that he would be able to stand for long the combined duties of Prime Minister and Leader of the House of Commons, and I cannot help thinking that after one session in that House, which would "save his face" with his extreme friends he would be glad to move into the House of Lords. I should imagine indeed that if he showed himself unwilling, when forming a Government, to become a Peer, the King might well ask him to give a pledge that he would go into the House of Lords within a certain time, say a year for instance.

'But if you and your friends declined to form a part of the Administration, the King would be obliged either (1) to accept Sir H. C. B.'s Government with the loss (I may without flattery say) of the most able and moderate men of the Liberal Party, or (2) he would have to seek for a Prime Minister elsewhere and where is he to be found? If Lord Spencer were to be sent for, Sir H. C. B. would be still more unwilling to leave the House of Commons, and I should doubt the former attempting to form a Government without the assistance of the latter. To whom then could the King turn? To Asquith, and if to him would he be able to form an Administration? I grieve to say that I should look upon Rosebery as out of the question for reasons which you and I know only too well. It appears to me therefore that unless you can suggest a way out of the difficulty, by mentioning someone besides Sir H. C. B., and Lord Spencer, that the King would find himself in a very unfortunate situation if you, Asquith and Sir E. Grey would not accept office. H.M. would I am sure welcome you as Lord Chancellor, Asquith as Chancellor of the Exchequer and Leader of the House of Commons, and Sir E. Grey as Foreign or Colonial Minister.

'I hope you will forgive me for having written so openly and unreservedly, and that you will not think me presumptuous for having done so.

'Yours sincerely,

KNOLLYS.'

The result of this correspondence, which Haldane sent to his two friends, was that he was invited to Balmoral, where he had long talks both with Lord Knollys and with the King. He found that the King was favourable to the proposals of the trio and regarded it as of great importance that they should be in the Liberal Government. He said that Sir Robert Reid's claims to the Chancellorship might stand in Haldane's way and that if they did he hoped that he would take the War Office.

The next stage in the negotiations was that on November 13 Asquith saw Campbell-Bannerman, who expressed himself willing, indeed eager, to have Grey at the Foreign Office, but said that he had decided that Sir Robert Reid should be his Chancellor. As to the proposal that he should go to the House of Lords he said this was the suggestion of 'that ingenious person Richard Burdon Haldane' and added that he would consent 'with reluctance and even with repugnance'. Asquith felt some hesitation in pressing for the

Regulas compact to his own advantage, but the position of Haldane and Grey was entirely different. Neither, as Haldane told Lord Knollys, was at all anxious for office except under conditions in which they felt they could render effective public service. Haldane was of course disappointed to learn that the Woolsack was not within his reach. This was the natural goal of the ambition of a distinguished lawyer, and as we have seen he had in mind plans for the development of the Privy Council as the Supreme Court of the Empire, to which he attached great importance. He was now making an income of £20,000 a year at the Bar and while he already had a sufficiency for his needs and money meant little to him, he was not disposed to sacrifice his income except for an object which he felt to be really worth while and under conditions which gave him a prospect of obtaining his object. Grey was equally determined to come in only on his own terms. So matters remained until December 4, when Mr. Balfour tendered his resignation to the King. That evening Grey called on Campbell-Bannerman and told him plainly that he would take no office in the Government unless C. B. went to the Lords and Asquith led in the Commons. The next day the King sent for Campbell-Bannerman and suggested to him that he should take a peerage to avoid the strain of leading both the Government and the House of Commons. To this C. B. returned a non-committal answer and kissed hands. On December 6 Lady Campbell-Bannerman came to town, and after consulting her C. B. decided definitely against going to the Lords. Grey was staying with Haldane in his rooms in Whitehall Court, and both were agreed that in the circumstances there must be no question of taking office. On December 7 Asquith was busy as a negotiator, and that afternoon, when Haldane was presiding over a meeting of the Technical Education Committee at South Kensington, two letters were brought to him, one from Campbell-Bannerman offering him the Attorney-Generalship, and the other was this from Asquith:

'I was empowered this morning to offer the Foreign Office to E. Grey and an offer of the War Office will soon be on its way to you. The Woolsack being, in spite of all my arguments and efforts, elsewhere, I judge from our talk the other day that this would be the place which you would like best, better e.g. than the Home Office.

'But on the other outstanding point—the leadership of the H. of C.—all my endeavours carried on ceaselessly for two days have proved vain. After considerable hesitation and ostensible, probably actual, wavering, C. B., has on the advice of his wife, declined to go at once to the House of Lords.

'This of course raises a situation of much gravity, and Grey, with whom I have had a long talk, is resolved to refuse office. I have thought the matter most carefully over during the last 48 hours from every point of view, and I have come to the conclusion, (as I told him) that it is my duty to accept. The conditions are in one respect fundamentally different from those which we, or at any rate I, contemplated when we talked in the autumn. The election is before and not behind us, and a Free Trade majority, still more an independent majority, is not a fact but at most a probability.

'I stand in a peculiar position which is not shared by either of you. If I refuse to go in, one of two consequences follows, either (1) the attempt to form a Govt. is given up (which I don't believe in the least would now happen), or (2) a weak Govt. would be formed entirely or almost entirely of one colour.

'In either event in my opinion the issue of the election would be put in the utmost peril. It would be said that we were at issue about Home Rule, the Colonies, the Empire, etc., etc., and the defection of the whole of our group would be regarded as conclusive evidence. The *tertius gaudens* at Dalmeny would look on with complacency. I cannot imagine more disastrous conditions on which to fight a Free Trade election.

'And the whole responsibility, I repeat, would be mine. I could not say after the offers made to you and Grey, that our group had been flouted, and the only ground I could take would be that I and not C. B. must from the first lead the new House of Commons. I could not to my own conscience or to the world justify such a position. If the election were over and Free Trade secure, different considerations would arise.

'This at any rate is my judgement, and I must act on it, tho' I cannot say what pain it gives me even to appear to sever myself from Grey. He knows this and reciprocates the feeling, and tho' we do not take the same view of our respective duties, I don't quarrel with him, nor he with me.

'I write this now, because I see no chance of seeing you to-day as I have to go to the country, and that you may have these considerations in your mind when you receive C. B.'s offer. I don't want in the least to attempt to influence your judgement; your position and Grey's, as regards this particular point, are necessarily different from mine. But I need not say what an enormous and immeasurable difference your co-operation would make to me.

'Whatever happens nothing can change our affection and confidence.'

With these letters in his pocket Haldane went to call on his old friend Mrs. Horner and she in a long talk agreed that Asquith was right and that it was his duty to the King, the country, and the party to take office. He and Grey then went to Acland, who argued very much on the same lines as Mrs. Horner. Finally, the two dined together and during dinner Grey agreed to come in provided Haldane was given an office in which he felt he could serve effectively. Armed with this Haldane went that night to see Campbell-Bannerman. Haldane had no desire to be a law officer and he told C. B. that he did not want to be Attorney-General. Campbell-Bannerman then offered him the Home Office. To this Haldane replied, 'What about the War Office?' 'Nobody', answered

C. B., 'will touch it with a pole.' 'Then give it to me,' Haldane replied, 'I will come as War Secretary if Grey takes the Foreign Office and I will ask him to call on you early tomorrow to tell you his decision, which may, I think, be favourable.' The next morning Grey saw Campbell-Bannerman and agreed to come in, and the same day Asquith wrote to Haldane:

'No words of mine can express what I feel; by your action during the last two days you have laid the party and the country and myself (most of all) under an unmeasured debt of gratitude. I have never spent such a distracting and agonising week. Everything that a man could do I believe I did to achieve the common purposes, under conditions which none of us could have foreseen. Grey at the F.O. is in itself a great thing; but the one thing I minded most, and regret most, is the Woolsack. The rest can wait. On a review of the whole affair, I am satisfied that more could not have been accomplished, and there was such a real risk of losing everything.

'The W.O. is a great opportunity, and every soldier I have met for the last fortnight has expressed the hope that what now is might be. The one thing that has dictated my action has been that the election was before, and not behind us.'

So the new Government was completed and on December 11 Haldane went to the palace and kissed hands as Secretary of State for War. Campbell-Bannerman liked Haldane no better than Haldane liked him. He was wont to refer to him as 'Master Haldane' and wrongly regarded him as the prime mover in an intrigue against himself. In fact, as I have shown, Grey was, if anything, the more determined of the two, and neither throughout this business had any thought for personal advantage to themselves. Both had solely the public interest in view and both yielded solely because they were persuaded that it was in the public interest that they should take office. Campbell-Bannerman would hardly have been human if he had not chuckled over the thought of one whom he regarded as at best a very luke-warm friend going to an office which had been the grave of Parliamentary reputations, and he is reported to have said: 'We shall now see how Schopenhauer gets on in the Kailyard.'[1]

In fact Schopenhauer enjoyed himself in the Kailyard from the first. A fortnight after his first appearance in the War Office he wrote to Gosse to regret having to cancel a meeting at lunch: 'I too am plunged in grief. Yet as soon as the elections are over and I am, if I am, back in this troubled sphere, I see possibilities of luncheons. I will make a confession of fickleness. I thought I loved the law, but out of sight out of mind. I am enjoying myself simply hugely. The dear generals are angels, no other name is good enough for these simple honourable souls. I have already made changes, which might have tried them and they gulp them down. Now I know what it is to live. It is the best of fun, though my solemn predecessors, not being Scotsmen, never saw it. You never saw such a band of reformers as I am trying to hold back. If I could only get three years I could do something.'

It was a real grief to Haldane that all this meant a definite break with Lord Rosebery, for whom he had a very real regard and even affection. After his own retirement from active politics he wrote this appreciation of the man whom he had hoped to serve as his leader:

'I met Rosebery first in the course of the General Election of 1885, when he helped me in East Lothian. By degrees he drew me to himself and I think took a real liking for me. I began to see him and his wife constantly, and finally came into terms of great political intimacy with him. He consulted me about his plans, and I sometimes remonstrated over these

[1]Lord Haldane included in his autobiography (p. 113 *et seq.*) a memorandum which he dictated to Mrs. Horner early in 1906, giving his account of the events of this week, which he described as one of the most disagreeable of his life. This memorandum gives the story in detail. There are one or two minor inaccuracies as to times and dates, which have been corrected here.

and proposed others to him. When the conflict between Rosebery and Harcourt became very acute it was thought that matters had been solved when Rosebery was called to be Prime Minister after Gladstone. But this proved to be not so. The fault was Rosebery's. In some ways he was magnificent as the foremost figure. He had a most powerful personality and great platform eloquence. He was so formidable that he was beyond the reach of London society on the one hand, and of the opposition of colleagues on the other. But he could not keep a Cabinet together. He was lacking in distinct plans, and even in definite purposes. He got discouraged and was turned away from his task by the fear of sleeplessness and by minor disappointments. Although Asquith and Grey and I stuck by him tightly we did so at the peril of our political lives, because we never knew when he would retire altogether and leave us in the lurch. He would make no sacrifice of himself. With all these disadvantages he was none the less, after Mr. Gladstone, the first figure of the time in the political world. Obviously our task as Liberals was a very difficult one. We got Rosebery to resume political activity in 1900 at Chesterfield, where he made a great speech, but immediately after he went off to Gastein from which he only returned when he heard that, having broken with Campbell-Bannerman over his attacks on the generals in the conduct of the South African War, we were acting independently and giving a dinner to Asquith, who had somewhat uncertainly responded to our appeal. But we had reckoned without Rosebery, who arrived hot-foot from Gastein and suddenly arranged a luncheon at the City Liberal Club, where he anticipated our function for the evening by making a speech early in the afternoon. Had it not been for *The Times*, which, with great insight, reported both Rosebery and Asquith verbatim, we should have been in a great difficulty because he had not backed us up in what he said. So things went on. In the earlier stages, as I have said, I saw Rosebery constantly, more, I think, than any other politician. When he was Prime Minister I used to be with him in the mornings, and I knew more of his plans than I suspect the Members of his Cabinet did. I worked out many schemes for him, and sometimes he gave help in putting them into effect. Anyhow, things went on so. But the break was inevitable, and it came in the autumn of 1905 when it was evident we could not rely on Rosebery's leadership any more.'

Chapter VIII

CAMPBELL-BANNERMAN'S GOVERNMENT— THE MILITARY CONVERSATIONS WITH FRANCE

1906

The General Election of January 1906 resulted in such a victory for the Liberals as not even the most optimistic member of the party had expected. They swept Lancashire, Balfour being defeated in Manchester, and returned with 377 members, a clear majority on the whole House; while the Chamberlainites were reduced to 109. Haldane had an easy triumph in Haddingtonshire, where Mrs. Lawrie insisted on his still making Monkrigg his headquarters. His majority leaped up from 378 in 1900 to 1,180, in spite of the fact that his electioneering was much interrupted by public business. On the eve of the poll he was delighted to receive from Lord Rayleigh a letter announcing his election as Fellow of the Royal Society.

The triumph of 1906 had the effect of solidifying the Liberal Party. Balfour had expected that its two wings would separate before long and bring the Government down, for he was well aware that the Liberal Imperialists had had no great confidence in Campbell-Bannerman. But his great victory gave C. B. just the confidence and assurance which he needed and he made an admirable leader of the House. Both Haldane and Grey admitted that they had been wrong and they served him with a loyalty which in the end turned to affection. The relations between Haldane and his chief were naturally, in view of what had passed, not very easy at first. C. B. had no understanding of or sympathy with Haldane's philosophy, which he held to have no bearing on the practical problems of life. His nickname for his Minister of War was 'Schopenhauer'. But he took a very keen interest in the Army and his friend Lord Haliburton, who kept touch with the civil side of the War Office, informed him of what was passing there, and he was as delighted with, as he was surprised at, Haldane's success. When in March 1906 Haldane made his first big speech as War Minister, outlining his policy, Campbell-Bannerman came to him and said: 'That was not only a splendid speech but an historical speech.' And as Haldane's plans developed the Prime Minister confessed to a friend:'I had no idea "Schopenhauer" would cut such a figure in the barrack yard.' So one of the chief difficulties which Haldane had supposed would confront him in the Cabinet disappeared.

Of his part in that Cabinet and of some of his chief colleagues he left notes which may be here put together.

'In the Liberal Cabinet from 1905 to 1915 I played a part which was much more at close quarters with individuals than with the Cabinet as a whole. I was not really good in that Cabinet, partly from temperament, and partly because I found it difficult to get really interested in its detailed work. I was myself taken up almost entirely with the large task of reorganising the Army for possible war. I should have liked to have extended that work to the Navy, and did the best I could, but the Government was not really interested in those things, and the result was that there was very little opportunity for this sort of scientific consideration in Cabinet deliberations. Our relations with Germany were of course of a critical kind, and my ties to Grey gave me much opportunity of speaking with him, but here there were difficulties because I was suspected by the public of being pro-German. In truth, all I wanted was to make my countrymen see that there was a problem of German character raising questions of a very dangerous kind, and that the organising power of Germany had to be understood before we could make ourselves safe. This was not so merely in military matters. In commerce and industry, in regard to which I also had special means of making myself acquainted with the progress of German advances, the danger appeared to me not less. What I saw of Ballin, of Sir Ernest Cassel and of German commercial magnates whom I met at the latter's house, made me think that there was a peril here really greater than that of war, in which we could always fall back on sea power. Science had been developed and applied in Germany as it had not been with us, and it was very difficult to get my colleagues to realise this, and to avoid, when I approached it, being put down as a pro-German enthusiast. Anyhow it was organisation for war and organisation of industry which were the two subjects which fascinated me during the ten years of Liberal Cabinet life, and I did not succeed in educating my colleagues, although I got the Army re-organised, the Navy influenced and more universities founded.

'About 1882 I met at Lincoln's Inn Herbert Henry Asquith. He had come from Balliol where he had swept everything before him. He was three years older than I was, but we became very intimate friends. He lived at Hampstead with his first wife and their children. Hers was a beautiful spirit, and among my letters is one which he wrote to me on her death, and which shews how fully he realised this. London society had, however, always a great attraction for him, and by degrees, particularly after his second marriage, he went more and more into that society and was somewhat diverted from the sterner mode of life with which he and I were familiar. For in the earlier years we rarely failed to dine together two or three times a week, generally at some restaurant, where we carried on earnest conversations about politics, and made plans. We were both rising at the Bar, but to Asquith eminence in the law at no time presented any attraction. From the beginning he meant to be Prime Minister. For this position nature had endowed him to a great extent, but only to some extent. He had the best intellectual apparatus, understanding and judgment, that I ever saw in any man. He was a serious person in those days. His photograph makes him look like a stern Nonconformist. I remember passing along the Horse Guards with him when he touched my arm and pointed to the figure of John Bright in front of us—"There", he said, "is the only man in public life who has risen to eminence without being corrupted by London society." In 1885 I got into the House of Commons as Member for East Lothian. I had more daring than Asquith and took the risk,—a considerable one,—of entering Parliament while still a Junior. Next year Asquith followed my example, and I introduced him to East Fife where he had a secure seat for many years. He had not been long in the House of Commons before he made a brilliant speech, and this, coupled with his great Oxford reputation, turned the attention to him not only of his leaders but of the public. His diction was faultless, and his voice was a powerful one. He rarely made a bad point, and it was a surprise to nobody when in 1892 Mr. Gladstone made him Home Secretary. But before that time he, and Grey, and Arthur Acland, and Sydney Buxton and I, had formed an organisation of young Liberal Members which had much of the future in its hands. We acted with a good deal of independence, and we shaped policy by our influence. Asquith did not originate much. He was not a man of imagination, but when we had worked anything out we always chose him to state it for us,—a thing he did to perfection.

'Grey I came to know through the House of Commons in the session of 1886 when we were both young members. The attraction was mutual and I became the intimate friend of himself and his wife. I was constantly at Falloden and they were often at Cloan. He was gifted by nature with a noble presence and a fine voice. He also expressed himself very well and he had a first rate judgment with the caution character-

HALDANE, ASQUITH AND CURZON
UNIVERSITY OF MANCHESTER, 1908

istic of an older man. He was less formidable than Asquith and he was lacking in the range of knowledge which came to Asquith from an intellectual curiosity that was lacking in Grey. But Grey was a first-rate statesman and he had a quality of character which Asquith did not possess. He was my most intimate political friend, and whenever a crisis public or private affected our lives we came together. He was always resolute and calm in an emergency. He had no prejudices, class or otherwise, and always approached every problem of public or private life with the question "what is right?" and having decided on his answer he held unswervingly to his convictions. He and I passed together through many testing times and with each test my admiration for him increased.

'Another remarkable figure with whom I came much in contact was John, Lord Morley. I knew him intimately for 38 years. But although Morley was one of the most interesting people I have ever known, and perhaps the greatest critic of life of my time, he was not really cut out for public administration. When he was Secretary for India he was not easy to work with. We were at that time reforming the Army on modern principles, and one would have expected that Morley would have come and consulted with us about what he himself was doing. Great soldiers were there to give him advice, but he would not have it. He insisted on consulting Lord Middleton and Lord Roberts. The result was that he drifted into the hands of Lord Kitchener, who made an Army in India that was efficient in some respects but was lacking in all modern equipment of transport. Results were disastrous when it had to take the field in Mesopotamia during the Great War. Morley would never willingly allow a colleague to suggest anything to him, and he was not a really good judge of men. Although he had a great respect for Lord Kitchener, he was determined when Lord Minto went from the Vice-Royalty that Lord Kitchener should not succeed him. King Edward was equally determined that Lord Kitchener should. I remember one day Morley saying to me, "The King has summoned me to an audience to-morrow at half-past eleven, and I frankly say to you I dread it. I am constitutionally not well fitted for fighting with Sovereigns." I, who was myself on the best of terms with King Edward, said to him: "I think I can avert anything disagreeable. I will ask for an audience an hour before you on Army things and I may say something that will change the subject." I did so and said to the King, after I had disposed of the formal business for which I had asked the audience, "There is Morley; he and Kitchener don't know each other; don't you think, Sir, that it would be well to put off any decision about the Vice-Royalty until Morley and Kitchener do get to know one another; could not there be a dinner arranged at which they could meet?" "Excellent," said King Edward, "I will settle that with him." I met Morley that afternoon and he said that he had had a very easy interview with King Edward, and he told me of a dinner to take place in the Carlton Restaurant in a private room. The guests were Lord Knollys, Lord Esher, Morley, Kitchener and myself. Unfortunately Kitchener took just the wrong way with Morley. Instead of saying "I am a soldier, a plain soldier", and then going on tactfully to develop that he would do as a soldier just the things Morley wanted, he proceeded to say that he had been much impressed with Morley's policy and with the necessity for a new order of things conforming to it in India, and produced on Morley's mind the impression that he was a weaker man than he really was. The result was that as Morley went out he said to me: "That man shall not be Viceroy of India." Poor Kitchener did not know he had got on so badly. But King Edward died within three weeks and the question therefore never became acute. Lord Hardinge was appointed with the concurrence of King George. Yet whatever Morley was not as an administrator, in social intercourse he reached the very highest level.

His talk was wonderful when he was at his best, as he generally was. The conversations which he held with me used to range over the whole field of human affairs. His platform speeches were far superior to his House of Commons orations. The reason was that he had generally more time to prepare them. I remember his coming to stay with us at Cloan before delivering a speech at Perth. He took three days to prepare it during which we were constantly hunting up quotations for him. When the time came I took him to Perth by special train and conducted him to the Hall. At that time I did not understand him as well as I did later, and I was so foolish as to tell the twenty or thirty Liberal Associations which were attending the meeting armed with Addresses that they need not present them formally but only hand them in. I told Morley this, thinking I should earn his commendation, but instead he was very angry and said it was ruining the whole magnificence of the Meeting, and I had hastily to countermand my directions so that they were formally presented. It was a fine speech ending with a quotation from Burns.

'Morley was never trained in Philosophy, though as Editor of the *Fortnightly Review* and the *Pall Mall* he had been closely in contact with the greatest men of his time in this country. The result was that, particularly in reminiscences, there was no one who could be at once so critical and so appreciative. In some ways, though not in all, he had a great insight into what the public wanted. When Campbell-Bannerman formed his Government in which he and I were both Secretaries of State he said to me: "This is the first middle-class Cabinet and I am far from sure that it is going to satisfy the public that the traditions of our Constitution will be preserved." He was a difficult colleague, constantly threatening resignation. Still he was a very great addition to the Cabinet, and his moral influence enabled us to carry on. He was, I think, ambitious, and would have liked to be Prime Minister, and I doubt whether he ever understood why he was not suited for this position and how it was that it went to Asquith.

'Lloyd George had boundless energy and quick intelligence and a really remarkable gift for sensing the drift of public opinion, but he was really an illiterate with an unbalanced mind. I never had faith in his ability to think anything out or to stick to the conclusion he arrived at. Splendid at getting out of a corner he had no prevision of coming situations. He took no interest in my first Cabinet in Imperial Defence except to urge me to make greater economies than I thought possible.'

The new Government being firmly established as the result of the election, letters of welcome and congratulation poured in upon Haldane. Those interested in Army reform had been in considerable anxiety as to what a Liberal victory at the polls would mean for them and they heaved a sigh of relief when a Secretary of State was appointed whose attitude during the South African War and whose public statements on imperial defence they remembered with gratitude and approval. Lord Esher wrote, immediately the announcement of Haldane's appointment was made, to say what pleasure the news gave him, and added, 'the King is delighted'. Lord Roberts, Lord Wolseley, Sir John Fisher, the First Sea Lord of the Admiralty, were the chief of a number of soldiers and sailors who sent messages of welcome, and there was a very cordial and generous letter from his predecessor, Mr. Arnold Foster. All this was very pleasant but Haldane was well aware that few if any of these were members of his party and he did not overestimate the practical value of their support in the solution of his problems.

As to those problems, he had made up his mind to come to no conclusions until he had given himself ample time to study them. He has told the story of his first meeting with his Army Council but it is good enough to stand repetition. The generals were accustomed to ministers who had come into office with schemes which they had advocated in Parliament and the Press, and they had had ample experience of the difficulties of fitting a general plan to the exigencies of practical administration. The military members of the Army Council therefore presented themselves to their new chief and said that they would like to have some general idea of the reforms which he proposed to submit to Parliament. 'My reply', wrote Haldane, 'was that I was a young and blushing virgin just united to a bronzed warrior and that it was not expected by the public that any result of the union should appear until at least nine months had passed.'

Despite this quip, which delighted King Edward when it was passed on to him, he was ready to give his Army Council some general idea of what was in his mind. On January 1, 1906, he sent them what he called a 'rough note' for their consideration. After suggesting that home defence was primarily a naval question, the next step, he said, was to determine the objects for which the military forces of the Crown exist. 'In this connection I feel that it is difficult to improve on the definition which the Localisation Committee of 1872 laid down for its own guidance. "The sole object of any military system in peace", so runs the Committee's Report, "is to provide for a state of war; and the test of any peace organisation must be its power:

' "1st, to place in the field immediately on the outbreak of war, in the highest state of efficiency, as large a force as is possible with the peace military expenditure;

' "2nd, to maintain that force throughout the continuance of hostilities undiminished in numbers and efficiency."

'As regards the purpose of the Army, what is obviously required is a highly organised and well equipped force which can be transported with the least possible delay to any part of the world where it is required.'

He then went on to suggest some general lines on which the Army Reserve, the Militia, and the Volunteers should be brought into the general scheme of imperial defence.

'The general nature of these observations will be apparent. It strikes my mind that the problem of the future re-organisation of the British Army can only be considered as a whole, and that it is fatal to try to deal with the parts of which one entire force is made up without first determining their co-ordination on broad principles according to which they are to be fitted into each other in the scheme as a whole. It is better to take time for this, and meantime to suspend piecemeal reforms, then to start work with a clear conception of what is to be ultimately worked out.'

This note delighted the military members of the Army Council. One of the leading spirits in the Localization Committee had been Colonel (afterwards Field-Marshal) Lord Wolseley, and in 1886, when Wolseley was adjutant-general, he directed the Intelligence Department to prepare a scheme for the mobilization of two army corps and the necessary line of communication troops for war outside Great Britain and Ireland. This was the first conception of an organized British expeditionary force, but it remained no more than a conception for almost simultaneously Lord Salisbury's Government yielded to a panic that we were exposed to invasion by France, and Mr. Stanhope, the War Minister, announced a vast scheme for the defence of London by the erection of fortifications on the southern edge of the North Downs, which cost a huge sum. In 1891 Mr. Stanhope issued a secret memorandum which defined the functions of the Army. These functions were:

(*a*) to support the civil power effectively in all parts of the United Kingdom;

(*b*) to find the troops required for India;

(*c*) to find the garrisons of our fortresses and coaling stations abroad;

(*d*) after providing for these requirements to be able to mobilize rapidly for home defence two army corps of regular troops and one partly composed of Regulars and partly of

Militia, and to organize the auxiliary forces, for the defence of London and for the defensible positions in advance and for the defence of mercantile ports;

(e) subject to the foregoing considerations and to their financial obligations, to aim at being able in case of necessity to send abroad two complete army corps with cavalry division and line of communication. But it will be distinctly understood that the possibility of the employment of an army corps in the field in any European war is sufficiently improbable to make it the primary duty of the military authorities to organize our forces efficiently for the defence of this country.

Right up to the South African War Lord Wolseley made continuous efforts to get this ridiculous policy changed for one more in keeping with the realities of the problem of imperial defence, but in vain. As vainly the blue-water school pointed out that if we lost command of the sea no enemy need trouble to invade us and that if we had command of the sea no serious invasion was possible; therefore the beginning and end of home defence was an adequate navy. The Stanhope memorandum held the field and all attempts by the soldiers to get from successive governments a more realistic statement of military policy had failed. Now a new Secretary of State had come and in his first note he had put the Stanhope memorandum in the waste-paper basket and given his Army Council a target which they felt worthy of their aim. This and his readiness to learn, while his immediate predecessors had been prone to teach, made Haldane at once *persona grata* with his generals. He wrote to Spender: 'I am enjoying myself hugely. The work of thinking out and executing organisation delights me. My Generals are like angels. They concur with me in a decision to arrest all schemes for new expenditure until we have thought out what the Army as a whole is to be, and we are already engaged in working from the top downwards, instead of beginning with details.'

Haldane had his first consultations with Lord Esher, who as chairman of the Esher Committee was very familiar with the organization and the personnel of the War Office, and on his advice he invited Colonel Ellison, who had been secretary of the Esher Committee, to be his military private secretary. Ellison, who had had some experience of previous attempts at Army reform, inquired of Lord Esher whether Haldane was coming into office with a preconceived plan, and on getting an assurance that the new minister had no plan, he accepted the appointment. The two men suited each other admirably. Haldane's object was to find principles on which to base his proposals and this exactly suited Ellison's trend of mind. He told his new secretary that he knew nothing of the elements of military organization and wished to be instructed. He took him down with him to Monkrigg and there, Ellison says, 'during the daytime he was engaged in canvassing and it was not until after dinner that we got busy with military affairs and then we were often at it till one or two a.m. Hour after hour we would walk backwards and forwards in a big billiard room, Mr. Haldane on one side of the table smoking the best cigars obtainable, I on the other.'

While they were so engaged an event occurred which gave a definite turn to the search for principles and plans. While at Monkrigg Haldane received this letter from Sir E. Grey:

'FOREIGN OFFICE
Jan. 8. 1906
'MY DEAR RICHARD,
    'Persistent reports and little indications keep reaching me that Germany means to attack France in the spring. I don't think these are more than the precautions and flourishes that Germany would naturally make apropos of the Morocco Conference. But they are not altogether to be disregarded. A situation might arise presently in which popular feeling might compel the Government to go to the help of France and you might suddenly be asked what you could do. Fisher says he is

ready, by which I take it he means that his ships are so placed that he can drive the German Fleet off the sea and into shelter at any time. I don't want you to give any definite answer in a hurry but I think you should be preparing one.

Yours ever

E. GREY.'

What had happened was this. Under Lord Lansdowne's agreement with France, which had resulted in the *Entente Cordiale* of 1904, we had promised France a free hand in Morocco in exchange for a free hand for ourselves in Egypt. In the autumn of 1905 Germany had somewhat roughly claimed a voice in Moroccan affairs, and as a result of this an international conference had been arranged to take place at Algeciras to seek an agreement. During the preparations for this conference Germany's attitude became definitely truculent and France definitely alarmed. As a result of the Russo-Japanese War Russia, France's only ally, was out of action, and the French Government was very naturally apprehensive that Germany would make the most of a golden opportunity. The new British Government had not yet had any occasion to make a pronouncement on foreign policy and the French were uncertain whether it would be prepared to honour Lord Lansdowne's agreement.

In these circumstances, the French Military Attaché, Major Huguet, unofficially approached Colonel Repington, then military correspondent to *The Times* and told him of the anxieties of the French Government. Repington passed on this conversation to Sir Edward Grey, and also told Esher, who was a member of the Committee of Imperial Defence, Sir George Clarke, the secretary of that committee, and Sir John Fisher, what had passed. Grey was engaged in his election campaign in Northumberland at the time, but he came up to town and after a talk with his own officials at the Foreign Office he saw Sir John Fisher and Lord Esher and then wrote his letter of January 8 to Haldane. He and Haldane arranged to meet at Berwick on January 12, and after a long talk both agreed that in the situation it might become necessary for us to implement our *entente* with France, and that naval and military plans for that eventuality should be prepared. Grey asked whether it would not be possible for our General Staff to make provisional plans for intervention on the Continent in aid of France as a precaution, without committing the Government. Haldane replied that this could easily be done and both were agreed that it should be done. Grey at once wrote to the Prime Minister to give him his views and on the very eve of his poll Haldane went up to London and saw Sir Henry Campbell-Bannerman, who gave Haldane permission to set his General Staff to work, on the express understanding that it should be stated in writing that the conversations were not to go beyond the limits of purely General Staff work and in no way committed the Government to action. Haldane thereupon saw Sir N. Lyttelton, the Chief of the General Staff, and General Grierson, the Director of Military Operations, and authorized the latter to get into touch with the French Military Attaché.

So began the 'military conversations' which resulted eventually in our war plan of 1914. Unfortunately these conversations took a wrong turn from the start. The Committee of Imperial Defence started by Balfour was a comparatively new thing and neither ministers, soldiers, nor sailors had yet learned to use it. No member of the new Government had ever attended one of its meetings. The armed power of Great Britain is, or was in 1906, essentially amphibious and any plans for action on the Continent of Europe should have been joint naval and military plans prepared under the direction of the Committee of Imperial Defence, but this body was not then equipped for such work. Sir John Fisher, the First Sea Lord, was a masterful person with his own views and he was not disposed to tolerate any military, or for that matter any French, interference. He did not believe in the employment of a military expeditionary force on the Continent of Europe and his plan was for joint naval and military attacks upon the coast of Schleswig-Holstein, a plan which both the French and our General Staff regarded as impracticable. So, as Haldane was to discover later, the Admiralty went one way and the General Staff another. He was himself quite clear as to what was right, for in his first note to his Army Council, dated January 1906, he said: 'In comparing such countries as England and Germany, in points of power and defence, a mistake is often made of comparing the English Army with the German Army. These exist for wholly different purposes, and cannot be compared. The principal comparison in fighting strength is between the Navy plus the Army in the one case, and the Army plus the Navy in the other.' He was not at the time sufficiently familiar with the machinery of government to realize that others did not take that commonsense view, and it took him some time to discover that there was no real co-operation or understanding between the Admiralty and the War Office.

The military conversations were begun in the first instance both with France and Belgium. On January 16 Grierson opened official negotiations with Huguet, and on the same day he wrote to Lt.-Colonel Barnadiston, our Military Attaché in Brussels: 'You may tell the Chief of Staff that we are prepared to put in the field in this case 4 cavalry brigades, 2 army corps and a division of mounted infantry and you know from our conversations the general lines on which you should go. The total numbers will be about 105,000 and we shall ferry them over to the French coast, Calais—Boulogne —Dieppe—Havre, railing them afterwards if necessary to Belgium, and then when command of the sea is assured changing our base to Antwerp.'

Grierson's calculation was that it would take thirty-two days to deliver those 105,000 men in France, but at a meeting of the Committee of Imperial Defence it was stated that it would take us two months to mobilize and transport to France 80,000 men fully equipped for continental warfare, and on January 15 Sir Edward Grey had written to Sir Francis Bertie our Ambassador at Paris: 'As to taking precautions beforehand in case war should come, it appears that Fisher has long ago taken the French Naval Attaché in hand, and no doubt has all naval plans prepared. I have now got Haldane's consent to General Grierson being in direct communication with the French Military Attaché, but I am told that 80,000 men with good guns is all we can put into the field in Europe to meet first class troops, that won't save France unless she can save herself. We can protect ourselves, of course, as we are more supreme at sea than we have ever been.'

Eighty thousand men in two months was very far from meeting the views of the French military authorities, who were asking for some help in the first week. Belgium dropped out of these conversations at an early stage, for the Belgian Government did not wish to give France or Germany any pretext for accusing her of a breach of neutrality. So the conversations were continued with France alone and Haldane's immediate problem became how to provide the largest possible force which could be mobilized rapidly and transported quickly to France, if the need to support that country on the Continent were to arise. The general policy which he had already adumbrated to the Army Council had swiftly been given a precise object. Haldane took Ellision with him to Cloan to think out the general principles on which his policy should be based.

On becoming Secretary of State for War he had decided that he must have larger and more convenient quarters than his flat in Whitehall Court provided and he took 28 Queen Anne's Gate, one of those delightful houses overlooking St. James's Park, and enlisted the help of Mrs. Horner and of his sister in the decorating and furnishing of it. It remained his London house until his death.

Chapter IX

THE CREATION OF THE EXPEDITIONARY FORCE

1906 to 1907

While Haldane had succeeded at once in establishing friendly relations with his Army Council he made himself no less welcome to the younger officers, both in the War Office and throughout the army, in whom the South African War had created a new spirit of professional keenness. To these he paid his tribute in his first speech in the House as Secretary of State for War:

'The men one comes across, the new school of young officers, entitled to the appellation of men of science just as much as engineers or chemists—were to me a revelation; and the whole question of the organisation of the Army is fraught with an interest which, I think, is not behind that of the study of any other scientific problem.

'A new school of officers has arisen since the South African War, a thinking school of officers who desire to see the full efficiency which comes from new organisation and no surplus energy running to waste.'

The men in question responded at once to this compliment and gave him their best. The new minister recognized that a great deal of spade-work had been done by his predecessors. If Mr. Brodrick's army corps scheme had proved to be unrealizable it had at least established the principle that the organization of the Army in peace should have some relation to its organization for war. Up to the time of the South African War the army at home had been distributed in districts, in which the number and nature of the troops was determined mainly by the barrack accommodation available. Throughout the long period of Victorian small wars it had been the practice to create a field force *ad hoc*, and generals, staffs, and troops were, in the main, brought together for the first time when the force was mobilized. It was now agreed that that was all wrong, and that the troops should be organized in peace as they would be in war and trained by those who would lead them in the field. Mr. Arnold Foster had adopted most of the recommendations of the Esher Committee, the War Office had been reorganized, the Army Council created, and the embryo of a General Staff was in existence. The Army had been provided with a service dress, and the equipment of the artillery with a new gun and of the infantry with a new rifle was nearing completion. Most important of all, great strides had been made in the practical training of the Army for war. To all this, and especially to Balfour's creation of the Committee of Imperial Defence, Haldane paid his tribute, while expressing the vain hope that the Army might be removed from the field of party politics. As Sir George Clarke had pointed out, it was a simple matter for the Admiralty to strike a ship off the active list and put it on a maintenance basis, but changes in the Army affected too many persons and interests to escape opposition.

Haldane at once recognized that his first difficulty would be with his own party. The triumphant Liberals had come into office burning with zeal for social reform, and the only way in which they could find the money to implement their schemes was by cutting down the defence estimates. Very few of them took any other interest in the Army and Haldane saw at once that no scheme of his had any chance of acceptance by the new House unless it proposed serious economies. His immediate task was to combine saving with efficiency, and of this he did not despair. With Ellison as his military and Mr. Charles Harris as his financial devil he set about a search for superfluities which might be abolished without injury to the general scheme which he had in mind. He was fortunate in finding these when the time came for him to present his estimates to the House.

He made his speech introducing his first estimates on March 8. After reminding the House that he had been only three months in office, he told members that he came to them with no preconceived plan and he asked for time to work out a plan based on sound principles. One of these principles he stated. In the previous year Mr. Balfour had announced his faith in the blue-water school. With this Haldane expressed his complete agreement:

'I came to office in December and being of a curious and enquiring mind and having taken a great interest in Blue Water principles, I set to work to see whether, following out the policy of my predecessors, I could not find some things in our army organisation which were inconsistent with these principles and which therefore might be gently removed. I found that distinguished soldiers, whom I consulted, were of exactly the same mind. They said "let us think clearly and act strongly".'

He went on to tell the House that he had discovered that a number of the forts erected for the defence of London under the Stanhope scheme were still being maintained at considerable expense; that there were still in existence a number of coast defence batteries with obsolete guns, in places where they served no useful purpose, that we maintained a garrison in St. Helena which had no justification, and a Chinese regiment with British officers at Weihaiwei, 'originally a naval base, now, I believe, a watering-place'. All these were to go, and he promised the House to continue his inquiries on these lines. This delighted the Liberals, and having got these into a good humour he went on to expound the consequences of faith in the blue-water school and to hint at the reforms which were in his mind.

'It must be remembered that this country is in quite a different position from that of any foreign nation. If Germany or France go to war they have conscription, and they are in this position—that in time of peace they must keep up a vast military organisation. They have one war to contemplate on a large scale, and that is with their neighbours across the border. They have to be ready to mobilise and to fight within perhaps ten days from the time of the order being given. Therefore they must be ready. It is absolutely necessary that their reserves should be trained up to the eyes and ready when called upon to take the field at once. But the British Army is not like that. We live on an island and our coasts are completely defended by our Fleet. Our Army is wanted for purposes abroad and overseas. It is necessarily a professional Army; we could not get such an Army by conscription. It must be of high quality; but because of the limited nature of its functions —to strike at a distance—it ought to be of strictly limited dimensions. Have we ever thought, scientifically and clearly, what these dimensions ought to be? I do not think so. I know that certain things have been worked out, but I do not think the whole problem has been dealt with in its entirety. Here is an island, the striking force of which does not exist for the defence of these coasts—it does not exist merely for our own insular interests. This island is the centre of an Empire consisting of nearly 12,000,000 square miles and including some 400,000,000 of population, and we have to protect the distant shores of the Empire from the attack of the invader. We want, therefore, an Army which is very mobile and capable of rapid transport. For fighting which has to be at a distance and cannot be against large masses of men it ought to be on a strictly limited scale, and perfect rather in quality than expanded in quantity. There never has been enough careful thinking about this problem. If the Army is not wanted for home defence, then its size is something which is capable of being calculated. The size of the expeditionary force is the principal ingredient in the present cost of the Army.'

This was his most successful speech in the House on Army reform. He was dealing in the main with generalities, which he handled like a master; his reference to the work of his predecessors pleased the Opposition, his promise of economies his own party. His later speeches were necessarily loaded with detail and this and his rapid delivery—he was the despair of all except the very best of shorthand writers—made it difficult to follow with comfort. He was loaded with congratulations, but he was fully aware that unless he produced something more substantial in the way of economy enthusiasm on his side of the House would dry up. He had explained that he found himself faced with automatic increases, the legacy of his predecessors, amounting to £800,000, and despite this he had reduced the estimates by £17,000. It was a beginning, but his party expected much more.

Happily, in April an agreement was reached at Algeciras. Germany, finding that Britain was resolute in support of France, drew in her horns, and Haldane was given leisure to proceed with his plans. These took shape more quickly than he had anticipated. Military opinion was almost unanimous that a divisional organization was best suited to the circumstances of our Army. It was agreed that there should be big divisions, big as compared with those of the South African War, actually of the same size as those of France and Germany. It then became a question of how many of these divisions could be formed from the troops quartered in Great Britain, and it was found that there were rather more than enough for one cavalry division and six divisions, but not enough for seven. It was therefore decided that the expeditionary force should consist of a cavalry division, and six divisions complete in all respects and capable of rapid organization, and that the troops at home should be given a corresponding organization in time of peace. It was further agreed that in the interests of economy everything redundant to this expeditionary force should be lopped off.

Rumours got about that Haldane was proposing to disband ten battalions of infantry, including two battalions of Guards, to reduce the colonial garrisons, and to make a large reduction in the artillery. Immediately protests poured in. The King wrote on March 23: 'I understand that Mr. Haldane contemplates making many reductions of troops in the Colonies, but I hope he will clearly understand that I cannot give my sanction to the reduction of any garrison in South Africa. It is too small as it is, and for training troops the best country we possess.' A few days later the King returned to the charge and noted on a dispatch from the Governor of Natal: 'My strong conviction is that the garrisons of South Africa and Egypt should be strengthened, not only for political reasons, but because the above-named countries are so admirably adapted to the drilling and manœuvring of troops, as there is so much space. The garrisons of Gibraltar and Malta should be denuded of troops as much as possible; in fact it would be far better if both places were handed over to the Royal Navy and garrisoned by Royal Marines, and of course a certain force of Royal Artillery.'

This was good sound sense, but the difficulties in the way were great. Haldane replied that there was very inadequate barrack accommodation in South Africa and that providing it would be a very costly business: '. . . . it is difficult to know where to place troops in South Africa. Natal is ruled out strategically and the Admiralty will not take over Gibraltar and Malta.' Haldane had described Trinity College, Dublin, as 'the ark of the Covenant', the Guards if not in the Holy of Holies, were in a sanctuary into which outsiders were not welcomed. The report that Haldane proposed to move two battalions from the Guards Brigade at Aldershot to London, and abolish the third battalions of the Coldstream and Scots Guards aroused a stream of protests. Esher records: 'In the course of the discussion which took place yesterday Sir John French told Haldane that if reductions are absolutely necessary, much as he would dislike it, he would far rather see four batteries of artillery reduced, than lose the Brigade of Guards from a force which he would have to command in the field. Mr. Arnold Foster and Mr Brodrick both protested, the latter describing a reduction of the artillery as a national calamity. In these circumstances Haldane decided to go down to the House rather sooner than he had originally intended and make public his plan for the reorganisation of the Regular Army.' He spoke on July 12 in Committee on the Army Estimates:

'Since I have been at the War Office I have been approached by many soldiers—by many of the modern type of officers to whom I have referred—who have said to me: "No soldier but would like more money and more men, and the more he had the more he would make of them. But we recognise that the nation demands retrenchment, and we know the grounds upon which it is held to be necessary. We do not dispute those grounds; we are prepared to agree with them. Yet this much we say to you—use the power, if you can obtain it from this new Parliament, full of vigour and life, to re-organise the Army in such a fashion that it shall be an Army shaped for the only purpose for which an Army is needed— for the purpose of war. We hate war. We would that we saw the day when the curse of war was averted from us, when it was no longer necessary to prepare forces for our defence. But till that day comes it is our duty to see that every penny spent on the Army is spent on its fighting efficiency." That is the view of the Army Council. That is the view of soldiers of every shade of politics—some of them in this House—who have come to me and said—"Do not lose this great oppor- tunity for asking Parliament to reorganise us—it may be in a drastic and searching fashion—but to reorganise us in such a way that we shall be efficient for war." That is the keynote of the attempt at Army Reform, of the proposals of my col- leagues and myself, which I have to-day to lay before the House of Commons.

'Indeed economy and efficiency are not incompatible things. Look at the great industrial concerns, the railways and big manufacturing establishments—how are they made to pay their dividends? Why, by going through every item of their accounts and asking why and for what reason has each particular sum of money been spent, and what justification there is for every item. We have been living laborious days in the War Office during the last few months. I am afraid the eight hours movement shows no sign of reaching that great Department, and more than that, we have put the Army lately on a very frugal and somewhat niggardly administration; but the result has been that we have been able to go through the Army piece by piece and bit by bit, inquiring why that bit is there, whether it is sound, whether there is any excess, ay, and what is equally important, whether there is any deficiency. We have applied to the Army the same procedure that an accountant would apply in investigating the affairs of a business; we have gone through it bit by bit, and asked in what condition that bit is, and what justification there is for the money spent upon it. We have put, as regards every officer and man, and every pound spent, the determining question, What does that officer, that man, that money mean, tested by the standard of efficiency in war?'

He went on to reaffirm his faith in the blue-water school. 'The first purpose for which we want any army is for overseas war. The Fleet defends our coasts.' Therefore the Army at home should be organized as an expeditionary force which could be promptly sent overseas to any part of the world where it was needed. He then announced that his expeditionary force would consist of a cavalry division and six divisions, with a total of 5,546 officers and 154,074 men, as compared with a previous maximum of 100,000 men, and, despite this increase for the one purpose for which the army at home would be required in war, he proposed to effect large economies by reducing the Regular Army by 20,000 men. This was to be done 'by rigidly adhering to the policy of writing off everything that is useless for war purposes, by applying strictly the principle of organization for war, by maintaining that organization so that it shall exist in time of peace not merely on paper but in reality'.

His so-called reductions in the artillery, upon which Mr. Brodrick had commented severely in *The Times*, he explained in a passage which delighted the Liberal benches: 'Now I come to a mystery, a great mystery, the mystery of the existing condition of our artillery system. Let us see how it stands. Mr. Brodrick, in his letter, said our proposals as regards the artillery portended a national calamity. That seems to me to show, what I came to suspect in the course of the searching investigation which I have had to make into this matter, that the late Government never knew how they stood as regards artillery. You gave the nation new field-guns and new horse-guns. They are excellent guns. The reports I have on all hands are most satisfactory as to their efficiency. But there is one thing which it does not seem to have occurred to you to give us, and that was men to mobilise them. Would the Committee believe it, out of 93 batteries of field artillery which we have at home at the present time, if to-day we were called upon to mobilise them—there is no secrecy about these figures, I dare say the general staffs of foreign nations have already found them out—you could only mobilise 42. Only 42 out of 93. All these guns will have been delivered complete by the end of the financial year, but your programme of 93 complete field batteries, of which we have heard so much has only resulted in this, that if we went to war at the present time we could, by using our last man, put just 42 of them into the field. Why was this? It seems to have been forgotten that the new guns were quick-firing guns, and used a great deal more ammunition than the old-fashioned 15-pounders; and the result of requiring more ammunition, of course, is that your ammunition columns have to be longer than is the case at the present time, and require many more men to mobilise. These batteries would have required at the lowest estimate 10,000 more men than you had available for the purpose.'

He proposed to bring home six batteries from South Africa, where they were not wanted and where they cost more to maintain than they would at home. This would give ninety-nine batteries at home and of these sixty-three would be required for the expeditionary force, and these were capable of prompt mobilization, complete with their ammunition columns, which were to be manned largely by Militia Garrison Artillery men. The remaining thirty-six were to be reserve batteries, of which eighteen, reduced to two-gun batteries, would be used to train the Militiamen required for the ammunition columns. He pointed out that, while he was not abolishing a single battery, he was increasing the number of batteries available on mobilization by twenty-one, and at the same time effecting a saving. This fairly took the wind out of Mr. Brodrick's sails.

As to the infantry, he had in March told the House of his belief in the Cardwell system, which required a balance between the formations abroad and those at home, which supplied them with drafts. This had delighted Campbell-Bannerman, a convinced disciple of Cardwell, and was in the Liberal tradition, for had not Cardwell been Gladstone's War Minister? He had pointed out that owing to increases in colonial garrisons, arising largely out of the South African War, the Cardwell system was out of joint, we had 83,300 infantry of the line abroad and only 61,000 at home. This produced administrative difficulties, while the cost of soldiers abroad was very much higher than at home. He now announced that he proposed to adjust the balance by reducing the colonial establishment by three battalions, and bring home two from Malta and one from Gibraltar. He proposed to abolish the third and fourth battalions of the Northumberland Fusiliers, the Royal Warwickshire Regiment, and the

Manchester Regiment, which had been added on the expansion of the Army during the South African War, all of which were much below strength.

He then came to the Guards. Under the Cardwell system the number of line battalions at home was regulated by the number which they had to maintain abroad. This was the main factor which fixed the size of his expeditionary force. He could not reduce any more line battalions at home, but the third battalions of the Coldstream and the Scots Guards were not required for his six divisions. 'The first consideration is not only efficiency but efficiency tempered with justice.' It would not have been fair, it would not have been possible to make the whole of the reduction in the infantry of the line! The 3rd Scots Guards was to go at once, the 3rd Coldstream was to go to Egypt and would not be reduced as long as it was required there. Eventually the political situation required the maintenance of a strong garrison in Egypt and this saved the 3rd Coldstream, the Guards undertaking to find a battalion for Egypt permanently.

As to the auxiliary forces he said, 'His Majesty's Government have deemed it to be their duty to put to the auxiliary forces precisely the same question as they have put to the Regular Army. That is: "What purpose do you serve in war?" But before I enter upon this branch of my subject I want the Committee to understand the difficulties which confront the reformer right through the whole organisation of the Army. There has been a want of plan, a want of method, and things have grown haphazardly, you do not know how or why.' He was in process of finding out the answer to this question.

A crowded House had listened to this speech with close attention. Two days before Lord Roberts had spoken in the House of Lords on the state of the Army, and the Algeciras crisis was sufficiently fresh to make the problem of defence real and actual. The experts were surprised and delighted at the size of the expeditionary force and the promise that it should be complete to the last detail. The Liberals were pleased that increased efficiency was to be combined with substantial economies and were ready to back their War Minister with their formidable majority. There were rumblings from the other side from some of the followers of Lord Roberts, who were to form the National Service League, but Balfour restrained these. 'We', he said, 'had failed to produce an acceptable scheme of Army reform. Haldane must be given his chance.' King Edward was appeased by the promise that the three battalions which were to be brought home from South Africa would be replaced by a cavalry regiment and if necessary by another, cavalry being of more use than infantry in South Africa. The scheme went through and on July 30 Haldane published his memorandum giving the details of his 'New Model' army.

His next step was to extend to the Army generally the General Staff, which till then had existed only in the War Office. He wrote himself the memorandum which introduced the order bringing this about, and in this he insisted that a general staff is essentially a war staff and that every member of it should keep the possibility of war and the requirements of war constantly before his mind, and that one of its main purposes was to ensure uniformity of thought and practice in this. It was not the business of the General Staff to interfere in matters of administration, which should be left to specialists in administration, and in a final paragraph, with an eye ever on an imperial policy of defence, hinted at a future development.

'Further, provided the General Staff can avoid the suspicion of wishing to interfere in purely administrative matters, there is no reason why its influence should not extend ultimately far beyond these shores and India. The self-governing Colonies will, it is certain, never brook interference in matters connected with the administration and the finance of their own military forces. But it is, perhaps, not too much to hope that they may in time welcome the assistance of a body of highly-trained experts, drawn from all parts of the Empire, whose concern is mainly the war organisation and the war training of the Imperial forces as a whole. Should such an ideal ever be realised, the new General Staff will become a real bond of union between the widely-scattered military forces of the Empire, giving to them all common ideas even in matters of detail, so that if ever the necessity should arise, they could readily be concentrated to form a really homogeneous Imperial Army.'

The War Office staff got to work at once to apply the organization of the expeditionary force to the Army at home and to prepare mobilization tables. On January 1, 1907, the Army Council issued an order providing for the formation in Great Britain of a cavalry division and six divisions complete with commanders and staffs. When the Army Estimates for 1907-8 were presented to Parliament they showed a saving of £2,000,000. Haldane had got over his first fence.

In June he had gone down to Oxford to receive the honorary degree of D.C.L., and while he was there a letter came to him from the Foreign Office enclosing a report from Colonel Trench, our Military Attaché in Berlin, of a conversation which he had had with the Emperor William after the spring parade of the Potsdam garrison: ' "Trench," the Emperor said, "what is the serial number of the army Scheme you're busy with in England just now? How can you have any organization when the Army is managed by civilians? Look at the state they are in in France! Saturated with *delation*! The Left exposes the Right because they go to church, and the Right reports the Left because they don't go! And these are your Allies! You make a difficult position. I send my greetings to my regiment [the Royal Dragoons] on the anniversary of Waterloo, but with your *entente cordiale* I'm sure they are in a fix and don't know what to do." The Emperor repeated to me a conversation I understand he had with his Royal Highness the Duke of Connaught: "He tells me that Haldane knows German well and has studied the German Army; but what good is that? One must see for oneself; he only knows what he reads and is told. I believe our army has a reputation for being well organised. He should write to his colleague here that he is coming over, and come and see the army for himself. We would be very glad to see him." '

Haldane was therefore not surprised to receive a formal invitation from the German Ambassador to go to Berlin as the emperor's guest for the occasion of the dedication of colours on August 30, and the autumn parade of the Guards Corps on September 1. Haldane at once consulted Grey and Campbell-Bannerman and then approached the King. He pointed out that it would be of real assistance to him to get first-hand knowledge of the principles and methods of the German military organization and that he hoped at the same time to be able to do something to make our relations with Germany easier. The King quite approved of a visit to Germany but said that he did not think that a military parade was a suitable occasion for the first appearance of a war minister, who could only wear civilian uniform. To this Haldane replied that he proposed to go in a frock coat and top hat and had no intention of getting on a horse. Riding was not one of his accomplishments. (Later in life he kept a cob for shooting, which knew its way about and took him where it wanted without much guidance from its master.) This satisfied the King, who invited him to come and visit him at Marienbad, before going on to Berlin. As he was about to leave England a diplomatic flutter arose. The French Press pointed out that September 2 was celebrated in Germany as 'Sedan Day', and, jumping to the conclusion that Haldane was going to take part in these celebrations, took offence. He had forgotten the date of Sedan, but he was at pains to ascertain that September 2, 1906, being a Sunday the celebration would take place on August 31, and that the two functions to which he was invited on

August 30 and September 1 had no connection with Sedan. It was too late to make a change but he undertook to make a point of calling officially on the French Ambassador in Berlin and of explaining to him the purpose of his visit and how it had come about.

Haldane arrived at Marienbad with Ellison on August 27. 'The King', he wrote to his mother, 'sent for me as soon as I arrived. He is full of cordiality and is really interested in our schemes. He took me out for a long motor drive with him alone through the woods towards Carlsbad. We stopped at a little restaurant in the forest and had coffee in the open at a rustic table. I was able, in a quiet talk, to explain to him many of my plans, particularly about the Volunteers, which he had not fully grasped before. He quite agrees with the general lines of my scheme and has promised me his support. Last night there was a man's dinner party, largely diplomatic, and to-day a luncheon party at which Prince Ferdinand of Bulgaria was present. The King shut me up in a room with him after lunch. He is on the brink of war with Greece and he was fishing for information as to the attitude of the British Government in the event of a Balkan row. I had to be cautious as the conversation was partly in German partly in French and it was delicate work. My advice to him was pacific, as you may imagine. When I said goodbye to the King, he asked me to send him a full account of my visit to Berlin.'

Haldane and Ellison reached Berlin late on the 29th, to be received royally. The 30th was mainly occupied with the ceremony of the presentation of the colours and the usual ceremonial visits. On August 31, while Sedan Day was being celebrated in Germany, he buried himself in the War Office. The German War Office was concerned solely with military administration and finance. The General Staff occupied a separate building. Haldane had made himself familiar with the work and organization of the General Staff. He made no attempt to pry into military secrets, but was anxious to learn something of the system of administration, more particularly in its financial aspects. 'I had a heavy evening', he wrote to his mother, 'at the Berlin War Office, where I was invited to examine for myself the organisation. Ellison and I did this in some detail. I had to catechise the officials in German about their work, but I got through pretty well, and I hear that they were impressed at my questions and by my command of their language.'

The rest of the story of this visit is best told by the account which Haldane sent to the King:

'The narrative which I sent on Saturday morning to Your Majesty extended to Friday evening. Next day several things happened. The French Government were so uneasy about my being present at the parade on Saturday that I took care to go only at some distance from the Emperor. I wore plain clothes, and drove among various civilian guests of His Majesty, including a number of ladies. But the Russian Military Attaché was so convinced that the parade had nothing to do with Sedan that he went to a prominent position. As we had conjectured, there was no more reference to "Sedan-tag" than to "Jena-tag"! Indeed, it became clear that such celebration as there had been of Sedan had taken place, not on the 1st September, but on the 31st August, the real day (the 2nd) being a Sunday.

'I thought it well to call on the French Ambassador in the afternoon and explain all this to him. He was cordial, and said there was nothing at all in the affair—that a mountain had been made out of a mole-hill, that his Government agreed that I could not get out of going, and that he himself was of opinion that the best relations between England and Germany meant improved relations between France and Germany, and that Your Majesty's visit had had a good effect. Lord Granville and I, at his request, sent an intimation to Reuter to the effect that I had called on the French Ambassador. He said his Government asked for this.

HALDANE IN BERLIN 1906

'I return to the parade. It took place at 8 in the morning, and I was there early. Notwithstanding my somewhat retired position, the Emperor galloped up, and I had an interview with him standing in the carriage. He was in excellent spirits and humour. "A splendid machine I have in this army, Mr. Haldane; now, isn't it so? And what could I do without it, situated as I am between the Russians and the French? But the French are your allies, so I beg pardon." I said that were I in His Majesty's place I should feel very comfortable with this machine, and that for my own part I enjoyed much more being behind it than I should had I to be in front of it. He laughed, and then talked of the organization of his War Office, which I had been inspecting the day before, and of the technical points in it. I had got a pretty good hold of the business side of this organization, and His Majesty was interested not the less because he had never gone very deeply into it himself. For, as he said, his teacher was General Bronsart von Schellendorff, who wrote about the Staff side of the war organization—not about the "intendantur"—which I had been inquiring into, with a view to improvements at home. Fortunately, I had read Bronsart von Schellendorff's book twice through, and also that of Clausewitz, on which it was founded, and His Majesty continued the conversation until he had to go, saying that it was odd that an English civilian should have read the things that only German and Japanese soldiers read. . . .

'In the afternoon a message from the Emperor arrived, with a present of various military atlases and tables which His Majesty thought would interest me, and I was bidden, along with Colonel Ellison, to dine at the Schloss. Before dinner Prince von Bülow called. I was out, but later met him at the Schloss, and had an excellent conversation with him. He began by alluding to the good effects produced by the meeting at Cronberg,[1] and said that the Emperor and he were thor-

[1] The King had met the Emperor at Cronberg on August 15.

oughly aware of the desire of Your Majesty and your Government to maintain the new relations with France in their integrity, that in the best German opinion this was no obstacle to building up close relations with Germany also. I said that this was our view also, and the only danger was trying to force everything at once. Too great haste was to be deprecated. He said that he entirely agreed, and quoted Prince Bismarck, who had laid it down that you cannot make a flower grow any sooner by putting fire to heat it. I said that none the less frequent and cordial interchanges of view were very important, and that even the smallest matters were not to be neglected. He alluded to my personal intimacy with Count Metternich[1] with pleasure. I begged him if there were any small matters which were too minute to take up officially, but which seemed unsatisfactory, to let me know of them in a private capacity through Count Metternich. This I did because I had discovered some soreness at restrictions which had been placed on the attendance of foreign military officers in England at manœuvres, and I had found out that there had been slight reprisals. I did not refer to these, but said that I had Your Majesty's instructions to give any assistance to German officers who were sent by the German Government to study. I said that while our Army was small compared with theirs, it had had great experience in the conduct of small expeditions, and that there was a good deal that was worth seeing. This brought Prince von Bülow to the question of the Navy. He said that it was natural that with the increase of German commerce Germany should wish to increase her fleet—from a sea-police point of view—but that they had neither the wish nor, having regard to the strain their great Army put on their resources, the power to build against us. I said that the best opinion in England fully understood this attitude and that we did not in the least misinterpret recent progress, nor would he misinterpret our resolve to maintain, for purely defensive

[1] The German ambassador in London.

purposes, our Navy at a Two-Power standard. Some day, I said, there might be rivalry somewhere, but I thought we might assume that if it ever happened it would not be for a great many years, and that our policy as a nation was at present strongly for Free Trade, so that the more Germany exported to Britain and British possessions the more we exported in exchange to them. He expressed himself pleased that I should say this, and said that he was confident that a couple of years' interchange of friendly communications in this spirit would produce a great development, and perhaps lead to the most pleasant relations for both of us with other Powers also. The conversation was both pleasant and interesting. I had seen Sir Edward Grey on my way to Marienbad, and knew what he thought I might properly say.

'After dinner I had an audience of the Emperor. He was most cordial, and spoke with pleasure of my interest in German literature. His Generals had told him that I knew the details of the development from after the battle of Jena of the economic and constitutional history better than they did, and this gave him pleasure. He had given instructions, hearing that I had been investigating the military organization with an interest that had not often been shown, that everything was to be shown to me. His sons, like himself, were keen soldiers. I said that it was in the blood, and that we in England were proud of His Majesty as being an Englishman as well as a German. He then said that he had been often misunderstood in England; that he had even made suggestions for the improvement of the Militia some years ago with keen desire to be of use, but that he feared no one had read them. By good fortune I was able to say with absolute truth that two months ago I had heard of the Emperor's suggestions from the Duke of Connaught; that I had obtained the original paper, prepared by His Majesty's General Staff, and with his own pencil-writing on it; that I had the plan proposed under investigation at this very time. His Majesty expressed himself as greatly pleased at this, and said that there was, he thought, yet another paper of his, about the operations in South Africa in 1900, though probably not so useful. The conversation then passed to the career of Frederick the Great.

'I had also a conversation with the Empress, to whom I gave Your Majesty's message of affectionate regard. Her Majesty was very friendly.

'After dinner the whole party went to the opera, where a stage box was assigned to Colonel Ellison and me and our two German officers. The Royal Family occupied the Royal box. Sunday was spent quietly in making calls. On Monday I went, by arrangement, to the house in the Tiergarten of the Great General Staff. After an hour and a half of explanations from General von Grundel, who had been detailed to show its organization, I returned the call of the Chief of the General Staff, von Moltke. We had half-an-hour's talk. He spoke with warm approval of our new organization of the English army into six great divisions instead of army corps, and said that their view was that this was what we should always have done in England, in order to make an army capable of easy transport with our fleet to distant theatres of war. Just as the army was the great thing with Germany so the fleet was with us, and they did not take "als uebel" that we should lay stress on keeping absolute command of the sea. They would do the same were they us. They must increase their fleet as a sea-police for their commerce, but the burden of expenditure would be too great for them if they were to try to rival ours, and also what was more important for them—keep their great army up. This was essential to them, and he thought they could defeat both France and Russia if attacked. But, small as our army was, they had profited by studying it. Nothing finer in recent military history had been displayed than the organization of Kitchener's Nile expedition. The Germans had had troubles in South-West Africa because their soldiers were not trained like ours for the conduct of distant expeditions, where self-reliance and initiative were even more important than scientific preparation. Our management of lines of communication with our base, too, in China was very fine. *Per contra*, we could have studied their organization with profit before our South African War. A war with England would be for them, as for us also, a fearful calamity, because it could not be short, whichever won, and would mean slow exhaustion while America—a very real danger this in his opinion—helped herself to the trade of both of us. Therefore it should not be contemplated.

'On arriving back at the hotel I found a telegram from the Emperor bidding me to lunch with him. I was in time to go. He and the Empress, the War Minister, von Einem, and four members of the Household were there. I sat next the Empress. After luncheon the Emperor took me away into his private room, and I had an hour-and-a-half's conversation. He was cordial, and talked sometimes in English and sometimes in German. He spoke of the French *entente*. He said that it would be wrong to infer that he had any critical thought about our *entente* with France. On the contrary, he believed that it might even facilitate good relations between France and Germany. He wished for these good relations, and was taking steps through gentlemen of high position in France to obtain them. Not one inch more of French territory would he ever covet. Alsace and Lorraine had originally been German and now even the least German of the two, Lorraine, because it preferred a Monarchy to a Republic, was welcoming him enthusiastically whenever he went there. That he should have gone to Tangier where both English and French welcomed him, was quite natural. He had desired no quarrel, and the whole fault was Delcassé's, who had wanted to pick a quarrel and bring England into it. I told His Majesty that if he would allow me to speak my mind freely I would do so. His Majesty assented, and I said to him that his attitude had caused great uneasiness throughout England, and that this, and not any notion of forming a tripartite alliance of France, Russia, and England against him, was the reason of the feeling there had been. As for our *entente* we had some time since difficulties with France over Newfoundland and Egypt, and we had made a good business arrangement ("gutes Geschäft") about these complicated matters, and had simply carried out our word to France. He said that he had no criticism to make on this, excepting that if we had only told him early there would have been no misunderstanding. Things were better now, but we had not always been pleasant to him and ready to meet him. He had asked Lord Salisbury to give him a coaling-station, had been curtly refused, and had therefore asked the Emperor of Russia for Kiao-chou.[1] His army was for defence, not for offence. As to Russia, he had no Himalayas between him and Russia—more was the pity. Now, what about our Two-Power standard! (All this was said with earnestness but in a friendly way, His Majesty laying his finger on my shoulder as he spoke. Sometimes the conversation was in German, but oftener in English.) I said that our fleet was like His Majesty's army. It was the "Wesen" of the nation, and the Two-Power standard, while it might be rigid and so awkward, was a way of expressing a deep national

[1]There is an illuminating note on this statement by the Emperor in *British Documents on the Origin of the War* (Gooch and Temperley, vol. III, p. 425) by Lord Onslow: 'The story I heard in Russia was that the two Emperors were playing tennis when in the intervals of the game the German Emperor turned round to the Russian Emperor and said: "I am afraid we shall have to occupy a Chinese port to get satisfaction for the murder of the missionaries. It will be a very tiresome undertaking, will it not? The Russian Emperor agreed vaguely and forgot all about it till he woke up one morning to find Kiao-chau occupied by the Germans, and they asserted that his specific consent was obtained!

'The next time the two Emperors met the Russians stipulated that there should be no political conversations *à deux*, the German Emperor did his best to steal a march on them and took the Russian for a *tête-à-tête* drive during which he tried to discuss politics but the Russian maintained an obstinate silence for two hours until the drive was over!'

tradition, sacred as the Gospel, and a Liberal Government would hold to it as firmly as a Conservative. Both countries were increasing in wealth, we, like Germany, very rapidly, and, if Germany built, we must build. But I added, there was an excellent opportunity for co-operation in other things. The present Liberal Government was Free Trade to the marrow of its bones, and would not encourage colonial preferences against other nations beyond what could not be avoided. We did not believe in them, and our creed was to increase our imports in order to increase our exports. There was a great opening for international Free Trade development, which would smooth other relations. The Emperor said he quite agreed. He was convinced that Free Trade was the true policy for Germany also. But Germany could not go so quick here as England could. I said that I had read Frederick List's great book defending a Protective policy for Germany, and knew that military and geographical considerations affected matters for that country. His Majesty remarked that Chamberlain's policy had caused him anxiety. Chamberlain was unfriendly to Germany. He had spoken slightingly of the German army, and when he (the Emperor) had tried at Sandringham to get on with him, he had found it difficult. I said that many of my countrymen had lived all their days in an island and were more apt to misunderstand Germany than those who had lived much there. Possibly this was so with Mr. Chamberlain. After all, perhaps Mr. Chamberlain thought we might some day have a real conflict over our trade. I myself thought it not likely, but did not disguise from myself that it was at least possible. But I saw no reason to dwell on what might well be wholly avoided with a little care on both sides. The undeveloped markets of the world were enormous, and we wanted no more of the surface of the globe than we had got. The Emperor said what he wanted was not territory but trade expansion. He quoted Goethe to the effect that if a nation wanted anything it must concentrate and act from within the sphere of its concentration. I said that the line of policy adopted by His Majesty would, if thoroughly followed out result in much good. There was a rivalry that was not only legitimate but beneficial. The Germans had got away from us over 50 millions per annum of chemical trade merely by better science and organization. "That," said the Emperor, "I delight to think, because it is legitimate and to the credit of my people." I agreed, and said that similarly we had taken away the best of the world's ship-building. Each nation had something to learn. The Emperor then passed to The Hague Conference, trusting that disarmament would not be proposed. If so, he could not go in. I observed that the word disarmament was unfortunately chosen. "The best testimony", said His Majesty, "to my earnest desire for peace, is that I have had no war, though I should have if I had not earnestly striven to avoid it."

'Throughout the conversation, which was long and animated, His Majesty was most cordial and agreeable. He expressed his wish that more English Ministers would come to Berlin, and more of those of the Royal Family whom he had made officers of his regiments. He mentioned His Royal Highness the Prince of Wales and Prince Christian, as two whom he should be glad to see in Germany. The Cronberg visit had, however, been a great pleasure to him.

'I left the Palace at 3.30, having gone there at 1.'

On sending in this account of his German visit to Buckingham Palace Haldane got this reply from Sir A. Davidson:

'The King has just received your diary letter and says he cannot sufficiently thank you for it. He has read it and re-read it and says each time he finds it more interesting. He is sending it on to the Prince of Wales. His Majesty says he is only in London for a few hours and is so busy that he is literally unable to write to you himself and that nothing short of this would have prevented him doing so, as he has read every word of your letter with the deepest interest.

'The King says that much of the conversation with the Emperor was travelling over old ground, but he is very glad you had this opportunity of discussion, and he is especially pleased with the way in which you handled and answered the topics and questions and criticisms advanced by the Emperor.

'The King says he looks forward to talking over with you the subjects of discussion, which you dealt with so admirably and with such excellent tact.

'Your knowledge of German of course stood you in excellent stead, and His Majesty said that this doubtless encouraged the Emperor and his ministers, as well as the many German officers and officials you met, to talk with you far more freely than they would otherwise have done. The King says that your reference to the Navy as being invariably kept at a two-power standard was of course simply an axiom, but it is evident that this is not so regarded (perhaps purposely) in London. The King is exceedingly pleased at the success of your visit which he attributes entirely to you personally, and His Majesty says that it is especially pleasing and gratifying to him to think that the knowledge you displayed of Germany and German military history, as well as of technical and military works, was so accurate and extensive, as to impress those you met in the way it evidently did.'

Before leaving for Berlin he had reinforced the War Office by bringing in two of the younger men, with whose minds he felt himself in tune. Esher had urged him to fetch Major-General Haig, then Inspector of Cavalry in India, home and add him to the General Staff, and in August he had installed Haig in the War Office as Director of Military Training, and also brought in Colonel Cowan to the Quartermaster-General's Department. On his return home he went for a short holiday to Cloan. While there he wrote to Esher:

'Thank you for your letter. I am writing to French to ask him to stay here 22nd to 24th as you suggest. But I hope you will come and stay with us for his visit, and that Lady Esher will come also. The Great General Staff has impressed me deeply, but I have been struck not less by what we have to learn from the peace organisation for War of the Intendantur and the German War Office generally. It is not understood here. It was new to Ellison, almost as much as to myself. We cannot drive things through all at once here. You know how strongly I hold that doctrine. The more haste the less speed. But not the less am I satisfied that we must begin to move in the direction of making brains and the modern spirit, and not seniority, the qualification for directing positions in the Army. Douglas Haig has impressed me greatly by the change for the better he has initiated even in his first fortnight. I had two strenuous days with him, and have left Douglas and Miles energetically co-operating with him.'

Lord and Lady Roberts also came to Cloan in September, and Haldane and the field-marshal had long talks but got no nearer to agreement. The field-marshal was firmly convinced that nothing short of compulsory service would make us safe, while Haldane was as fully convinced that this was impracticable politically and was by no means certain that it was advisable militarily. The sequel to this conflict of views was to come later. Haldane returned to the War Office in October to complete his scheme for the reorganization of the auxiliary forces, and towards the end of the year had to meet one of those minor storms which are the common lot of ministers. Complaints had reached the War Office of the condition of Piershill Barracks, Edinburgh, and a committee presided over by Sir Alfred Keogh, the very able Director of the Army Medical Service, had reported that the accommodation which the barracks provided was totally inadequate and their condition insanitary. The surroundings of Edinburgh were not ideal for the training of a cavalry regiment, and the Army Council was not sorry to have an excuse to remove it. But it happened that the regiment was the Scots

THE HORSE-THIEF.

Trooper Rosebery (of the Scots Greys). "HE'S AWA' WI' MA HORSE! AN' HIM A BRITHER SCOT!"

[Lord Rosebery is expected to take an active part in the National Meeting to be held at Edinburgh for the purpose of protesting against Mr. Haldane's proposed withdrawal of all cavalry from Scotland.]

"Punch," November 28, 1906.

HALDANE'S FIRST APPEARANCE IN 'PUNCH'

Greys, Scotland's only cavalry regiment, and as soon as there was a rumour of its removal the Scottish members and the Scottish Press were up in arms and Lord Rosebery took the field. The incident earned Haldane the honour of his first full-page cartoon in *Punch*. Eventually it was decided to rebuild the barracks, and Haldane learned that efficiency had not only to be tempered by justice but also by sentiment.

In December the new War Office in Whitehall was ready, an outward and visible sign of a new era in military adminis-tration. Haldane described his new room as 'very gorgeous, but not so comfortable as my old quarters in Pall Mall'.

Chapter X

THE MILITIA AND THE TERRITORIAL ARMY

1906 to 1908

Having got his scheme for the reorganization of the Regular Army approved Haldane had to tackle what was, politically, by far the most difficult part of his problem. The Regular Army was but a small part of the community and, having won the agreement of his generals, Haldane had found no great difficulty in meeting criticism effectively. But a far larger number of people were interested in the Militia and the Volunteers, and any scheme of reform which affected these would certainly meet many vested interests, old traditions, and old prejudices. In his first memorandum to his Army Council he had told them that the problem of the Army could only be considered as a whole, in which Regulars, Militia, and Volunteers were each given a co-ordinated part based on well-considered principles, and he had told Parliament that he was asking of each part of the auxiliary forces the same question as he was asking of each part of the Regular Army, 'What is your function in war?' This was a new line of approach to the auxiliary forces. The Regular Army took very little interest in the Volunteers, and, as Haldane said, there was a vague idea that a touch of ridicule attached to zeal about the auxiliary forces. The way to get over this was to assign to each a clearly defined place in the scheme of imperial defence. This was far from easy. The Militia, 'the old constitutional force', had its basis on the right of the State to call out all able-bodied men to defend our shores if they were threatened with invasion. Cardwell had said of it, 'its theory is conscription, its practice is voluntary enlistment'.

Cardwell had in 1872 removed the control of the Militia from the Lord-Lieutenants of counties to the Commander-in-Chief, and had defined its object as 'to maintain in the United Kingdom a trained body of men available in case of imminent national danger or great emergency to supplement the Regular Army in the defence of the country'. In such a case it could be embodied by proclamation, but it was not liable for service beyond our shores. The force had a long and honourable history and many of the county magnates, who almost to a man were opposed politically to Haldane, took an active interest in the force. It consisted almost entirely of batteries of artillery, companies of engineers, and battalions of infantry, without any higher organization, and had no supply service of its own.

The Yeomanry had its origin in the war with the French Republic and was the mounted equivalent of the Militia. It was organized only in regiments, which had been raised on the patriotic initiative of county gentlemen, who organized their tenant farmers. It could be employed for the suppression of riots, and, like the Militia, embodied for home defence.

The Volunteers dated in the main from the fear of invasion by France in 1858, when Tennyson trumpeted his 'Form, riflemen! Form!' It consisted mainly of batteries of artillery and companies of engineers, designed for coast defence, and a large number of infantry battalions, organized in brigades, but with hardly any of the services required to maintain an army in the field, and like the other auxiliary forces its rôle was home defence.

Now Haldane had started with the hypothesis that home defence was the business of the Navy and that the only part required of the auxiliary forces in that business would be ability to meet and defeat a raid on our shores, by a comparatively small hostile force which had escaped the vigilance of the Fleet. What he wanted from the auxiliary forces was the means of maintaining his Expeditionary Force when it went to war abroad, and the power of expanding it if need be. How were the auxiliary forces to be organized to enable them to undertake these tasks, how were they to be persuaded to fill this new rôle in the scheme of imperial defence?

These questions Haldane put to a committee which he formed in May 1906, and he persuaded Lord Esher to be its chairman. It was a formidable body composed of leaders of the Regular Army, the Militia, and the Volunteers, numbering forty-five in all.[1] It was too large and represented too many diverse interests for an agreed answer to Haldane's questions to be possible. It was given the nickname of the 'Duma', after Russia's contemporary attempt at a parliament, and in July it dispersed without presenting a report. But it had accomplished something. Haldane had from the first proposed to give the country gentlemen and other local personages who had taken an active interest in the Volunteers definite responsibilities in his new organization, and to put the administration in the hands of what he called county associations, taking the name of Cromwell's Associations of the Civil War. Esher reported to the King: 'The Committee have worked out in detail a plan for forming County Associations. They have allotted to these Associations certain functions of administration. They have kept command and inspection in the hands of the General Officers Commanding-in-Chief. They have defined the Territorial Army to be existing Yeomanry, Volunteers, Cadet Corps, and Rifle Clubs. They have excluded the Militia from the Territorial Army.'[2]

[1] Amongst its members were Lord Roberts, Lord Methuen, Sir Frederick Stopford, and Colonel Ellison as the representatives of the Regular Army; the Duke of Bedford, Lord Chesham, Lord Lovat, Lord Stanley, now the Earl of Derby, Lord Bingham, now Earl Lucan, Mr. Freeman Thomas, now the Marquis of Willingdon, and Mr. J. E. B. Seely, now Lord Mottistone.

[2] *Journals and Letters of Reginald, Viscount Esher*, vol. II, p. 108.

The Militia were intransigeant. They refused to be linked up with the Volunteers, and they refused with equal decision to be used to supply drafts for the Expeditionary Force. In no other way could Haldane find a use for them in his general scheme. He made two more attempts to bring them into line, and appointed another committee, composed mainly of Militia commanding officers, with the indispensable Esher again as chairman, and Lord Roberts, Haig, and Ellison as members, and when this failed to obtain an agreement he went in the autumn with Haig and Ellison to a meeting arranged by the late Earl of Derby at Knowsley with a number of representative Militia commanding officers, but he got no nearer to winning their consent to his plans. He then made up his mind that the existing Militia must go and be recreated in an entirely new form. It was to form a Special Reserve to feed the Regular Army. By this time it had become evident that the changes which he proposed were so many and so drastic that nothing short of an Act of Parliament would be required to give them effect. But first Haig and his staff were set to work out a complete reorganization of the Militia as a Special Reserve to feed the Expeditionary Force, and of the Yeomanry and Volunteers as a Territorial Army, composed of brigades and divisions similar to those of the Regular Army, to be administered by county associations. The whole scheme was now taking definite shape, the Regulars formed the Expeditionary Force, the Army Reserve and the new Special Reserve were to provide the men to maintain the Expeditionary Force in the field, the new Territorial Army was to provide the means of expansion outside the Regular forces. There remained one important gap to fill. Both the Regular and the Territorial Armies would require a large additional number of officers on mobilization, and there would certainly be a large wastage of officers in war. Where were these officers to come from? There were in existence a large number of rifle and cadet corps formed for the most part in the universities and public schools, which had as yet been given no definite place in the general plan, and Haldane, with his wide knowledge of educational authorities, had urged his Army Council to bring these into consultation before attempting to formulate a plan for them.

So yet another committee was set up, with Sir Edward Ward, the permanent Under-Secretary of the War Office, as chairman, Professor Bourne of Oxford, Colonel Edwards from Cambridge, Professor Beare of Edinburgh University, Dr. David, the Headmaster of Clifton, and Lord Lovat, who had for long advocated a scheme for using the public schools and universities as training-grounds for officers, and one or two professional advisers, as members. The committee advised the creation of officers' training corps organized in a senior division, to be provided by the universities, and a junior division, to be provided by the public schools, with a standardized system of training. These proposals were approved by Haldane and his Army Council and the scheme was then complete.

It had next to be embodied in a Bill for presentation to Parliament, and this work Haldane undertook himself, with the help of his former 'devils' at Lincoln's Inn, one of the chief of these being his old friend John Kemp. So with a final polish from the parliamentarian draughtsmen, the Territorial and Reserve Forces Bill took shape. It was ready by the end of the year and Haldane took it to the Prime Minister, who was surprised and delighted at the care and detail with which the plan had been prepared. He had been disposed to think that his philosopher colleague was apt to be vague, and he promised Haldane his support. The Bill then went to the King, who approved of it very cordially, but the Cabinet, or a considerable part of it, was doubtful. Liberal Ministers were deep in plans for social reform, old age pensions were on the table, and they were preparing for conflict with the House of Lords. Few of them attached much importance to a Bill dealing with the auxiliary forces, but the fact that Haldane had reduced the Army Estimates by two millions, and a little pressure from the King, won over the doubtful, the Bill was mentioned in the King's speech, and time was found for it owing to the lucky chance that another Bill was not ready.

On February 25, 1907, Haldane introduced his estimates, and in doing so outlined the proposals in his Bill, which, he announced, he would introduce immediately and bring up after Easter so as to give the House plenty of time for consideration. He at once boldly declared war on his Militia opponents. 'The professional Army must be kept alive; and accordingly by sure and slow degrees the Militia have been made the hewers of wood and the drawers of water to the Regular forces. Lord Lansdowne in a debate not long ago said: "The Militia have been plundered at one end by the Line and encroached on at the other by the Volunteers." The War Office has been powerless to remedy this serious state of affairs. It is essential to the War Office to get recruits for the Regular Line. We get 12,000 recruits a year for the Infantry of the Line from the Militia at present, and without the Militia we could not get them. These recruits go into the Militia young, and the Line takes them up when they reach the age at which they can go to the Line. The result is that under the existing system the War Office must control the Militia. It is impossible to get away from that, and if the Militia protests against it, the protest is met with the argument that the most important thing is to get the infantry of the Line sufficiently recruited, and if one has to suffer the Militia must go under.'

Then he turned to the Territorial Army, which he announced was to be organized in fourteen mounted brigades and fourteen divisions 'as complete in every detail as the first line'. He went on in a passage which was prophetic:

'We propose that if a great war were to break out, and the strength of the nation was called on, measured by the necessity of calling out all the Regular Reserve, the second line should be mobilised in its units, and be embodied for training for say six months. And our belief is that at the end of that time, and in this we are confirmed by high military authority, not only would they be enormously more efficient than the Yeomanry or Volunteer Force is at the present time, but that they would be ready, finding themselves in their units, to say—"We wish to go abroad and take our part in the theatre of war, to fight in the interests of the nation and for the defence of the Empire." It might be that they would not only go in their battalions but in their brigades, and even in divisions. If given the occasion I do not know that there is any limit to the spirit of our people when the necessity is upon them. At any rate they will have that opportunity.'

While waiting for the Bill to come to the House, Haldane went off for a short holiday to Germany with his old friend Professor Hume Brown, to Ilmenau, and thence to revisit his old haunts at Göttingen. Of this he wrote to his mother: 'Old Fraulein Schlote, who taught me German when I was here 33 years ago, entertained us with great hospitality. She is a great Goethe scholar and was delighted to see me. I went to Zirdal Strasse No. 1 where I used to lodge. The people were dead but the occupier showed me my old rooms. Alas it is a different Germany and a different Göttingen, there is less peace. The Göttingen papers have been chronicling my visit, claiming me as belonging to the University. This brings some disturbance, however the rulers and princes have discreetly left me alone.'

He came back for the second reading of his Bill on April 9, and, while he was piloting it through the House, he had to turn to another highly important development in his scheme of imperial defence. I have said that he had always been taken by Rosebery's proposal for an imperial *Kriegsverein*. It happened that an Imperial Conference attended by the colonial premiers met in London in April. In preparation for this

Haldane had got his General Staff to prepare a memorandum for the premiers on the possibility of assimilating war organization throughout the Empire. The memorandum pointed out the discrepancies which existed in the British and colonial forces and stressed the great advantage of uniformity in organization, equipment, and training. This memorandum was mainly the work of Haig. On the morning of April 23 Haldane went to the Colonial Office and met the colonial premiers. In a short speech he explained to them the principles on which the British Army was being reorganized and asked them to adopt similar principles. He ended by moving 'that it was necessary to form a General Staff selected from the forces of the Empire as a whole to study military science in all its branches, to collect and disseminate to the various Governments military information and intelligence, to undertake the preparation of schemes of defence on a common principle, and without in the least interfering in questions connected with command and administration, give advice at the request of the respective Governments, as to the training, education, and war organisation of the military forces of the Crown in every part of the Empire'. This was unanimously approved and in the evening Haldane went down to the House and carried the second reading of his Bill. The next morning he wrote to his mother from the War Office:

'Yesterday was a real event in the history of the British Army. We carried the proposal for an Imperial General Staff by acclamation in the Premiers' Conference. Mr. Deakin moved and Sir Wilfred Laurier seconded that the rule of secrecy be departed from and that my speech be circulated to the Empire as a military charter. Then in the evening we carried the second reading of my Army Bill by a huge majority. A great day and only 14 months since I came into this office. But much remains to be done. We are only at the beginning of our task. There is great enthusiasm in this office, and C. B. told me that he had made a hit in choosing his War Minister.'

There was certainly still much to be done. Balfour had been as good as his word and the opposition in the Commons was not serious, but the Lords, who had as yet passed but one Liberal measure, had to be met, and there the Militiamen led by the Duke of Bedford were in force. When and if the Bill passed the country magnates had to be induced to form and work on the county associations, and the Volunteers to accept their new organization.

The Bill passed its third reading in the Commons in June by a majority of 286 to 63, and when it went up to the Lords the opposition proved to be less serious than Haldane had expected. Lord Portsmouth, who had charge of the Bill, handled the House with great skill, ably helped by Lord Crewe, and it went through with only trifling amendments. So the first Army Bill to be submitted to Parliament since Cardwell's in 1872 became law. Haldane then devoted himself to touring the country with the object of explaining his scheme to county authorities and to Volunteer commanding officers, and winning their assent. Having prepared the ground in this way he approached the King with the suggestion that His Majesty should summon a meeting of Lord-Lieutenants to Buckingham Palace and impress upon them the importance of their co-operation in getting the new county associations to work. The King at once agreed and the meeting was held on October 26. Addressing the Lord-Lieutenants His Majesty said:

'My Lords and Gentlemen, I have summoned you, the Lieutenants of England, Scotland, and Wales, to acquaint you with the new duties and responsibilities which will now devolve upon you. I gave my consent, by a statute on the 2nd August, for the formation of a new Territorial Army, and the success which will, I trust, result, will mainly depend upon your efforts.

'Henceforth my Yeomanry and my Volunteers are to form the Territorial Army, over the destinies of which you and your County Associations are to watch; so to you are now delegated the duties of raising, equipping, and maintaining that portion of this force, the Imperial Army of the Second Line, which lies within the shores of this Kingdom. The command and training of this force will be entrusted to the Generals in the commands, and to the generals and other officers serving under them, so that the force may enjoy, in the fullest degree, in common with the Regular Army, those advantages which accrue from being instructed in the highest and most developed school of military thought.

'It is further intended that the Territorial Army shall receive that complete military organisation without which no army is competent to take the field. To accomplish this much will have to be done. Changes will have to be made in some corps which at present exist, and other corps which do not yet exist will have to be created.

'In the performance of this difficult task I have instructed the military authorities to render all the help that is in their power to give; but the ultimate success must depend upon the goodwill and public spirit of my loyal subjects, inspired and guided by you and your County Associations. Your duties will not be confined to raising, in your counties, the forces which the military authorities may require of you under the scheme that will hereafter be communicated to your Associations. You will be required to hand over these forces to the military authorities in a fit condition to take the field, whether for training or for war. It will also rest with you to provide and maintain rifle-ranges, drill-halls and such accommodation as is necessary for the safe custody of arms and equipment. Funds will be placed at your disposal by the Army Council for this and similar purposes. I look to you, my Lords and Gentlemen, through the instrumentality of your Associations, to protect the interests of the Reservists and old soldiers, who have worthily served their country in all parts of the world, and I ask you to enlist the sympathies of the owners and cultivators of the soil, to facilitate the provision of areas for the training of my troops.

'My Lords and Gentlemen,—The important duties and responsibilities which were formerly yours are being restored to you, and when you return hence to undertake this great and honourable task, I look to you to foster and direct, by your precept and example, the spirit of patriotic and voluntary effort which has for so long distinguished my loyal subjects. I hope that you will call to your aid all men who have at heart the interests of their country, and with a generous emulation will stimulate the efforts which you will make in your several counties. I have called you here to-day in order to express to you my confidence that you will employ your best endeavours to carry out the work with which you are entrusted. I have faith that the united efforts of my people will enable you to achieve success.'

The Duke of Norfolk, at the close of His Majesty's speech, promised on behalf of those present to carry out the scheme to the best of their ability.

The King's action created a deep impression and Haldane at once wrote to express to him his deep gratitude for the fine lead which he had given. Haldane very wisely decided to give plenty of time for the county associations to be formed and for the conversion of the Volunteers, and April 1, 1908, was fixed for the birth of the Territorial Army.

From the Territorials Haldane had suddenly to switch off to foreign affairs. The German Emperor had arranged a visit to the King at Windsor, where he arrived on November 11, and the King had insisted that Haldane should be there to meet him. The immediate bone of contention between Great Britain and Germany at the time was the Baghdad railway. As far back as 1899 Turkey had granted a concession to a German syndicate to build a railway from Konia to the Persian

Gulf. As work on this proceeded enthusiasm for the project grew in Germany and the 'Drang nach Osten' became a popular item in German foreign policy. *Pari passu* anxiety grew in England at the prospect of Germany obtaining a firm footing at the head of the Persian Gulf and controlling what would be the shortest rail route to India. The Emperor took great pride in the Baghdad railway, which he regarded as his own idea, and was anxious to come to an arrangement with us about it. On the evening of Haldane's arrival he took him aside and said that he was sorry that there was friction over the railroad and that he did not know what we wanted. Haldane answered that he could not speak for the Foreign Office, but as War Minister he knew that we wanted 'a gate' to protect India from troops coming down the railway, and that by a gate he meant control of the section nearest the Persian Gulf. 'I will give you the gate,' answered the Emperor. After dinner Haldane inquired of the Emperor whether he meant his offer seriously, as if so he would go to London at once and see Sir Edward Grey. At 7.30 the next morning a message came to Haldane from the Emperor that he had meant exactly what he said, which implied that in the interval he had consulted the ministers who were with him. Haldane at once went to the Foreign Office with this news. The rest of the story is best told in a memorandum which Haldane dictated the next day:

'I left Sir Edward Grey and Sir Charles Hardinge soon after 12 on Thursday 14th and went to Windsor.

'I made a copy in my own handwriting of the document we had discussed, and headed it as a note of a private conversation between Sir Edward Grey and myself.

'I received a communication from the Emperor's Secretary saying that the Emperor wished to see me at 7 that evening. I also heard that the Emperor had spoken to the King upon the subject of the Baghdad railway when they were out shooting. I thought it best to see the King, and I explained to him exactly what had happened, and how it came that I had been the bearer of a communication to the Foreign Office, and of information from that Office in return. The King approved and wished that the German Emperor should be informed of his approval.

'At 7 I saw the Emperor.

'I found him very enthusiastic about the possibility of an agreement, and eager to say that about the strategic question of the gate Germany would make no difficulty of any sort.

'I said to him that there was another part which would require attention. The footing on which we stood with Russia and France was now so friendly that it was impossible that we should discuss matters without keeping them informed, and that it was really essential that the discussion should go on *à quatre* instead of *à deux*.

'The Emperor expressed himself in a quite friendly spirit on this, but with considerable vehemence. He said he knew that Russia was opposed to the whole project, and would at once make difficulties. Also, he felt confident that France would at once proceed to make claims for further recognition about Morocco, in exchange for what she was asked to do about the railway. He said, further, that the concession was really a German affair, and that it was all very well for Germany to discuss the matter with a Power with which she was on as good terms as she was with England, but that her people would certainly object to her having *pourparlers* with France and Russia.

'I observed that difficulties which seemed serious if they were taken in abstract sometimes became much less so when the men of business had come in and discussed matters. And this might be the case when the business men had come in and ascertained what it was that France and Germany wanted. I had ascertained quite definitely that our view was that the question was a commercial one, in which Germany had special rights by virtue of her concession; and that, therefore, it was open to His Majesty, if he chose to proceed upon that footing, to say how much he would give up of his commercial advantages.

'The Emperor did not seem altogether happy; but he said he would examine the matter, and would communicate with me after dinner.

'Immediately before dinner, Herr von Schön came up to me and said that there had been a mistake: the Emperor had not known that he, Herr von Schön, had discussed the whole question of the Baghdad railway with M. Isvolsky before he himself had left St. Petersburgh, and that they were entirely at one and would have negotiated and signed an agreement had M. Isvolsky not been taken ill. He added that the Emperor considered that this altered the whole features of the difficulty, and made matters much more easy, and that after the theatrical performance, which was to follow the dinner party that night, the Emperor wished to see me in his private room.

'I went to the Emperor's private room at 1 o'clock in the morning, and the conversation lasted till 2.

'Herr von Schön and Count Metternich were present. The Emperor said that he had not known of M. Isvolsky's conversation with Herr von Schön, and that he was now of the opinion that there would not be the slightest difficulty with Russia. As regards France, he said there would be no difficulty either, because he had gathered from the French that they would have liked to come into the business, but would not do so unless we were ready to come in also. Now that matters were upon such a friendly footing, he did not anticipate any difficulty.

'At the earlier interview, before handing to the Emperor my note of the conversation, I had taken it piecemeal, and had begun after defining the necessity of going step by step with the concurrence of France and Russia, by reading out to him a sentence in which it was stated that the concession

was a German commercial concern, belonging to Germany.
—This pleased the Emperor very much, and he said that,
starting with that, the other points seemed to present no difficulty.—Finally I read out to him, at the earlier interview,
the whole of the note before handing it over, having in this
fashion explained it first piecemeal.

'The Emperor had considered the note with Herr von
Schön. I do not think he had shown it to Count Metternich.
But at the second interview we went carefully through it.

'The result was that the Emperor said that he completely
understood the necessity on our part of proceeding at every
step with the full knowledge and concurrence of the French
and Russian Governments; that in our position this was quite
legitimate; and that it was further in accordance with his
own wishes.

'Count Metternich, at an earlier stage in this second interview, had said that he did not think a Conference of the four
Powers was desirable. The project belonged to Germany, and
ought not to be thrown open in such a fashion.

'But I had explained that I did not think Sir Edward Grey
meant any more than this: that the business men should meet
in Berlin, and should define what each of them wanted. They
might not get what they wanted. The Emperor might not be
willing to concede things out of his commercial rights. But,
on the other hand, the difficulties might be diminished, and
even might all disappear.

'As a result, after a long discussion which lasted till 2 in the
morning, the Emperor said that he cordially concurred in the
note as a basis on which to proceed; that we were *ganz
einverstanden*; and that what he would like would be to get
on as quickly as possible. He was very hopeful, now, that good
business would come to all the four Powers concerned, and
he would ask Herr von Schön to proceed to London that day
to take the initiative by making a proposal from Germany,
which he understood Sir Edward Grey desired as a first step.

'By the end of this interview, Count Metternich's critical attitude had become so greatly modified that he observed that there should be no difficulty about a discussion in Berlin *à quatre* in the sense now made plain, and that it was not only legitimate but quite natural that we should wish to proceed in full consultation with France and Russia.'

Haldane was naturally enough delighted with his success in smoothing out an international difficulty. He wrote to his mother on November 16:

'Our relations with Germany have been put on a new footing and the French and the Russians cordially concur. We hope it will all work out without a hitch, but of course we can't be certain yet. The Foreign Office is unstinted in its expression of gratitude. Where they were faced by a stone wall your bear climbed over and extended a paw to the Emperor. Edward Grey was with me till nearly one this morning and came in again after breakfast. "You have done", he said "a tremendous piece of work for us. The Emperor thanked me effusively for a great service rendered, 'not only to me and my people but to your own!'" It was all very complicated and difficult but at the end the Emperor said there was no single point on which he and his ministers were not at one with me, and that as I had previously settled everything in writing with Grey, things should go smoothly.'

Haldane had of course sent a copy of his report to the King and in reply Lord Knollys wrote: 'The King desires me to thank you for your letter and to say he is very glad to hear that you had such a satisfactory conversation with the German Emperor, and Grey writes that since then the Emperor has been much more amenable about the Baghdad railway. The Emperor told the King that he had you with him till 2 a.m. on Friday morning and that the conversation had materially affected the course of affairs. The Emperor added that he thought you one of the most remarkable men he had ever come across.

'I think that when Lascelles retires you should be appointed Ambassador at Berlin in his place.'

Alas, as was so often to be the case negotiations with the Emperor proved to be an unreliable basis for policy. A few weeks later von Bülow, the German Chancellor, objected to the inclusion of France and Russia in discussions about the Baghdad railway and the agreement that Haldane had engineered fell to the ground. At the end of his official visit to the King the Emperor went off to stay with Colonel Stuart-Wortley at Highcliffe, and there he engaged in a conversation with his host, designed, as he put it, to remove misconceptions of his feelings towards England. This conversation was published with his approval in the *Daily Telegraph* a year later. Its patronizing tone caused deep offence in England and entirely obliterated the good effect of his visit, while in Germany the Emperor was charged with allowing his family sympathies to over-ride his duty to his country, and the publication produced a great political crisis.

The year 1907 had been even for Haldane one of exceptionally hard work, which had succeeded beyond his expectations. The Expeditionary Force had been created, the new divisions of the Regular Army were in being, the formation of the Imperial General Staff was well on its way to completion, the Territorial and Reserve Forces Act had received the Royal Assent, and his scheme for the conversion of the Militia and for the creation of the Territorial Army was in being. In such intervals as this work left him he had found time to give a remarkable Rectorial Address to the students of the University of Edinburgh, to receive one more honorary degree from Cambridge, and to take a leading part in the effort to improve our relations with Germany. He had, as was his way, absorbed himself almost entirely in the problem with which he was concerned, which did not happen to be the problem in which the bulk of his party and the larger part of the Cabinet were most interested. Those were concerned mainly with preparations for the inevitable conflict with the House of Lords, that the way might be cleared for their programme of social reform. He had no great opinion of the Government's Education Bill, indeed the only Liberal measures which had aroused his interest so far had been Campbell-Bannerman's proposal that responsible government should be conferred on the Transvaal, and Asquith's scheme for Old Age Pensions. His party had been pleased at the reductions he had made in the Army Estimates, but were asking for more, and many of the Cabinet were ready enough to listen to critics of his schemes, in the hope that in these criticisms would be found ways to force the War Minister to make more economies. Critics there were in plenty. Lord Roberts' National Service League was getting up steam and its members were stumping the country pointing out that Haldane's Territorial Army could not possibly be made fit to meet the regular troops of a Continental army, that it did not give us the security that we needed. General Wilson, then Commandant of the Staff College, and a disciple of Lord Roberts, believed that nothing short of an army on the Continental model would meet our needs, and poured ridicule on Haldane's scheme. Lord Roberts, who of course commanded great influence, led the attack in a speech in the House of Lords on March 12, 1908, in which he declared that the new Special Reserve would be incapable of maintaining the Expeditionary Force and that it was ridiculous to suppose that the Territorial Field Artillery could be made fit to meet a surprise invasion.

The equipment of the Territorial Army with field artillery had been amongst the most revolutionary of Haldane's changes. The Regular Army had been rearmed with new field-guns, and Haldane had had the field-guns of the South African War re-conditioned and converted into quick-firers to arm his Territorial batteries. It was a tradition of the Army that artillery and engineers were the scientific arms in which amateurs had no place, but the experience of the South African War had shown that new batteries could be created and trained effectively in a much shorter time than had been believed possible, and Haldane had influential support for his opinion that it would not be beyond the capacity of his Territorials to produce efficient batteries if they were given time for training on mobilization. Sir John French, who after giving up the Aldershot command had become Inspector-General, wrote to the King after Lord Roberts' speech giving it as his opinion that Territorial artillery could be made efficient. Haig, whom Haldane had moved from the Directorate of Military Training to that of Staff Duties, in which organization for war became his particular province, wrote to Haldane:

'WAR OFFICE

'DEAR MR HALDANE   18/3/08

'You will no doubt remember that two Batteries of the Lanarkshire Artillery Volunteers were turned out for special training last summer, and were brigaded with Regulars for about ten days at the Scottish manœuvres. The chief object of this was to enable us to form some opinion as to the standard of efficiency which Volunteer Artillery could reach under the conditions then existing. I attach a letter from Colonel May[1] who, as Assistant Director of Training, accompanied me specially to watch the work of this Artillery.

'I fully agree with what he writes, and am of opinion that what was done by these sections shows that Volunteer Artillery can become mobile enough, even under the old system of training, to take part in field operations. I did not, however, see this Artillery at practice, but Colonel Wing's[2] report on Allen's (Sheffield) Corps, 4th West Riding of Yorkshire, dated 9th August last, seems sufficient testimony on

[1] Afterwards Major-General Sir E. May, an artillery officer.

[2] Afterwards Major-General Wing, killed at Loos, 1915. Also an artillery man.

this head. His words are "the practice was very satisfactory". Wing is now Staff Officer for R.H. and Field Artillery to the Commander-in-chief at Aldershot, and his opinion is that of an expert of today. Copy of Wing's report is attached.

'In discussing the question of the standard of efficiency to which Volunteer Artillery can be brought, it seems highly important to notice the very great changes that are being made with the view of providing better means of training. Briefly put, they amount to the following:

'1. The Volunteer Artillery is now to be organised as *Field* instead of *Garrison*, and will be formed in Artillery Brigades with Q.F. guns.

'2. A Divisional Artillery Commander and Staff is provided to direct the training throughout the whole year.

'3. The training of the officers and N.C.O.'s of the Territorial Artillery by means of the Regular Training Brigades.

'4. The methodical association of Volunteer Artillery with Regulars at training centres and camps.

'Lastly there is the General Staff Officer in each Division of the Territorial Force, so that the results of what is being done will be closely watched, and proposals for improvement in organisation and training will be carefully thought out and put forward as necessity demands.

'For these reasons I deprecate any change in the policy of creating a 2nd-line Army complete in all arms and services.'

Haldane sent this letter to the King, but His Majesty had been much impressed by Lord Roberts' criticisms and he replied through Sir Arthur Davidson:

'The King has been seriously concerned to read in the recent debate in the House of Lords the severe strictures passed upon the composition, duties and allotment of the Artillery force in the new Territorial Army.

'So far as the King could judge, these adverse criticisms were not made from party motives but solely from a technical and military point of view, the whole gist and net result being comprised in the view that the actual defence of the shores of the country on invasion is intrusted to Territorial Artillery, and the gunners comprising the force are, from inadequate training, incompetent to fulfil the heavy and responsible task put upon them.

'Both before this debate and since it took place it has been several times represented by soldiers and others that the weak point of the Territorial scheme lies in the composition of the Artillery, and that the training given to untrained and unskilled men is wholly insufficient to enable them to carry out duties which require the careful, the most prolonged, and the most scientific training of any of the three arms.

'The King says he has of course no wish to enter into a technical argument on the merits or adequacy of the amount of training suggested for the Territorial Artillery, but His Majesty wishes to point out in the most forcible manner that a system of defence requiring the highest science, training, and skill, if placed in the hands of men only partially or inadequately fulfilling these requirements, can have but one result, and he trusts therefore that a modification of the scheme, so far as it concerns the training of the Territorial Artillery, may be forthcoming, and that the number of days' training which the Garrison Artillery have to undergo may be in accordance with expert military opinion.'

The King's help in launching the Territorial scheme had been so invaluable that the prospect of its withdrawal on a difference about the artillery was a very serious blow to Haldane, who wrote to His Majesty: 'Lord Roberts has fallen into an extraordinary blunder as to the character of the scheme and the length and nature of the artillery and other training proposed. He seems to imagine that the Government and their expert advisers proposed that the Territorial Force should be treated as having got sufficient training in peace time to enable them to meet a force of European picked troops without further preparation. Neither I, nor the Committee of Imperial Defence, nor the General Staff, all of whom collaborated in preparing the scheme, ever proposed anything so foolish. Under the provisions of the Territorial Forces Act the Territorial Army would go automatically into special war training on the calling out of the Regular Reserves. Thus the Territorial Force must always and will always have a special war training, and it is this which will make the Artillery sufficiently trained.' The King, who was at Biarritz, was not convinced, and it was not until Haldane had an opportunity of seeing him on his return home that he withdrew his opposition.

All this led to opposition of another kind. Sir Henry Campbell-Bannerman's health for some time had been shaky, his wife's death had been a heavy blow, and early in 1908 it became clear that he could not hold office much longer. In March he resigned and the King sent for Mr. Asquith to come to Biarritz to kiss hands, an arrangement the propriety of which provoked some discussion. Haldane wrote to his mother: 'I have just got the news that my old chief C. B. is going. I fear that he will not be alive much longer. We shall miss him. Whatever the wisdom or otherwise of the line he took in the South African War seven years ago, he had brought his party together out of the wilderness. He was a loyal leader and I owe a great deal to him. Asquith will succeed him. I have firmly decided to stay at the War Office and see my task through.'

The last letter Haldane had from Sir Henry, written at the end of the session 1907, ran: 'As this is the close of a Parliamentary chapter, let me most sincerely and warmly congratulate you upon the great success you have wrought out of your complicated problem and your worrying labours over it. It is a great triumph to have carried such a large body of opinion with you, and I hope you will have as much satisfaction while you proceed to carry out and superintend the working of the details of your *magnum opus*.'

It was a curious turn of the whirligig of politics that Haldane, who, a few years before, had been gravely distrustful of C. B.'s leadership, should now be regretting deeply his departure. The Prime Minister had been one of the few members of the Cabinet who had understood what Haldane was doing, and the War Minister was becoming daily more and more aware of the importance to himself of allies in the Cabinet, for he sensed that he would have to meet not only the attacks of the followers of Lord Roberts but also serious opposition from the Liberal ranks. When Parliament met for the session of 1908 an important group of Radical members proposed to move an amendment to the Address regretting that nothing had been said about economies in expenditure on armaments. This they had been induced to withdraw on the assurance that the Cabinet would give earnest consideration to the reduction of naval and military estimates.

The first consequence of this was that a sub-committee of the Cabinet composed of Mr. Lloyd George, then President of the Board of Trade, Mr. Harcourt, the first Commissioner of Works, and Mr. McKenna, Financial Secretary to the Treasury, had been appointed to examine and reduce the naval estimates, and this sub-committee proposed to cut them down by £1,300,000. Sir John Fisher, the First Sea Lord, was up in arms at once, and he received timely reinforcement from the German Emperor, who wrote an indiscreet letter to Lord Tweedmouth, the First Lord, of which *The Times* got wind. The letter provoked a storm and killed any attempt to reduce the expenditure on the Navy.

This was the position when Asquith formed his first government. The most important changes which he made were to make Mr. Lloyd George his successor as Chancellor of the Exchequer, to bring Mr. Winston Churchill into the Cabinet, as President of the Board of Trade, and send Mr. McKenna to the Admiralty. Morley went to the House of Lords. The economists of the reconstructed Cabinet, baulked of their desire to reduce naval expenditure, turned with avidity upon the Army and yet another sub-committee, composed this time of Mr. Lloyd George, Mr. Winston Churchill, and Mr. Harcourt, was appointed to enforce economies. This involved a long struggle for Haldane which went on throughout the summer.

The Committee of Imperial Defence had examined Lord Roberts upon the question of the liability of this country to invasion, and had found in favour of the blue-water school. This and the criticisms of the experts upon Haldane's scheme were paraded by the economists, who maintained that an expeditionary force was an unnecessary luxury, and that the War Minister's plan did not in fact provide for a force which could intervene effectively either on the North-West Frontier of India or on the continent of Europe. A drastic reorganization of the Army, with which Mr. Churchill is credited, was proposed to replace Haldane's plan. The Navy was to be charged with defence against attack upon our shores, the garrisons of India and Egypt were to be financed by those countries, depots being organized at home to train the necessary troops for these. A small expeditionary force of 10,000 regulars and a brigade of Guards were to be maintained at home. It was claimed that this would result in a saving of £10,000,000.

Haldane was now under a cross-fire; on the one hand he had to meet the arguments of those who asserted that nothing short of compulsory service for home defence would make us safe, on the other the attacks of those who agreed with him that home defence could be left to the Navy, but considered his Army scheme to be both extravagant and incomplete. While this struggle was in its early stages the advocates of compulsory service received a reinforcement from abroad. M. Clemenceau, then Prime Minister of France, paid a visit to England at the end of April, and Asquith got Haldane to meet him at dinner. Of this meeting Haldane wrote: 'I met Clemenceau, the French Prime Minister, at Asquith's last night. He is a really remarkable man and a dour political fighter. One of the objects of his visit was to stir us up to create a great field army, founded on compulsory service, which could take the field along with the French against the powerful German Army. I had an hour's talk with him, and found him to be very well informed, he had been following our army reforms closely, but he wanted much more from us. I explained to him that the two things which were essential to us were a supreme navy and the maintenance of our foreign garrisons, particularly in India. No country had ever been able to bear the burden of maintaining a very large navy and a very large army. I said that for myself I was determined that the bulk of our strength should be concentrated on the preservation of naval superiority, and on developing as far as possible its organisation. As to the Army, no country had ever proposed to conscript 120,000 men to serve for long periods abroad, and compulsory service would make it more than doubtful whether we could obtain the volunteers to keep our Army in India and our other garrisons at the requisite strength. These considerations made conscription both politically and militarily impracticable for us. All that remained for us to do as regards the Army was to organise from the troops at home, required to keep up our foreign garrisons, as large an Expeditionary Force as possible, finely equipped and so organised as to be capable of rapid mobilisation and transport. This I had done and we had a force ready to co-operate with an ally on the Continent, if necessary. If we maintained a large and costly army at home, down would go the resources and money which we could pour into the Navy and that I would not stand for. He was not impressed but then no Frenchman has ever understood what the Navy means to us.'

With these arguments Haldane was confident that he could defeat the conscriptionists. His relations with Lord Roberts were very friendly and both the field-marshal and his wife came to stay with him at Cloan and to see him in London. In May Lord Roberts wrote to him: 'I feel that though we differ as to the means which should be adopted, we have the same end in view, the formation of an efficient army for Home Defence. My hope and my belief are that by putting the difficulties of raising a vast amount of Territorial Artillery plainly before you, I am helping you to gain the object you have at heart, on the accomplishment of which no one is more alive than I am to the great difficulties with which you have to contend.' The points of view of the two men were poles apart. Lord Roberts was advocating compulsory service to save us from invasion, Haldane regarded home defence as but a very secondary function of the Army.

The opposition to him within the Cabinet threw upon him a great deal of additional work just at the time when he was launching his Territorial Army. However, he was not without allies. His soldiers were very loyal to him, *The Times* supported him cordially, Esher was a tower of strength, and helped to put matters right with the King. Haldane went to Buckingham Palace soon after the King's return from Biarritz, and of this he wrote to his mother: 'I have just come from breakfasting with the King. We were quite alone in a small room. I had a most agreeable interview and everything is smooth now. I explained to him about the Territorial Artillery. He quite understands. He is as keen as ever about the Territorial Army and agreed to my suggestion that the battalions have colours, and he told me that he would like to give as many as possible of these himself, when the time came. We had a very simple breakfast, not so good as at home.'

This support decided Haldane to stick to his guns and fight the economists to the last. He knew that he could rely upon Asquith, Crewe, and Grey, and he hoped to win over the waverers and the uninterested if he could meet successfully the contentions of the sub-committee which was hunting him. The climax of the struggle came at the end of June, and of this Sir Charles Harris, who continued to be Haldane's right hand in matters of finance at the War Office, writes: 'A critical moment in the history of his main army reforms was when the Cabinet Committee, of which the leading lights were L. G., Winston and Lulu Harcourt, challenged the whole thing as an extravagance, though it was saving some millions annually. At that time the test question was what reinforcements we could send to and maintain in India in case of an attack by Russia on the North-West Frontier. Haldane and I spent a sweltering King's Birthday in the War Office in our shirt-sleeves, with printers' boys waiting for copy, and on the following Monday the main engagement took place in the Cabinet Committee. In the upshot a Treasury man was told off to follow me back to the War Office and see if he could not pick holes in my figures. If he could not Haldane had won, and in fact we made good our case.'

While the struggle went on till the end of July this was the turning-point, and at the end of June he was able to write to his mother: 'I am glad to say that I am near the top of the great mountain which has been in my way. I have come to a preliminary agreement with the Chancellor of the Exchequer which frees my hands for the present and relieves me of immediate anxiety. I took the bull by the horns and acted firmly.'

Haldane had won a hard fight. Guerilla warfare with the economists went on for some weeks, but the War Minister's arguments, like those of the First Sea Lord, were reinforced by the German Emperor, who on the announcement of the annexation by Austria of Bosnia and Herzegovina, announced that he would stand by his ally 'in shining armour', and this was followed in October by the publication in the *Daily Telegraph* of his talk with Colonel Stuart Wortly.

While this was going on in the Cabinet a great deal of strenuous work was being done at the War Office, where

Haldane made some important changes. General the Hon. Sir N. Lyttelton vacated the post of Chief of the Imperial General Staff, and in his place Haldane appointed Lt.-General Sir W. G. Nicholson, whom he had made Quartermaster-General on coming to the War Office. Major-General H. Miles, who had been Director of Recruiting and Organization, became Quartermaster-General, and Ellison took Miles's place with the rank of brigadier-general. On the formation of Asquith's Government Lord Lucas, affectionately known as 'Bron', who had been Haldane's private secretary, became Parliamentary Under-Secretary and the representative of the War Office in the Lords, in place of Lord Portsmouth, and Mr. F. D. Acland had succeeded Mr. Buchanan as Financial Secretary.

This new team backed Haldane even more enthusiastically than had the old one. On April 1 the Territorial Army and the Officers' Training Corps came formally into being, and its direction was transferred from the Department of the Adjutant-General to the Parliamentary Under-Secretary, and there were in consequence incessant demands upon the Secretary of State to attend meetings up and down the country called to inaugurate the scheme locally. Haldane was determined that the organization of his Territorials should be as complete as it could be made and he encouraged his very able Director of the Army Medical Service, Surgeon-General Sir Alfred Keogh, to arrange for the mobilization of the medical resources of the country in the event of war. Sir Alfred not only greatly improved the regular medical service of the Army, but he persuaded numbers of doctors and surgeons to join the Territorials, he organized a network of hospitals covering the whole country, ready to deal with the casualties of war, established a Territorial Army Nursing Service, and created the Voluntary Aid Detachments.

In July Haldane went to Manchester for the inauguration of Lord Morley as Chancellor of the University. The Chancellor had for this occasion the nomination of three candidates for honorary doctorates, and the three Morley chose were Balfour, Curzon, and Haldane. Haldane welcomed these university honours, not only as a mark of appreciation for his public services, but because they gave him a standing in the universities which he could use to forward his Officers' Training Corps scheme. He made use of the ceremonies at Manchester for this purpose, and at a crowded meeting of the university got its approval of the formation of a contingent of the Senior Division of the Officers' Training Corps. A few weeks before he had done the same at both Oxford and Cambridge, and the Manchester meeting was followed by one with the university of London. All of these promised him support.

Nearly every one of his week-ends throughout the spring and early summer had been taken up by meetings of this kind, and he was very weary towards the close of the session. At the end of July he got away for a visit to the Desboroughs at Taplow. Of this he wrote to his mother:

'I spent a very pleasant week-end with the Desboroughs at their lovely place at Taplow in very pleasant company. The King was there. He took me out for a walk and was very affectionate. He knew all about my difficulties with 'the Cabinet and urged me not to give way. He is now really keen about the Territorial Army, and there are few matters in which Royal influence can be more effective. He had a photograph taken of himself and the house party on the lawn and insisted that I should be lying on the grass talking to him. He arranged the position of my feet so that they should not be out of focus and appear too big. It is a great comfort to have him behind me in my struggle.'

On the adjournment of the House he went off for a holiday to Austria and on his return home was called to Balmoral as minister in attendance. From there he wrote to his mother: 'It is a great thing for me to have got professional backing. The King naturally notices what the soldiers have to say

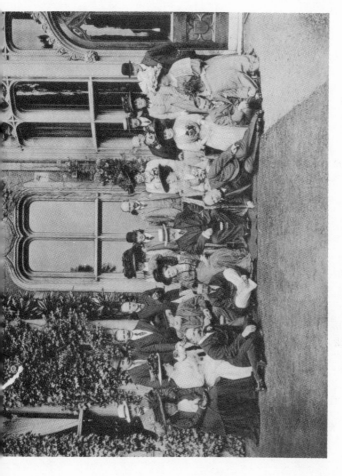

HOUSE PARTY AT TAPLOW COURT, JULY 1908

Back row: Count Mensdorff, Prince Francis of Teck, the Hon. G. Keppel, the Hon. A. Lytelton, the Hon. Mrs. A. Lytelton, Mr. Hwfa Williams, Lord Hugh Cecil, the Hon. Mrs. G. Keppel, Sir E. Cassel, Sir. A. Davidson, Mrs. Hwfa Williams, Lord Revelstoke

Middle row: Consuelo, Duchess of Manchester, Mrs. W. James, Earl of Wemyss, Countess of Wemyss, His Majesty King Edward VII, Lady Desborough, Lady Norreys, Lady Cynthia Graham

Front row: Lord Desborough, Lord Valletort, Mr. Haldane, Mr. William James

about my reforms, and he has been told that he has at last got an army to put in the field larger than ever before known in British history and as scientifically organised as that of the Kaiser. He and a good many other people are astonished that a Liberal Government has done this, and as he is well aware that I have had to fight for it in the Cabinet he is more affectionate than ever. He told me yesterday that mine was an extraordinary achievement. He is quite unnecessarily anxious about my health and urges on me the importance of my staying in the War Office. He persuaded me to take to some sport for exercise, so I chose to go trout-fishing. He was much amused for it was a bright sunny day and he was sure that I would catch nothing. However my old skill had not deserted me and I got a basket of 14, which he is to have for breakfast this morning. I had a splendid days' exercise moreover and a long walk home from the Gelder Burn. I chose it because no one fishes there now. The Prince Consort used to go there years ago!'

When Parliament reassembled for the autumn Haldane found the minds of his colleagues fully occupied with the coming struggle with the House of Lords. The Peers had thrown out the Licensing Bill and had destroyed the Scottish Small Landholders' Bill, and the Scottish Land Values Bill. One of the few measures which to Haldane's satisfaction had got through was the Irish Universities Bill, which was very much as he had planned it originally. All this meant that the War Office was left in peace, but it made the political outlook very uncertain. On December 11 Asquith declared war on the Lords in a speech at the National Liberal Club, in which he said: 'To put this plainly, the present system enables the leaders of the party which has been defeated and repudiated by the electors at the polls, to determine through the House of Lords what shall and what shall not be the legislation of the country. The question I want to put to you and to my fellow Liberals is this: "Is this state of things to continue?"'

Of this Haldane wrote to his mother: 'Asquith did not tell much in his speech last night. We shall not dissolve at present, but I do not think that we shall be in a great while. Our Budget we must bring in and we cannot go on with the House of Lords in its present attitude.

'Anyhow I think I shall have pretty well accomplished my present task. It has taken all my strength and has made it impossible for me to take much part in the general work of the Government. It has been worth while to concentrate on this effort. The public do not yet know how much has been done. Nothing could have been better than the way in which all branches of the War Office have pulled together to complete a great task. Since October a great deal of ground has been covered.'

Chapter XI

MR. LLOYD GEORGE'S BUDGET—DEATH OF KING EDWARD

1909 to 1910

As it happened conflict with the House of Lords was not the first business which occupied the attention of the Cabinet and the public at the beginning of 1909. Hardly had the new year begun when one of those naval scares to which we were periodically liable swept the country. Sir John Fisher's 'all-big-gun' battleship, the *Dreadnought*, had a superiority in armament which made the older type of battleship out of date. The consequences of this development were serious for us. It began a race in naval armaments in which we had but a short start. Germany had in April 1908 announced a new naval programme, and it was asserted that if we kept to our rate of building and Germany completed her programme with capital ships of the new type she would be approaching equality with us by 1912. The Admiralty proposed to answer the German challenge by laying down eight dreadnoughts, and 'We want eight and we won't wait' became a Conservative electioneering slogan. The demand alarmed the economists, and Mr. McKenna, then First Lord, was involved in just such another struggle with Mr. Lloyd George and Mr. Winston Churchill—both of whom threatened resignation if six dreadnoughts were included in the current programme—as Haldane had been engaged in over the Army Estimates in the previous year. There was for some weeks an atmosphere of crisis, which was eventually settled by agreement that four ships should be laid down in 1909 and powers taken to lay down four more, if necessary early in 1910. This compromise was only reached with difficulty, the economists objecting to an Admiralty note on the draft estimates which appeared to imply that all eight ships would be laid down in the current year. Haldane, who had endeavoured to act as an intermediary in this dispute and got raps from both sides, received on February 27 letters from Mr. Asquith and Mr. Lloyd George. Asquith's ran: 'I told Lloyd George to send you on McKenna's letter with any suggestions he had to make. The obvious objection to McKenna's proposed "note" to the estimates is that it expressly treats the whole 8 ships as in this year's programme, tho' no money is to be spent this year on the last 4. This is not in accordance with the Cabinet decision. The note should state that in addition to the 4 actually provided in the year's programme, power will be taken by Act of Parliament to anticipate the ordering of the next 4 ships so that they can be laid down if necessary at the commencement of the next financial year. It is a question not really of substance, but of form.' Mr. Lloyd George, however, appeared to regard it as a matter of very real substance, for he wrote: 'The P.M. wishes me to send the enclosed along to you. It represents with perfect accuracy the decision arrived at by the Cabinet after weeks of anxious debate and deliberation. I do trust that McKenna will not be allowed to restart the whole trouble in an aggravated form. His suggested note to the estimates is purely an intimation that the Cabinet are committed to a programme of 8 this year, but that they mean to postpone payment of the expenditure on the last 4 to the financial year 1910–11. It would be quite out of the question for those, who opposed a programme of 6, to assent to this interpretation of the Cabinet decision.

'We went out of our way to avert a crisis and split which would inevitably weaken the Liberal forces. You will admit that we went further to meet the Admiralty views than McKenna came to meet ours. But if every concession that we

make is to be used as a means of manœuvring us into something much worse than the proposal we originally fought,
the situation is hopeless.'

In the event Asquith got his compromise accepted, but the
anxiety and friction which the German naval programme
had aroused was allayed, not removed. This conflict had the
effect of diverting the attention of the economists from the
War Office, and in the lull which followed a settlement of
the naval problem Haldane got his estimates accepted by the
Cabinet. Nor was this his only piece of good fortune. London was being thrilled by a play by Major Du Maurier, a
younger brother of Sir Gerald, called *The Englishman's Home*,
which presented dramatically the consequences of failure to
prepare effectively against the dangers of invasion. The play
was designed by the author to help Lord Roberts' campaign,
but it had the result of giving a valuable fillip to recruiting for
the Territorial Army. Haldane also found an unexpected ally
in Lord Northcliffe, who was induced by Lord Esher to start
a campaign on behalf of the Territorials in the *Daily Mail*.

The result of this was that when he introduced his fourth
estimates in the House on March 4 he had a very satisfactory
story to tell. Recruiting for the Regular Army was going up.
The old Militia had practically disappeared, and in its place
had come the Special Reserve, which already numbered over
70,000 men out of an establishment of 80,000, while after an
existence of only eleven months the Territorials had enlisted
240,000 men, and the Officers Training Corps 17,000. He announced that plans were well advanced for providing the
Expeditionary Force with a new howitzer and an increased
number of howitzer batteries. He was able to say that not only
were his six divisions of Regulars at home complete, but that
a seventh was being organized from troops in the Mediterranean. The War Office was carrying out experiments in the
use of mechanical transport, and a committee was at work
investigating the possibilities of the use of aircraft for military

purposes. Lord Roberts had said in the House of Lords that we required in the Second Line a million men in order to provide, in the absence of the Regular Army abroad, sufficient troops to find garrisons for our coast fortresses and to supply sufficient men to make invasion on a large scale impossible. Haldane concluded his statement with his first reasoned answer in Parliament to the proposals of the National Service League:

'What is the object for which the Army exists? There are two views; one that the Army is for defence—passive defence —the other that the Army with our command of the sea, takes and makes a frontier on the enemy's coast-line, where you seek him out. That is the mode of defence that has been our characteristic defence throughout our history, and it is most important that we should have a clear idea that that is the strategical principle on which the Army is based. To go in for an immense and costly defence force must weaken the Regular Army. Ancient Rome fell into the mistake of not balancing these two things, defence and the power of initiative, and unable to withstand the stress laid upon her, Rome fell.

'This is a mistake in one way. We ourselves in our history have made mistakes in another way. Anyone who studies the admirable book by Mr. Fortescue[1] and the writings of the late Colonel Henderson, will see what would come to this country if we gave up the command of the sea and an overseas army that could make that command effective. A home defence force no larger than is necessary to make impossible invasion is the foundation of British strategy. This is a practical question. An admirable article in the *Contemporary Review* last month written by a naval expert whose name I do not know, but who is somebody who knows his work thoroughly, points out the enormous difficulties of invasion in the fullest technical details, and shows how with an invading army of 200,000 or 150,000 men or even less, the fleets

[1]Sir John Fortescue, *The History of the British Army*.

would form a target that could not escape a navy which had command of the sea. He shows that what is desirable is that we should so home-defend ourselves as to make it necessary that the invading force should be so big that it would form a certain target to such naval defence. If we bear that in mind, then it seems to me that we must come to one conclusion, that for a country like ours, which is an Empire to be defended at a distance, naval power is never effective without an overseas army power to work with it.

'Our first duty is to take care that the home defence force does not drag back and starve the power of the first line.

'This brings me to compulsory service. I am looking at these things for the moment, not from the idealist point of view, but from the strategic point of view, and from my strategic point of view I have to say that if you go in for building up a large home defence army, particularly on a semi-Regular and compulsory basis, you will starve inevitably your Regular Army of both men and money. I am not drawing conjectures but am speaking from the study of such books as Mr. Fortescue's. The greatest harm you can do is to forget your great strategic principle that the offensive is the true mode of defence, and that you must keep the oversea line of your Regular Army intact and strong. If we adopted any different system, if we departed from that—and there is danger in some counsels—we should do two things. We should inevitably substitute in people's minds for the true theory the idea that the army of this country should be squatted along the sea shore with their bayonets fixed. The second thing we should do would be to make the Regular Army bankrupt of men. Our great overseas army must recruit on a voluntary basis, consisting of men who engage for seven years with the colours and five in the Reserve. That army is recruited from enthusiasts. We know that in Continental countries they have the greatest difficulty in getting volunteers for service abroad, whereas with us it is perfectly easy. It is that phase of a military career that appeals most to a lot of men who are under no compulsion for military service.

'Depending as we do on getting every year to join the Regular Army and the Special Reserve about 56,000 recruits, who must take voluntary enlistment for oversea service, it would be an action of deadly peril to put that stream of recruits in danger by applying compulsory measures to young men between the ages of 17 and 21, who are just the people who give us the stream of recruits. To apply compulsion in time of peace to that field would be gravely to imperil the stream of life of the Regular Army; if there is ever substantially a danger to that stream of life, strategically situated as we are we ought not to run the risk. If that be true, that rules out a great many propositions that have been made. I am not talking of other things. Were the nation in deadly peril everybody would come forward, and not only so but nobody would be concerned to dispute that if the country were invaded or in danger of being invaded, it would be the legal as well as the moral duty of every man to bear arms and repell the invader. That was laid down in 1635 by the great St. John, one of the great defenders of the Commonwealth, and as late as 1803 it formed the preamble of the Act of Parliament under which the *levée en masse* was to be made in case Napoleon invaded this country. It rests on the common law of the land. We are not disputing that, although opposed to compulsion. What we are contesting is that it is a good thing to apply compulsion in time of peace to young men who otherwise came forward to our Regular and Territorial Forces. It may be very right that the national duty to serve in times of supreme emergency should be recognised in our education. I have been in the East End of London and have been struck and impressed with what I saw of the Boys' Brigades there. I have been in the slum regions and have seen in the area round the homes from which the boys have come all that one would wish not to see; and yet these young fellows are splendid specimens of humanity, and have become so by athletic exercises and physical drill, and are of the very type out of which you could very quickly organise a great reserve in time of national necessity. It may be right for the schools to do that, but what I say is that the War Office ought not to touch them. Conscription I am against, not on any sentimental grounds or any ground except strategical grounds, which are enough for me. I am against any interference with the present system of voluntary recruiting for an island like ours, and that is the policy of the War Office.'

The House was pleased with this statement and he got his estimates through without difficulty.

With War Office business now running smoothly and his new creations all developing satisfactorily Haldane was able to turn his attention to other matters, and one of the first of these was his old love, the development of university education. At the Prime Minister's request he accepted the chairmanship of yet another Royal Commission on the University of London. The immediate object of this was to define the relationship which should exist between the new Imperial College of Science and Technology and the university, but at Haldane's suggestion the terms of reference were widened into an inquiry into the working of the university and the development of advanced education in London. This commission reported in 1913 and its recommendations led eventually to the preparation of new statutes for the university and the provision of the new site for its headquarters in Bloomsbury, for the commission recommended that the university should have for its headquarters 'permanent buildings appropriate in design to its dignity and importance, adequate in extent and specially constructed for its purpose, situated conveniently for the work it has to do, bearing its name and under its control'. It was not until 1936 that this recommendation was realized by the opening of the new offices of the university behind the British Museum.

Not long after he had started his commission on its task
Haldane was called back to deal with yet another naval crisis.
In April Lord Charles Beresford had addressed a letter to the
Prime Minister which was in effect a severe attack upon Sir
John Fisher's administration. The chief grounds of this attack
were that the organization and distribution of the Fleet in
home waters was defective, and no adequate machinery
existed in the Admiralty for the scientific preparation of war
plans. On getting this letter Mr. Asquith at once appointed a
sub-committee of the Committee of Imperial Defence to investigate Lord Charles's charges, with himself as chairman,
and he invited Haldane to be a member. The sub-committee
found that the charges were not established, but concluded:
'the Committee have been impressed with the differences of
opinion, amongst officers of high rank and professional at-
tainments, regarding important principles of naval strategy
and tactics, and they look forward with much confidence to
the further development of a Naval War Staff, from which
the naval members of the Board and the Flag Officers and
their staffs at sea may be expected to derive considerable
benefit.'

Haldane had in fact a good deal of sympathy with this part
of Lord Charles's criticisms. He was far from happy about the
system in the Admiralty. Sir John Fisher, an autocrat, kept
his plans to himself, and there were no general and accepted
principles of naval strategy, still less any agreement between
the Admiralty and the War Office on the major problems of
imperial defence. Haldane got Haig to draft a paper for him
on the subject of the organization and functions of a naval
war staff.

This Haldane sent to Sir Charles Ottley, who had followed
Sir George Clarke as secretary of the Committee of Imperial
Defence. Ottley replied:

'I am grateful to you for allowing me to see the paper on
the Naval War Staff.

'The writer is unquestionably right in insisting on the importance of a clear definition of the purpose for which the War College exists. The primary object to be attained is the supply of a large body of trained officers from whose ranks the Staff appointments of the Admiralty and at sea will in future be selected. I am very thankful to say this is now recognised at Whitehall, and a Fleet circular will be promulgated in the course of the next few days I hope, giving effect to this proposal.

'The Staff of the Committee of Imperial Defence have for the past eighteen months given unremitting attention to this question, which indeed lies at the root of any rational advance towards the ideal which we are striving for (viz. the creation of an efficient Naval War Staff). The unfortunate domestic squabbles between high naval officers have prevented much progress hitherto, it is scarcely too much to say that for the six months during which the Beresford Enquiry was proceeding the entire thinking machinery of the Admiralty was concentrated on that question, and every other matter was necessarily shelved. Even now those who believe in the importance of the early creation of a Naval War Staff are an insignificant minority of the officers of the Fleet. The vast majority don't realise what such a Staff means; not one naval officer out of fifty has any knowledge of what the British Fleet will have to do in war, or how it will do it.

'With a strong and capable Board such as we have at present and more particularly with a man of Sir John Fisher's brilliant ability, the danger of this state of ignorance is perhaps not great, but the inconvenience of half-a-dozen schools of thought inside the navy, one of which preaches a doctrine which the others regard as 'retrograde' need not be insisted upon. I wrote most strongly a few weeks ago to Sir J. Fisher to point this out, and I then begged him to put the coping stone to his great work as a naval reformer by initiating a true Naval War Staff. The result of our efforts will be the

Fleet Circular to which I alluded just now. More than this we cannot expect just at present I am afraid. After all, there is something to be said for the attitude of these who say: "The existing system has produced men as able as Sir A. K. Wilson, Sir J. Fisher, Prince Louis of Battenburg, and some 3,000 of the very finest sea officers in the world. Why tamper with it?" Only those who have seen the great machine of Admiralty Administration from the inside, and who have had an opportunity of comparing its working with the working of other similar naval organisations in foreign countries can give a reasoned answer to that question. The first and most immediate necessity is therefore I think to spread the light, and this will be the function of the War College. It will perhaps be a slow process, but (if we can give effect to the proposals in our circular): before ten years are over every staff officer in every flagship, and every officer on the Admiralty Staff and in the N.I.D. will have been trained in the War College. With such a body of enlightened naval opinion so highly placed I am confident in the future. Everything else will come. The vital question remains, What is the War College to teach? That is so urgent a matter that I should hope the Admiralty will e'er long appoint a Committee to decide it. The curriculum might well be laid down by a little committee of men like Captain G. A. Ballard, Prince Louis, Sir Reginald Custance (if he will bury his hatchet) and one or two others. But on that question Combatant Naval Officers (not the civilian element at the Admiralty) must decide.

'I am strongly of opinion that the Broad Outlines of our national policy of Defence, as fixed by the C.I.D., must be used as the basis of the curriculum. At present the service at large knows nothing definite of the enormous responsibilities which the Admiralty has (very rightly and necessarily) accepted. Yet these responsibilities are our Bible in the Navy. Take for example the guarantee we have given to every corner of the Empire "against organised invasion". That's a responsibility! Is not a staff composed of the most brilliant brains in the Empire urgently needed to equip the fleet to fulfil that tremendous responsibility? And last, but not least, arises the question of co-ordination of effort between H.M.'s fighting forces by sea and land. Surely a free interchange of views, a free permission to soldiers and sailors to attend lectures given in the sister institutions at Camberley and Portsmouth is a fundamental necessity. The history of our past efforts at warlike co-operation between the British Navy and Army is one long record of almost unbroken mistakes, due to misunderstandings and lack of cordial co-operation. Yet if ever there was a nation which needed to utilise its sea and land forces as a single tempered weapon Great Britain is such. I hear (for it is my business to hear everything and say nothing) that the widest divergences of policy are taught at Camberley and at Portsmouth; why even at Portsmouth itself there is no clear guidance given from the Admiralty on the Broad Questions.

'Hitherto there has been some excuse for this because the national policy of Defence has until recently been inchoate and undefined. But your labours here and those of the two preceding Governments have changed all this. We now have certain first principles quite clearly and authoritatively laid down here by the supreme authority of the Government. One of the most urgent needs now is to communicate these broad principles to *both* services and to insist that both shall preach the new gospel. The soldiers are just as heterodox as the sailors.

'A series of six articles has been written by Thursfield on the "Naval War Staff" question, which will I suppose appear e'er long in *The Times*. I have read these articles and agree in the main with all that has been said: indeed I may say that to some extent they were inspired by me; *no* rather let me say that in conversation with Thursfield I have made no secret of my own strong views on this question. But, as to the expedience of *publishing* these articles I am by no means so clear. I dread any appearance of a seeming desire to carp, criticise, or coerce the Admiralty, or to put them in a corner, with a white sheet and a candle. The Board are still smarting under what they conceive to have been an undeserved criticism (in the last para. of the Beresford Enquiry Report). They are in a hypersensitive mood, and from something that I heard at the Admiralty a few days ago, I am afraid that they did not at all relish the "Naval War College" paper prepared by a military officer, of which you now so kindly send me a copy.

'As a matter of personal opinion I disagree very strongly with a good deal that the anonymous military officer has written on this question, while I cordially endorse his general thesis (which is I take it that the Naval War College requires a complete reorganisation).

'e.g. The Problems (set out in the appendix) seem to me to be in several instances based on an entire ignorance of the fundamental tenets of British Naval Strategy. Can anything be more preposterous than to suggest to the Admiralty to set down its officers to discuss "A problem dealing with war with Germany breaking out suddenly, when a *large proportion of our fleet* is absent in the Mediterranean". The entire history of recent naval re-distribution is a negation of such an idea. *When* the German Fleet goes to the Mediterranean, *then* the British Fleet may *pro rata* be expected to quietly move into that sea also. But, where the carcase is, there are the eagles is the principle from which no sane Board of Admiralty will depart.

'I don't want to be drawn into a critical analysis of the military paper on the Naval War College, but I do think it worth while indicating the sort of effect that this kind of proposal may be expected to have on a rather hypersensitive Admiralty Board.

'Still the general idea of the paper is excellent.'

Haldane was very far from satisfied with this and contemplated asking the Prime Minister to send him to the Admiralty when an opportunity for a change arose, that he might do there what he had done at the War Office.

The immediate result of the settlement of the dispute over shipbuilding was to bring the quarrel of the Liberals with the House of Lords to a head. The Liberals insisted that if money were to be found for dreadnoughts money should also be found for social reform, and the consequence was Mr. Lloyd George's Budget for 1909. This at once aroused furious opposition which was not diminished by the Chancellor of the Exchequer's outspoken and occasionally vituperative criticism of his opponents. The rival parties lost no opportunity of giving expression to their feelings, and Haldane soon had his experience of the change of atmosphere. The Committee of Imperial Defence was in process of preparing the War Book, which prescribed the action to be taken by every Government department in the event of a national emergency, and some of the measures proposed required new clauses in the Army Annual Bill, the measure by which Parliament brings the military forces of the Crown into being each year. By this Bill the power of the military authorities to billet troops was confined to billeting upon licensed victuallers, but clearly something more than this would be required if the Regular and Territorial Armies were to be mobilized. Therefore one of the most important changes in the Bill which Haldane proposed was to take powers under specified conditions and on specified terms to billet troops in private houses. This invasion of the rights of the citizen offered a sufficient excuse for obstruction, much of which came from private members who, outside the House, were advocating compulsory service. It took an all-night sitting to get the Bill through, and of this Haldane wrote to his mother:

'I got to bed at 6.45 a.m. having managed after a long fight, 3.45 p.m. to 6.20 a.m. to carry through the most important

Army Annual Bill which has been passed for a generation. It included changes which are essential if our scheme of defence is to work. Most of my opponents knew this in their heart of hearts, but the Opposition in its present temper was looking for a chance to make itself objectionable and lighted on my Bill. The Tories, the Irish, the Labour men and even some Liberals combined to produce the maximum of obstruction. Sir Charles Dilke was one of the leaders of the attack, but I drove him home to his bed for I knew every line of my Bill and beat him badly in argument. The Generals say that no Secretary of State before my time has performed such legislative feats. They have got from Parliament now all they ever dreamed, but it leaves their Secretary of State feeling the want of a few days rest.'

From this effort he went off again with Professor Hume Brown for ten days to Ilmenau and took his recreation in talking philosophy and in long walks in the hills. He came back to meet another attack in the House of Lords upon his organization of the Army. His relations with Lord Roberts continued to be very friendly, though the two were no nearer agreement, but there were peers of the Opposition who jumped at the chance of using the field-marshal's prestige for party purposes, and there was a degree of bitterness in the debate unusual in the Upper House, an indication that tempers were badly frayed. However, Balfour and Lord Lansdowne were as good as their word, and the malcontents got no encouragement from the front Opposition bench. Three days after the debate the King asked Haldane to come to Windsor. 'I went down to spend the afternoon with the King and returned after dinner. You will be interested to hear that he sent for his friends in the Army after Lord Roberts' speech. They told him that I had substituted a new order of things for the old and that Lord Roberts did not really understand what the changes in organization meant in military efficiency. They told the King that he now possessed the finest army the country had ever had in time of peace. I see Esher's hand in this, he has been a very stalwart ally. The result was that I had nearly three hours' talk with the King and he was most cordial and affectionate. He advised me to lay papers on the table of the House explaining what had been done and this I mean to do. He told me that he had been to Aldershot to see for himself and had heard nothing but approval of the changes I had made. The only thing he criticised was my hat, which he said I must have inherited from Goethe. It had been twice to Ilmenau with me.

'He is keenly interested in the forthcoming presentation of colours to the Territorials and he very rightly said that they should be paid their travelling and other necessary expenses for the occasion. Recruiting for the Territorials is still booming, we have now more than 260,000 men, and the presentation of the colours will give it a fresh fillip.'

This ceremony took place in Windsor Park on June 19 when the King presented colours to 108 Territorial battalions. Haldane and his sister were asked to dine and sleep at Windsor for the occasion, the compliment to his sister delighting him. 'The ceremony on Saturday was really splendid,' he wrote to his mother. 'The King was greatly pleased with his new army. Fortunately it was beautifully fine till all was over. It was a curious experience to stand beside the King and watch the outcome of three years of strenuous days and nights of missionary enterprise; and of long hours of work in the War Office and in Parliament. I have had splendid backing and from no one more than from the King. It was a peculiar pleasure that he should see the magnificent result. I have been fortunate in that the things for which I have worked most strenuously, the Universities and the Army, took outward and visible form, which does not often happen to the work of politicians. On Sunday the King and Queen took Bay [Miss Haldane] and me out for a tea picnic in the Park. The Queen made tea herself and spilt it plentifully.'

In July the King went to Knowsley to review and give colours to the West Lancashire Division, and followed this next day by doing the same for the East Lancashire Division at Worsley Park, Lord Ellesmere's seat, Haldane being with him on both occasions. These public demonstrations that the Territorial Army was in being under royal auspices did much to silence such opposition as remained.

In the latter part of July another Colonial Conference assembled in London. In the interval since the last meeting the colonies had become dominions and were, under the inspiration of the conference of 1907, taking a much more active interest in the problems of imperial defence. Haldane's General Staff now had ready a complete scheme for military cooperation throughout the empire, which proposed uniformity in equipment, organization, and system of training. It was obviously necessary, if this uniformity was to be accepted by the dominions, that there should be first agreed principles of training and organization formulated for the British Army. On these the General Staff in the War Office, mainly under Haig's direction, had been for some time at work. There was not much difficulty in getting agreement upon a system of training for war, and Part I of the Field Service Regulations duly appeared. But over Part II, which dealt with the system of administration and organization to be adopted in war, there was a long battle. This part of the Field Service Regulations dealt mainly with the functions of the departments of the Adjutant-General and the Quartermaster-General, and these high functionaries were not too ready to listen to a comparatively junior member of the General Staff like Haig telling them what they ought to do. Haig, who was in deadly earnest and realized the vital importance of system, was not over-tactful in insisting on his points, and Haldane, who realized that the prime cause of the administrative scandals of the South African War was lack of system, had to bring him reinforcement, and in the event the second part of the Field

Service Regulations was ready in time for the dominions to consider it. So for the first time the Army was given definite plans for organization and administration in war, plans which stood the test of the years 1914–18.

It happened that Lord Kitchener's time as commander-in-chief in India came to an end in the autumn of 1909. It was no secret that he aspired to succeed Lord Minto as viceroy. Lord Morley, the Secretary of State for India was opposed to this on the grounds that important political developments in India were in contemplation and a soldier viceroy would not be qualified to bring these into being. As it was important to make use of Kitchener, Haldane proposed to the King that he should be offered the post of commander-in-chief in the Mediterranean, which position the Duke of Connaught was about to vacate, and with the King's consent Haldane wrote to Kitchener:

'Changes are at present under discussion with regard to the organisation for defence of the forces of the Empire. The discussion indicates convergence on developments in which your great ability and experience may hereafter be of high value to this country should it be possible for you to place them at our disposal.

'What I am now about to ask you to take into consideration will not, I think, interfere with the period of rest from hard work—amounting to a year or a year and a half at least —which I gather you wish to reserve. Moreover, in this letter I am merely writing tentatively and informally, with the purpose of ascertaining what you might hereafter be prepared to consider, rather than with the desire to make a definite proposition. I may, however, add that not only are the Prime Minister and my principal colleagues in the Cabinet cognisant of what I am doing, but that I have gone over the substance of it with Mr. Balfour, who is anxious to lay the foundations of continuity in Military policy.

'The Government proposes, in development of the concep-

tion of an Imperial General Staff, and of the other propositions which were accepted in principle by the Colonial Conference in 1907, to ask the self-governing Dominions and the
other parts of the Empire, to co-operate in fashioning common plans, not only for the organisation of their own local
forces (this has been done at home and in India) but for possible concentration in a period of great emergency. At present there is no general scheme providing for the mobilisation of the 1,200,000 trained or partially trained officers and
men in the Empire. I enclose for your private information
papers which indicate in outline and tentatively what we have
in mind. These papers have been before the Committee of
Imperial Defence. The new Mediterranean Command, including as it does the British Force in Egypt, ought, we think,
to be made of greater importance in connection with this
plan than it is at present. The Duke of Connaught is likely to
relinquish this command before long, and its organisation
and details, including arrangements for the defence of Egypt,
may then be reconsidered with a view to development. It is
not possible to be more specific just now, and besides this we
should desire to have your considered advice before settling
several questions. Moreover, the affairs of the Command can
be carried on for a time, after the Duke leaves it, without the
new Commander-in-chief assuming the reins on the spot.
The question that I should like you to consider quite informally is whether it would be agreeable to you should the Government hereafter find itself in a position to offer you the
post of Commander-in-chief in the Mediterranean, with a
seat on the Committee of Imperial Defence and the Presidency
of the Selection Board when you are in London. I think you
would have it for some months every year. While it is our
earnest hope that you will be favourably disposed towards
this idea I may add that quite independently of whether or
not you accept it I shall propose to the King the offer to you
in November of a Field-Marshal's baton.

'I am of course only in a position to begin the negotiation of arrangements, but if I had your sanction I would again see Mr. Balfour with a view to making certain that all our plans commended themselves to him, so that continuity of policy might be made as secure as possible. From what I have hinted to you you will gather that I do not anticipate difficulty under this head.

'I may in conclusion add that what I have tentatively suggested in this letter commends itself to the King, as well as to the Prime Minister, Lord Morley, Lord Crewe, and Sir Edward Grey. It is not merely that we are full of appreciation of the splendid services you have rendered in India, but that we feel that the best chances of success in the difficult enterprise of making plans for the organisation of the combined Military Forces of the Empire, in any spot where they may be required, and to such an extent as the circumstances of each country will admit of, depend on our being so fortunate as to secure your co-operation in a prominent position. We think that the Mediterranean Command would be in your hands capable of being developed into an instrument of power.'

Kitchener wanted a holiday and was not at all attracted by the offer, but when the King expressed the hope that he would accept he wrote: 'If the Government play the King we poor soldiers are done and can only obey, at least such are my principles.' Actually he never took up the post, which soon after the King's death was changed to that of Inspector-General of Overseas Forces. But one result of Haldane's letter was that Kitchener agreed to visit Australia and New Zealand and advise those Dominions on the organization of their forces, and this proved to be a valuable reinforcement to Haldane's plans. At the end of July another Imperial Conference had met at which Haldane presented his scheme, now complete, for the organization of the military services of the Empire and the dominions agreed unanimously to accept uniformity of organization, training, and equipment, with the mother country, and to a regular interchange of British and dominion officers. As one outward and visible sign of this agreement the British Chief of the General Staff became the Chief of the Imperial General Staff.

This reform, which has attracted very little public attention, is second in importance only to Haldane's organization of the Expeditionary Force in its effect on the conduct of the war, when it came, for it enabled the dominions to take their part far more promptly and effectively than could otherwise have been the case, and for the war the dominions provided and maintained two cavalry and ten infantry divisions and a number of additional contingents, and sent overseas more than 1,200,000 men. Since the Statute of Westminster became effective, it is commonly said that the Crown is the one link that keeps the Empire together, but Haldane fashioned a second link which has important moral and sentimental values. Nearly every military unit in the dominions is to-day linked to a regular unit of the British Army, and the establishment of a common tradition of service and of practice endures and is the stronger because it is entirely voluntary.

Lord Roberts' campaign for compulsory service, his statements in the House of Lords, and in speeches up and down the country, that we were not in a position to defend ourselves against invasion, combined with Lord Charles Beresford's attacks upon Fisher's naval administration, coming at a time of great political excitement over the conflict of the Liberal Government with the House of Lords, served to produce a general feeling of nervousness in the country. This in turn produced a crop of spy stories, most of them sufficiently ridiculous, but, in the state of public feeling, they had to be examined seriously. One paper announced that it had discovered that Germans had many thousands of rifles stored in the cellars of a bank near Charing Cross to be used for arming the German reservists in this country. The rifles proved to

be military weapons of an old pattern which had been purchased by the Miniature Rifle Association for conversion.
Well-authenticated stories of airships flying over the country
by night turned out to be experiments by a commercial firm
for advertising purposes. It happened in the summer that a
naval display in the Thames had been arranged and a member
of Parliament suggested that this would give the Germans a
splendid opportunity for bottling up a large part of our fleet.
Erskine Childers' *Riddle of the Sands*, one of the best spy
stories ever written, had a great vogue, and was the parent of
many ingenious suggestions for surprise attacks by the Germans. The Kaiser used one of these to make a joke of our
nervousness, and suggested that a special type of mine should
be designed which could be carried in packing-cases in cargo-
vessels and dropped overboard in the estuary of the Thames
or in the Solent, when we had a considerable part of the
Fleet assembled in either place. The Kaiser's jest had some
circulation in Berlin and was taken seriously when it drifted
across the North Sea. It reached Balfour, who sent the papers
on to the War Office and Haldane replied:

'DEAR BALFOUR

'Thank you for the papers. These things have to be investigated at once. No Minister ought to neglect the investigation of dubious reports, and it is good of you to have
helped in this case.

'I saw Grey and Fisher without delay, and have reconstructed the materials—here they are—

'1. The Kaiser takes in Romeike's press cuttings.

'2. Therefore he read Sir George Armstrong's gloomy letter to the *Globe* of a week ago pointing out the risk we ran,
on the occasion of the Thames Review, of a German assault.

'3. The temptation to make a Teutonic joke was too great,
and he chaffed someone at the Embassy in Berlin, and referred to the "packing cases". (This needless to say he did not

do by desire of his General Staff that the kindly warning should be given, for that is not their way.)

'4. Grey heard nothing of this from Berlin, because they treated it as chaff.

'5. Lord Leith went to Bridgeman when the tale reached him, most properly.

'6. Bridgeman went to Fisher's room (this Fisher told me this morning) and asked him to see Lord L. Fisher replied "I am too busy to waste my time over this cock and bull story!"

'7. Bridgeman being a polite man, and knowing Lord L. well, did not like to say this, but told Lord L. that Sir John had been informed and was fully acquainted with the situation and Lord L. took him to mean that no shred of confirmation had come to Fisher of any sort or kind. Still it is well that they should all be informed, improbable as is the whole story.'

So this 'cock-and-bull story' involved the Foreign Minister, the Secretary of State for War, the leader of the Opposition, and the First Sea Lord.

The prevalence of spy-mania worried Haldane a good deal. 'Lord Roberts' repeated statements that we are in danger of invasion and are not prepared to meet it, while made with the honest intention of strengthening our military forces, are doing a good deal of mischief. You would hardly believe the number of circumstantial stories which reach the War Office of German plans to seize our dockyards, block up the fleet, and in other ways prepare for an invasion *en masse*. The stories themselves are almost always ridiculous, but they are the index of a dangerous state of nervousness which if it is allowed to grow might lead to a public outcry against our sending the Expeditionary Force, which we have created with such pains, overseas when it was needed to go. Worse still is the effect on the public mind that Germany is the enemy, which renders any attempt to improve relations increasingly difficult. The King is a good deal worried about this, and I told him that I would myself back up Lord Roberts' proposal for Compulsory Service in order to restore confidence and banish the German bogy if I were not convinced that it was both impracticable and dangerous.'

Before the House adjourned for the summer recess the strain of these years of exceptionally heavy work had begun to have its effect upon Haldane, whose eyes were inflamed and were giving him a good deal of anxiety. His doctor ordered him complete rest, so he took no part in the platform warfare, which raged up and down the country during the summer and autumn, between the 'Budget Protest League' and the supporters of the Government led by Mr. Lloyd George. By the second week of October he had recovered sufficiently to be able to take his turn as minister in attendance at Balmoral, where he followed Asquith, who had sounded the King on his attitude on the conflict with the Lords. From Balmoral he wrote to his mother: 'I had two long talks with the King yesterday. My relations with him are delightful. He is full of gratitude for the way his army has been transformed. The recent manœuvres have impressed him greatly and I find that he knows all the details. This has made it easy for me to get through several tasks with which Asquith was charged and which he had been unable to settle. I am more than ever impressed with the King's sound judgement and good sense in as difficult a position as any monarch has ever been placed in. I find it hard to believe that the Lords will go to extremes, but if they do we may indeed be thankful that we have on the throne one who will stand between them and revolution. He again scolded me about my health and ordered me to stop work to-day. I was sent out trout fishing with the Master of the Household and Campbell the piper. I was not as lucky as I was last year and only got two and a half brace.'

Soon after his return to London he went to Birmingham to receive, in company with his brother John, an honorary degree from the university. Of this he wrote: 'Yesterday was a fine ceremony. I think the nicest thing they said about anybody was said about Johnny: "There are those living whose lives have been preserved by his scientific work, some of it done at the peril of his own life." It was remarkable enough that two brothers should receive honorary degrees at the same time, but still more unusual was the conjunction of a brother, sister and brother-in-law, Arthur Balfour, Mrs. Sidgwick, and Lord Rayleigh. Arthur Balfour and I travelled down together, closely guarded by Scotland Yard detectives, to protect us from suffragettes!'

When Parliament reassembled the long struggle over the Budget in the House of Commons ended on November 4, when it was passed by a majority of 379 to 149, only to be thrown out by the House of Lords on November 30. Parliament was dissolved on December 3 and the General Election was fixed for the middle of January.

In this election Haldane was able to take little part. Before Parliament was dissolved his eyes were again giving him trouble and this soon became acute, and was accompanied by a severe attack of rheumatism. He had therefore to leave the battle to his friends, for his doctor forbade him to read or write, and for several weeks he had to lie with his eyes bandaged. Miss Haldane took her brother's place with energy and skill, and Asquith and other friends came to speak for him. On the eve of the poll he was well enough to address a big meeting at Haddington and was able to be present to hear that he was returned with a majority of 745, which, seeing how small a part he had been able to take in the election, was a very satisfactory majority.

The result of the election was disappointing to both the chief political parties. The Liberals were still the largest party in the House, but their majority over the Conservatives was only two, and while they could be certain of the support of the Labour members on the Budget, there were eighty-two Irish Nationalists to reckon with. The Irish had expressed strong objection to certain items in the financial Bill and might seize the opportunity to voice their perennial grievance of the over-taxation of Ireland. The Liberals were therefore left in an unpleasant dependence on the Irish vote. The Conservatives on the other hand could not construe the result of the election as a mandate for a second rejection of the Budget by the Lords. There was a clear English and Scottish majority in favour of the Budget. The result was to leave the political situation nebulous and anxious.

On his return to London, Haldane plunged immediately into negotiations with his Cabinet colleagues on future policy. There was considerable divergence of opinion. The Irish were reported to be seeking a definite pledge of immediate legislation to curtail the powers of the Lords and so clear the way for Home Rule. No one in the Government was prepared to give such a pledge. Some were for an immediate appeal to the country with the understanding that if it were successful the King should be asked to use the royal prerogative to create 300 peers, as a preliminary to the reform of the Second Chamber. These thought that capital could be made out of the disturbances to the finances of the country caused by the rejection of the Budget. Others were for keeping the question of ultimate reform of the Lords distinct from the immediate issue of limiting the powers of the Upper House, and for proceeding at once with the Bill, which became known as 'the Parliament Bill'.

As usual Haldane and Grey found themselves to be in agreement; both were in favour of proceeding at once with the Budget, both declared themselves to be Second-Chamber men and both were in favour of proceeding at once with reform of the existing Second Chamber.

'It was inevitable', Haldane wrote at the end of February, 'that after a turn of office with a huge majority the swing of the pendulum should bring about some loss of seats, but I believe that the country is firmly with us in the desire to prevent the House of Lords from hamstringing permanently a Liberal majority. The right course for us is to proceed with the Budget. I do not believe that Redmond will throw it out for he will realise that this will be taken in Ireland as an alliance with his country's enemies and will postpone indefinitely any chance of Home Rule. Nor do I believe that the Lords will venture again to throw out the budget. This would force a dissolution on the least favourable grounds to them and they must see that this is so. Having got the budget through we should proceed with a well considered measure for the reconstruction of the second chamber. This has for years past been a plank in the Liberal platform, and now circumstances have made it the question of the hour. The events of the last year have made it clear that a second chamber which commands public support and respect is an essential element in the Constitution, and we shall be failing in our duty to the country if we do not proceed to amend an obvious defect in our parliamentary organisation.'

Until the attitude of the Irish on the budget was known the position of the Government was very shaky.

On February 3 Haldane had an audience of the King just before His Majesty left for Biarritz. 'The King wished me to see him yesterday. I went to the Palace and had a delightful talk with him for over an hour. He said the result of the election was inconclusive and he could not possibly consider the creation of peers without a much more definite expression of opinion from the country. I told him that I had every hope that it would not be necessary to proceed to that extreme, which he evidently dreads. He then turned the conversation to Kitchener and the Viceroyalty. He is eager to have Kitchener. I gave him Morley's reasons for preferring Hardinge. He was not convinced but said he would await Kitchener's return about the end of April. I then told him what was in my mind about creating an Inspector-Generalship of overseas forces as a necessary complement to the decision of the

Imperial Conference. In this he was keenly interested and he asked me many questions about the prospect of the Dominions making a useful contribution to Imperial Defence. As I was taking leave he said: "This Government may not last. I say nothing of some of my Ministers but I wish you may be very long my Minister." '

The absorption of his colleagues and of his party in the political situation had for Haldane the happy result, in the uncertain state of his health, of easing his work at the War Office. He slipped through an increase in the Army Estimates without any difficulty, and had no difficulty in meeting the usual attacks in the Commons on the Territorial Army and the voluntary system. He was able to announce that the strength of the Territorials was 280,000 and that the Special Reserve was up to its establishment. He also informed the House that a Flying Corps was now in existence for the Army, that we had at Aldershot one small dirigible, and that two others, one the result of a public subscription raised by the *Morning Post*, were coming over from France. There was now little excitement or even interest in the Commons over Army reform, the battle-ground had shifted to the Upper Chamber, where the supporters of Lord Roberts still maintained that the Territorials were not fitted to defend the country, and the friends of the old Militia lost no opportunity of expressing their resentment. There Lord Lucas ably held the fort.

As usual the resultant of the conflict of opinion in the Cabinet as to the best solution of the crisis was compromise. It was agreed to proceed with the resolutions limiting the powers of the Lords, which became known as the Veto, and then to introduce the Budget. The Resolutions were passed by substantial majorities, and on April 20 Haldane's forecast proved correct, the Irish went into the lobby with the Liberals when the Budget Bill came on, and on April 28 it was accepted without a division by the Lords. No immediate appeal to the country was now in question, but the House rose for the Easter recess in an atmosphere of political storm and uncertainty, for the major question of the future of the House of Lords was still in the air.

Haldane planned a holiday in his favourite Ilmenau with Professor Hume Brown, but his departure was delayed by two notes which he received on the same day from Lord Knollys and Lord Morley. Lord Knollys said that the King was due back from Biarritz on April 27 and had directed him to meet Lord Kitchener, who was due in London on the 25th, and arrange for him to come to the palace on April 28, when the King proposed to present to him the baton of field-marshal and broach the question of the viceroyalty. Morley, who had the same information, wrote in some agitation. He feared that the King would precipitate matters. His objection to Kitchener as viceroy was due to the fear that the appointment of a soldier would be taken in India as a declaration that we meant to rule with the sword. He did not know Kitchener and wanted time to make his acquaintance before making up his mind. On getting these letters Haldane at once saw Asquith and suggested that he should see the King before Kitchener was received and point out the reasons for not being in a hurry over the viceroyalty. Asquith agreed to this, Haldane made the necessary arrangements with Lord Knollys, and Kitchener's audience passed off without any reference to India. Morley, who was curiously nervous of entering into an argument with the monarch, wrote: 'You once saved the life of a favourite dog of mine. I am as grateful to you now for what you have done for me.'

Devotion to dogs was one of the links between the two men. Haldane was too fond of dogs to keep them in London, but there were always dogs at Cloan, and his daily letter to his mother usually had in it some advice about them or asked for news of them. Just at this time he was much perturbed because a very special favourite had taken to killing sheep and he was as much exercised over the reform of the beloved culprit as he was over the Viceroyalty of India. On April 29 he had his last interview with King Edward: 'The King has relieved me for a fortnight's holiday. I had a difficult but fairly successful interview with him this morning. Morley had been received before me, this did not put the King in a good humour, for he is still quite set on sending Kitchener to India. I did my best to smooth matters for Morley with some success. I promised the King to bring Morley and Kitchener together and the King in the meantime won't rush the issue. He was not looking as well as I hoped to find him after his holiday. He seemed to be short of breath and for the first time that I can remember was not smoking while we talked. The Professor and I leave for Ilmenau to-night.'

The holiday was a very short one. The news of the King's sudden illness and death on May 6 brought him home in haste. 'I am back', he wrote on May 9, 'with a heavy heart. The relation between my King and myself was not a usual one as between Minister and Sovereign and something personal is snapped. He was one of the few outside the professional soldiers who understood what I was trying to do for his army, and without his constant support and advice I could not have done what I have done. He never allowed his dislike of the Kaiser and his ways to interfere with the great object of making our relations with Germany easier, and I believe, had he lived, we might together have made as firm a friendship as, largely due to his influence, we have now with France. Ten years ago no one would have ventured to prophesy that France would be our devoted friend and friendship with Germany is not really as difficult to-day as friendship with France was then. I have written a letter to the new King just saying what I felt of his father.'

This is the letter to King George:

'Mr Haldane presents his humble duty to your Majesty and ventures to take the liberty of allowing himself a few words of reference to your Majesty's great sorrow. His dear Master had created in Mr Haldane a sense of devotion and attachment such that he asks that he may be permitted for a moment to write in a fashion which might otherwise seem to be an intrusion on your Majesty's personal grief. The King that is no more stood as few of his predecessors for the great mission of England in the world. In his personality, so strong and direct, lay as it came more and more to seem to Mr Haldane, the symbol of our mission to the peoples of this country, of this Empire, of the earth. He was beloved first by his subjects and especially by his Ministers, who stood to him in a relation in which they sought, as well as offered to him, counsel.

'And so it is that there has come into the life of Mr Haldane a sense of deep personal sorrow and of profound feeling for your Majesty at this moment of sudden severance of the closest ties. Your Majesty has thought much and often of the ideals which have from the first guided the great sovereigns of this great country, and Mr Haldane knows that the consciousness of these ideals, and a firm faith in them are the source of strength to your Majesty at this momentous time.

'As generation succeeds generation their ideals change, but what is of essential and continuous purpose in them remains yet always the same, and is a rock on which Mr Haldane feels that your Majesty has long since sought to plant your feet. It is his hope and faith that to you will be given the strength to carry yet further the great mission in the world which is your Majesty's inheritance.'

Chapter XII

THE NATIONAL SERVICE LEAGUE—
NEGOTIATIONS FOR AN AGREEMENT WITH
GERMANY

1911 to 1912

The death of King Edward had an immediate effect upon the political situation. It was generally agreed that it would be wrong to confront the new monarch with a constitutional crisis and a truce was declared by mutual agreement, during which the leaders of the Government and of the Opposition met in conference to seek a solution. But the truce affected only the major question of the relations of the Commons with the Upper House, and the large number of peers who were opposed to Haldane's military policy felt themselves free to give vent to their displeasure with him and with the Government in general. Immediately on the re-assembling of Parliament attacks upon Haldane in the Lords began and between June 13 and July 18 there were no fewer than seven debates on Army affairs. As before, the leaders of the Opposition stood aloof with the one exception of Lord Middleton, the leaders of the attacks being, besides the former Secretary of State for War, the Duke of Bedford, Lord Derby and Lord Lovat. The ground of attack was in the main the old one that the Territorial Army was not and could not be made fit to protect the country against invasion, and to this was added the charge that Haldane had drastically reduced the strength of the Regular Army. The first of these charges, backed by Lord Roberts' active campaign in the country and by the propaganda of the National Service League, was the more serious and Haldane realized that a reply in a more popular form than speeches in Parliament was needed.

The National Service League had in 1909 had a bill formulating its proposals to apply compulsory service to the Territorial Force introduced into the House of Lords and had worked out a detailed scheme. This was to produce a home defence army of 400,000 men at an increase to the previous estimates of less than £4,000,000 a year and the object of this force was declared to be to provide for the security of the country against invasion in such a way as to enable the Expeditionary Force and the Navy to be sent away from the United Kingdom without delay in case of necessity.

Haldane had in 1909 appointed Sir Ian Hamilton to be Adjutant-General in succession to General Douglas and in June 1910, when Lord Kitchener had definitely refused the appointment, he nominated him to be first Inspector-General of Overseas Forces. Sir Ian was a firm believer in the voluntary system and he had a fluent pen, so Haldane asked him while he was still Adjutant-General and therefore the member of the Army Council responsible for man-power, to state the case against compulsory service in a popular form, and at the same time he got his financial expert, Charles Harris, to examine the budget of the National Service League. The result was a book by Sir Ian entitled *Compulsory Service* and to this Haldane wrote an introduction. In this he elaborated the arguments he had already presented to the House of Commons. His case was built up on the fundamental fact that command of the sea was vital to our existence. If we had command of the sea invasion on a scale which would necessitate such a force as the National Service League proposed would be impossible; if we had not command of the sea we should starve. With Harris's figures to support him, he showed that the proposals of the National Service League would mean an addition not of four but of eight millions to the estimates. 'If this somewhat substantial sum is to be found by the public, I should prefer to spend the money on increasing the Navy still further and in adding to the establishment of the Regular Army a new division.' Be it remembered that the proposals of the National Service League were to provide for home defence and included no proposals for the expansion of the Expeditionary Force.

The appearance of *Compulsory Service* provoked Lord Roberts to rejoin with *Fallacies and Facts: An Answer to 'Compulsory Service'* and in this he asked why Mr. Haldane had chosen Sir Ian Hamilton, who had been Adjutant-General for but a brief period, why instead did he not give us the opinion of his chief military adviser, General Sir William Nicholson, Chief of the Imperial General Staff? Nicholson had been, in India, a close associate and friend of Lord Roberts and was known to have been in favour of compulsory service, while General Wilson, who had been an active supporter of Lord Roberts's campaign, and believed that nothing short of a military system analogous to that of the great Continental armies would suffice for us, had recently left the position of Commandant of the Staff College to become Director of Military Operations. Lord Roberts had therefore good reason to believe that the General Staff was on his side. To meet this challenge a second edition of *Compulsory Service* was produced, which included a memorandum by Sir Arthur Wilson, who had succeeded Fisher as First Sea Lord, giving an authoritative opinion that if the Navy were maintained at adequate strength the risk of invasion was small.

Sir Arthur Wilson said:

'The really serious danger that this country has to guard against in war is not invasion but interruption to our trade and destruction of our merchant shipping.

'The strength of our Fleet is determined by what is necessary to protect our trade, and if it is sufficient for that it will be almost necessarily sufficient to prevent invasion, since the same disposition of the ships to a great extent answers both purposes.

'The main object aimed at by our Fleet, whether for the defence of commerce or for any other purpose, is to prevent any ship of the enemy from getting to sea far enough to do any mischief before she is brought to action. Any disposition which is even moderately successful in attaining this object will most certainly be effective in preventing a large fleet of transports, than which nothing is more vulnerable or more difficult to hide, from reaching our shores.

'To realise the difficulty which an enemy would have in bringing such a fleet of transports to our coast and disembarking an army, it is necessary to remember that all the ships operating in home waters, whether they are in the North Sea, the Channel, or elsewhere, are in wireless communication with the Admiralty and with the Commander-in-chief, so that if a fleet of transports is sighted anywhere by a single cruiser, or even by a merchant ship, if she is fitted with wireless, every ship which happened to be in a position to intercept the transports would at once get an order to concentrate as necessary for the purpose, whether she was at sea or in harbour.

'It is further necessary to remember that even supposing by some extraordinary lucky chance the transports were able to reach our coasts without being detected, their presence must be known when they arrive there; and long before half the troops could be landed the transports would be attacked and sunk by submarines, which are stationed along the coast for that purpose.

'Is it possible to entice part of our fleet away by any stratagem? Possibly. But even if he succeeds in drawing off half our fleet, the other half, in conjunction with destroyers and submarines, would be quite sufficient to sink the greater part of his transports, even if supported by the strongest fleet he could collect. The fleets would engage each other while the destroyers and submarines torpedoed the transports.

'Finally, even if he reached the coast in safety, he would

see that it was quite impossible to guard his transports against the attacks of submarines while he was landing his troops; and it was quite certain that a superior force would be brought to attack him before the landing could be completed.

'Taking all these facts into consideration, he would probably decide, as the Admiralty have done, that an invasion on even the moderate scale of 70,000 men is practically impossible.'

In order to add to this the reinforcement of military opinion Haldane sent *Compulsory Service* to Sir John French and to Sir Douglas Haig, then Chief of the General Staff in India. French wrote: 'I agree entirely with your introduction. I have recently inspected the 1st London, South Midland, North Midland, and West Lancashire divisions. In each case the whole division was concentrated. The artillery of the North Midland division was firing away in Lancashire when I went to see them. The progress these troops are making (both infantry and artillery) is quite wonderful. The difference in spirit and earnestness from the old Volunteers is in my opinion entirely due to the fact that you have given them a real organisation. What struck me more than anything else was the behaviour and bearing of the men in camp, bivouac, on the march and in the field. There is evidence of a force and power which will never be found in any but volunteer soldiers. Our policy should be to strengthen your Expeditionary Force, not to create a conscript army.'

Haig wrote from Calcutta: 'I have read your preface to *Compulsory Service* with the greatest interest. You could not have put the case better or in a way to be more easily grasped by the average citizen.

'Every soldier will be glad to hear that you are to remain on at the War Office. It would be very disheartening to have any radical change in military organisation now.

'All that is wanted is to continue to build on the foundation which you have so surely laid. Nor should any fundamental change be allowed in the organisation and administration of the army for war, as now laid down in the Field Service Regulations, because all parts of the Empire, including India, are now trying to develop on these lines, and any change must now have a more disturbing effect than formerly.'

To clinch the matter Haldane authorized the General Staff to carry out an independent inquiry into the methods by which compulsory service could best be introduced and to report whether its introduction would be practicable and would increase our military strength. The investigation took some time, and eventually the General Staff reported early in 1912 that a change in our military system involving the introduction of compulsory service must inevitably take time, that in the interval before the new system was in working order there was danger of a breakdown of the voluntary system, such as would make it uncertain whether our overseas garrisons could be maintained, that the period of change must be a period of weakness such as might invite attack, and that in the existing uncertain and anxious state of Europe it would be most unwise to attempt such an experiment.

At that time a semi-official military quarterly called the *Army Review* was edited in the War Office under the direction of the Chief of the Imperial General Staff. The *Review* had opened its pages to the National Service League, which had presented the case for compulsory service. In the number of July 1912 there appeared an editorial reply to the National Service League. This was written by the then Director of Staff Duties, General Kiggell, at the request of the Chief of the Imperial General Staff and without even a hint from Haldane that such an answer was desirable. In this article our defensive requirements were stated to be:

'1. A sufficient navy to secure us both against invasion and to provide a reasonable degree of security for our ocean trade routes. The greater margin we can afford, over and above

that, the better no doubt, with due regard to other requiie-
ments, but that is a question for the Government concerned
in consultation with the Admiralty.

'2. A home defence force to deal with possible raids. In our
opinion, the Territorial Force, kept even approximately up
to strength, together with unallotted Regular troops and various Special Reserve Units not required, at any rate immediately, outside the United Kingdom, would suffice for so long
as we have a naval superiority, and so long as specially important points, within reach of possible raids, are adequately
fortified and garrisoned. The garrisons must include some
Regular artillery and specialists, the remaining requirements
being furnished from the home defence force now available.

'3. An Expeditionary Force highly trained, fully equipped,
with the best of everything and complete in every detail,
capable of being mobilised very rapidly, and of being transported without delay to wherever it may be wanted. As to
the size of this force, we shall add a few words further on in
this article.

'4. Adequate fortifications and garrisons for our coaling
stations and harbours in all parts of the world, to enable them
to resist raids and to hold out, if attacked, until we can relieve
them. If we are victorious in the main theatre of war, we shall
thereby ensure their relief automatically.

'Under this head we must include provision for periodical
relief of garrisons furnished from home. Under this head, too,
we must include the garrisons of India, and of our self-governing Dominions, which are all taking steps to provide for their
own home defence.

'5. Finally, we require a general agreement amongst the
leaders of public opinion, not only in the United Kingdom,
but in the Empire, as to the correct principles on which to
prepare for possible eventualities, and on which to act if action should become necessary; and we require that every possible means shall be taken to educate the public in these prin-

ciples. We recognise that this question of education is so important that we think it should be bracketed with a strong navy as forming the two most important factors in any scheme of defence, on which the success of that scheme must mainly depend. We acknowledge to the full the danger of a misguided public opinion, so much so that we realise many thinking men have been led to conclude that in itself it provides a justification for the National Service League's proposals. To such we can only say, with all respect, that we fear they are misguiding, instead of educating, public opinion by urging that the existing organisation for home defence is insufficient for our requirements, when, in fact, we have reasonable grounds for believing that it is sufficient. As a nation we flatter ourselves that our instincts are sound. Will not the view —as we believe the only sound view—appeal to the national instincts that it is better to put our efforts into preventing the possibility of an invasion rather than into measures to defeat an invasion which we have needlessly allowed to become possible? Do not our instincts already run in the direction of sea power? Is it impossible, then, to educate the people into accepting the view that money proposed to be spent on home defence forces, beyond what we require to deal with raids, would be better spent on the Navy, if the Navy is not strong enough already? That is the first step in education. The next is that, having made the Navy so strong, that invasion is practically impossible, having done what we can to secure our ocean trade routes and to enable our oversea possessions to defend themselves in case of necessity, and having provided the necessary measures of home defence, we still require something further—viz., a sufficient and efficient land force, capable of seeking out the enemy—instead of waiting here for an enemy who cannot come—and of forcing him to make peace.'

So the proposals of the National Service League were ruled out, not, as Haldane's enemies were to say later, in the interests of his party, but on the best available naval and military advice. To a correspondent who wrote to ask him whether he did not think that compulsory service might be necessary if we were engaged in a great war, he answered: 'I agree that compulsion may be necessary if we have to fight for our existence during a great war, but compulsion in war is quite a different thing from compulsion during peace when recruiting for the first line ought to be the paramount consideration, and nothing should be done to impede it. In war the Government would take powers to keep the men serving with the colours in the ranks while the war lasted. In peace we have to let the men go when they have completed the term of their engagement, and it is a sheer gamble, which I am not prepared to take, to risk getting men to replace them in order to provide for a wholly unnecessary home defence army. The change of military system, while we have to provide and maintain large garrisons overseas, must involve a period of weakness and can therefore only be made safely when a period of peace is reasonably certain, but public opinion is unlikely to favour compulsory service except when faced with a grave national emergency, and the change can then only be made with safety when the Government has the powers which would be accorded it in the event of a major war.'

In his introduction to *Compulsory Service* Haldane said the principles of home defence were defined by the Committee of Imperial Defence, and he went on with an account of what that committee was and what he hoped it would be:

'One of the advantages which followed on the foundation by Mr Balfour of the Committee of Imperial Defence was that the subjects assigned to that Committee began to be systematically and scientifically studied. The Committee affords to the Chiefs of the Staff at the Admiralty and at the War Office a meeting-place where they have a constant opportunity of bringing their operations into harmony, and of working out in detail objects and principles common to both services, which are to be followed by those who serve under them. But the Committee does more than this. Recently it has developed the scope of its procedure. The Foreign and Colonial Offices, the India Office, the Home Office, the Treasury, the Board of Trade, and the Post Office, are now, not only through their Ministerial Chiefs, but in the persons of the permanent heads of departments, called into council whenever occasion renders it useful. The organisation works largely through carefully chosen sub-committees, of which several are always sitting and collecting and investigating materials. When the main body assembles the Prime Minister presides, having summoned not only the permanent members, but colonial statesmen who may be in London and are concerned in the particular problem of defence which is under investigation. More and more each year the Committee is being transformed into a body, of which the Prime Minister is the controlling head, but which works mainly through experts. The Sub-Committees, which report to the main body, deal with work much of it so highly technical that it is necessarily carried out by experts. This work the highly qualified secretary, Rear-Admiral Sir Charles Ottley and his special staff, arrange, under the eye of the Prime Minister. With the Admiralty and the War Office the Secretary is in daily communication. The Defence Committee thus organised contains the germ of a Great General Staff for the Empire. The Admiralty consults it on problems that are more than merely naval. The Imperial General Staff of the Army is in constant relation with it over matters that concern the defences of the Empire. The Committee has now become a body which is in effect sitting and working, largely through the medium of its sub-committees and officials, almost as continuously as is the General Staff of the Army. If war were threatened it could develop into a War Council for the Prime Minister, the duty of which would be to furnish him, and through him his Ministers, with the expert knowledge required before policy could be settled in the Cabinet.'

Alas, when war came this Committee of Imperial Defence was not so used. Had it fulfilled the functions which Haldane wished, in 1910, that it should fulfil, many of the blunders that we made in 1914–15 would not have been made. Our preparations for the war were in many respects admirable, but we overlooked the need for an effective general headquarters for the Empire, and the man who foresaw that need was driven by obloquy from office.

Throughout the summer of 1910 Haldane was kept busy defending the voluntary system and in addressing meetings on behalf of the Territorial Force. At most of these meetings he slipped in a few words on our relations with Germany. Speaking at Warrington in the autumn he said:

'The nation has been in a somewhat "scarey" mood. We are preparing and overhauling our naval and military establishments, but we are doing that in no spirit of scare and in no spirit of hostility. Speaking from knowledge, I should say that our relations with the German Government have rarely been better than they are at this moment. There has been a real effort on the part of many distinguished Germans to understand and appreciate our point of view, and many of us, on the other hand, are making a real effort to appreciate and understand the point of view of Germany. There ought to be no rivalry. We are two great nations, to which the earth opens up a great field for commerce and industry, and my hope is that as time goes on, and as we come to know more of the great nation—great in wealth, in organisation, and in her splendid science and literature—we shall come to feel that we more and more ought to be associated with her in promoting the progress of the world. And, therefore, I no more think it is legitimate for us to criticise Germany for organising her fleet as she likes—and she is entitled to a great fleet, for she has a great commerce—than it is for Germany to take exception if we on our part overhaul our military and naval arrangements, and see to it that they are put upon a secure basis.'

A good many of these speeches were later used by his enemies as proof that he was blinded to the interests of his country by his affection for Germany.

In November he went to Aldershot to inspect the aircraft factory and made his first flight, in a frock coat and top hat, in airship *Beta*.

'*Beta*', he wrote to his mother, 'is a little airship of an old type and there is not much room to sit. You look down on the earth through the girders at your feet, but I soon conquered the feeling of giddiness. We made a short flight at 25 miles an hour and at a height of 500 feet. The factory is developing well under O'Gorman. We have now four airships and a fifth is under construction.'

Meantime the conference between the leaders of the Government and the Opposition had broken down and in December Asquith decided to go to the country on the issue of the relations between the two Houses. So Haldane went to Monkrigg for his last election. The result was to make little change in representation of parties, but as there was now no Budget question to make the support of the eighty-two Irish Nationalists doubtful the Liberals could count on a majority of 124. In January 1910 Haldane had completed twenty-five years as a member of Parliament and the Liberals of Haddingtonhad decided to celebrate the event. So in March his long services to the constituency were pleasantly rewarded by making him a freeman of Haddington and by presenting to him a service of plate. Hardly had this been done when his connection with the constituency came to an end. In October 1910 Morley had resigned from the India Office. Asquith asked Haldane to go there with a peerage, but Haldane felt that the position of the Territorial Force was not sufficiently secure to allow him to leave the War Office just yet and he told the Prime Minister that if a change at the War Office was to be made later on he would like to go to the Admiralty, where he wanted to organize a naval general staff. So Lord Crewe became Secretary of State for India, but not long after the meeting of the new Parliament Lord Crewe was taken ill. The struggle with the Lords was not yet over and it was known that a large number of the back-bench peers wanted to force the hands of their leaders, throw out the Parliament Bill, and force the Government to ask the King for a creation of peers on a large scale. Asquith naturally felt that in these circumstances it was important to fill adequately the place of Lord Crewe, as leader in the Lords, and in March he again pressed Haldane to take a peerage. 'I don't much like it,' he wrote to his mother, 'but it is not a question of liking but of duty. It appears unlikely that Crewe will be able for some time to come to stand any great strain of work and Morley is 73. Asquith feels that he must have some one in the Lords on whom he can rely. So I have agreed and I am to be Viscount Haldane of Cloan. I have, I think, just enough money if I live quietly. Asquith has agreed that I am to stay at the War Office and finish my work there, and going to the Lords will be a considerable relief from the hard labour of the front bench in the Commons.'

In this same spirit he accepted appointment as Lord of Appeal, an unusual promotion for one who had not held high judicial office. He felt that his main work in the War Office was done, and remained there rather as a watch-dog to see that there was no disturbance to his reforms than to initiate further. It happened that most of the Prime Ministers of the dominions had come to London for the ceremonial of the coronation and an Imperial Conference was held at which he was able to complete some of the details of his scheme for imperial co-operation in defence, and as a member of the Judicial Committee of the Imperial Council to get his plan for the reconstruction of the Supreme Courts of the Empire adopted.

The German Emperor had arranged to pay a state visit to King George V on his accession in May and Haldane, who never lost an opportunity of smoothing our relations with Germany, suggested to the German Embassy that he should give a dinner to the German generals who would come in the Emperor's suite in order that they might meet some of our generals. In reply he received a message that the Emperor would like instead to come and have lunch with him and to meet some people whom he might otherwise not come to know. Haldane's collection of guests to meet the Emperor was catholic. It included Lord Morley, Lord Kitchener, Lord Curzon, Mr. Ramsay MacDonald, then leader of the Labour Party, Admiral Sir Arthur Wilson, the First Sea Lord, Lord Moulton, Mr. Edmund Gosse, Mr. John Sargent, and Mr. Spender, the editor of the *Westminster Gazette*. 'The Emperor', he wrote to his mother, 'was in great good humour. He spoke to everyone, complimented me on my food and cigars and after lunch went upstairs to my den for a talk. He chaffed me on the small size of my house and then talked about the motor tour in which he is much interested. He is putting his brother Prince Henry in charge of the German side and urged me to get a Royal Prince to lead us. I told him that Coronation engagements would make this difficult, but I undertook to get some senior English General.'

The motor tour had been a scheme of King Edward's to promote friendly relations with Germany. It took the form of a challenge from the Kaiserliche Automobile Club to our Royal Automobile Club. Each club was to provide one hundred motor cars driven by their owners for a tour through Germany and England, which took the form of a test of reliability. In each English car there was to be a German officer as umpire, and an English officer in each German car. Haldane took great interest in the scheme and interested himself personally in the selection of the British officers. The tour in Germany was very successful and at Bremen the whole party was embarked on a North-German Lloyd liner to be met on arrival at Southampton with the news that Germany had sent the gunboat *Panther* to Agadir and that an international crisis of the first magnitude was developing. This was one of the blunders of the German Foreign Office, which, with strangely untimely iteration, wrecked all attempts on our side to improve relations between the two countries.

There had been disturbances in Morocco and the French had sent an expedition to Fez. Germany affected to believe that this went beyond the terms of the Algeciras agreement and sent the gunboat *Panther* to Agadir as a demonstration that she intended to protect German interests in North Africa. As a demonstration it was stupid, for Germany was not then ready to proceed to extremes, and the only result of the crisis was to bring Great Britain and France still closer together and to cause both to perfect their military preparations.

The crisis came at an unfortunate time for us and this probably influenced the German Foreign Office and made them believe that we would not venture to call their bluff. Political feeling was again excited and strained at home and Haldane found that he had been optimistic in supposing that he would have an easy time in the Lords. There Lord Lansdowne had introduced a Bill for the reform of the Upper Chamber for which Lord Curzon was said to be responsible. This the Government refused to accept, and after it was withdrawn the Parliament Bill came up from the Commons. There was a short truce for the Coronation, for which Haldane had to procure a coronet, and when Parliament resumed the Lords proceeded to emasculate the Bill. In the middle of July the Cabinet sent a formal minute to the King saying that they could not accept the Bill as amended in the Lords, and that if the Lords again rejected the Bill they must advise His Majesty to use his prerogative to make sufficient peers to make the passage of the Bill certain. The next day Asquith informed the leaders of the Opposition of the decision of the Cabinet. In the midst of the political tension which this caused a great strike of railway and transport workers was declared, and Haldane was kept busy arranging for the Army to assist in maintaining the essential services of the country. Fortunately both crises at home came to an end just before the crisis in foreign affairs reached its most acute stage. On August 11 the Lords passed the Parliament Bill by a majority of seventeen and a week later the strike was settled.

In the meantime anxiety as to Germany's intentions had grown in England, where the international situation was taken more seriously than it was in France. The French seem to have realized that Germany was not yet ready to provoke a European war, but the then somewhat unusual spectacle of Mr. Lloyd George beating the patriotic drum loudly in the City caused excitement, and General Wilson, in charge of the Intelligence Department of the War Office, used the alarm cleverly to expose gaps in our programme of mobilization which required to be filled. Haldane was persuaded that the situation was so threatening that he asked the Prime Minister to call a special meeting of the sub-committee of the Committee of Imperial Defence to consider what our action should be if Germany attacked France.

This meeting took place on August 23 and is described by Mr. Winston Churchill in his *War Crisis*, vol. I.

In the morning General Wilson, as Director of Military Operations, expounded the military plans for coming to the help of France, the chief points being that we should mobilize on the same day as the French and ship the whole of our Expeditionary Force to a position on the left wing of the French Army as rapidly as possible. In the afternoon Sir Arthur Wilson put forward an entirely different plan. He opposed the sending of the Expeditionary Force to the Continent, said our main action should be naval and our army be used to make raids in conjunction with the Navy on the German coast. There was thus a grave difference on policy between the Army and the Navy, and it appeared that one result of this difference was that the Admiralty was not in a position to supply transports for the Expeditionary Force as and when the War Office wanted them. There were three important results of this meeting of the Committee of Imperial Defence. The first of these was that the General Staff plan was accepted and the Admiralty directed to prepare at once for the necessary transports. Asquith wrote to Haldane: 'Sir Arthur Wilson's plan can only be described as puerile and I have dismissed it at once as wholly impracticable. The impression left on me after consideration of the whole discussion is (1) That in principle the General Staff scheme is the only alternative; (2) that it should be limited in the first instance to the dispatch of four divisions. Grey agrees with me and so, I think, does Winston.'

Haldane then and in 1914 was in favour of sending all six divisions to France, but he discovered that the arrangements for speeding up the mobilization of the Expeditionary Force were not yet completed and that the fourth and sixth divisions could not be ready at the same time as the other four. He therefore cancelled the Army manœuvres and used the money saved to fill the gaps in the scheme of mobilization. So the immediate result of the German threat was to enable us to perfect our military plans and to draw us and France still closer together.

A second result of this episode was a threat of a Cabinet crisis. Lord Morley and several other members of the Cabinet who were not members of the Committee of Imperial Defence had no idea that our arrangements for possible co-operation had gone as far as they had, and protested that they were being committed to war on the Continent. Colour was given to this complaint by reports which had reached some members of the Cabinet that General Wilson, who till recently had been Commandant at the Staff College and was as keen a politician as he was soldier, had openly condemned the Government's preparations for war and had advocated the immediate support of France on the Continent in the greatest possible strength as the only possible solution of our military problem. In the schemes which he gave his students to work out Germany appeared as the enemy without disguise. Spender got news of this and complained to Haldane of the dangerous effect of this on our relations with Germany. Haldane replied: 'I should like before long to have a talk with you about war staffs. I do not think any nation can hold its own without a war staff. In Germany the influence of the General Staff is the outcome of the national spirit; there was the same dominating military influence in Scharnhorst's days before the General Staff had been created. I do not think that here either our General Staff or the Committee of Imperial Defence exercises anything like the influence supposed; I can only say that they have done more than any other instruments, of which I know, to redeem military policy from confusion and ineptitude. It is quite true that abuses may arise. You told me of some at the Staff College and my information, when I obtained it, confirmed your impressions. If you went there now you would find that all that sort of thing, which is not really the necessary outcome of the system, has been firmly stamped on and policy is not taught or discussed at the Staff College. The officers there are now trained to look upon the Government of the day as the only body which can or ought to lay down policy. But we can expand these ideas and discuss them when we meet.'

Haldane had sent General Robertson to the Staff College with definite instructions that the business of the college was to teach the application of the principles approved by the General Staff and to keep clear of policy. This soothed some of the anxieties which had been aroused and on the major question, that it was the merest prudence to have hypothetical plans for co-operation with the French, Asquith, Haldane, Grey, Crewe, and McKenna stood firm. When Morley and his friends were assured that the plans were accompanied by an explicit engagement that they committed neither government to action before the event, and when Germany, finding that we were standing resolutely by France, drew in her horns and began to look for a line of retreat, the danger of a split in the Cabinet passed off.

The third consequence was that the differences between the Admiralty and the War Office brought to a head Haldane's distrust of the Admiralty's methods of preparing for war, and he decided that drastic action was necessary. After careful consideration he wrote to Asquith:

'MY DEAR A.

'You have recognised that the position disclosed at the meeting of the Committee of Defence on August 23rd is highly dangerous. By good fortune we have discovered the danger in time, but had war come upon us last month, as it very nearly did, the grave divergence of policy between the admirals and the generals might well have involved us in disaster. The fact is that the Admirals live in a world of their own. The Fisher method, which Wilson appears to follow, that war plans should be locked in the brain of the First Sea Lord, is out of date and impracticable. Our problems of defence are far too numerous and complex to be treated in that way. They can only be solved correctly by a properly organised and scientifically trained War Staff, working in the closest co-operation with the military General Staff under the general direction of the War Office. Wilson's so-called plan disclosed an ignorance of elementary military principles which is startling.

'I have after mature consideration come to the conclusion that this is, in the existing state of Europe, the gravest problem which confronts the Government to-day and that unless it is tackled resolutely I cannot remain in office. Five years experience of the War Office has taught me how to handle the generals and get the best out of them and I believe that the experience makes me the person best qualified to go

to the Admiralty and carry through as thorough a reorganisation there as I have carried out at the War Office. In any
event I am determined that things at the Admiralty shall not
remain any longer as they are.'

It happened that Mr. Winston Churchill was also eager to
go to the Admiralty and Asquith, who was in Scotland, asked
him and Haldane to come up and talk over the matter. Of
this meeting Haldane wrote to Grey:

'I have not told you of my visit to Archerfield on Thursday
and the discussion about the Navy. I went there to meet
Winston. I saw Asquith first and he said that Winston was
immensely keen to go himself to the Admiralty. I said that, as
far as I was concerned, the prospect of moving my house and
of the yacht, were distasteful. But it was not a question of his
or my likings. It was the gravest issue the Government had in
front—a problem more urgent than that of any social reform, and the only real point was how the existing situation
could be changed. Germany had studied our naval psychology, and the old Fisher cry of "Seek out and destroy the
enemy's fleet; this is the objective of the British Navy and
has been ever since the Seven Years War and before it". This
cry has been heard by Germany who were meeting it with
the Kiel Canal and by other highly scientific methods. What
was needed was a new objective for the Navy here, if it was
to be really effective. The Admiralty, which was very conservative, must have a better intellectual basis. To build up an
adequate War Staff was a very difficult thing. If the Admirals
were hostile they could make it an affair of mere words. The
essence of such a scheme was the spirit and earnestness in taking thought of the heads. Such a state of things could not be
brought about by *driving* these powerful Admirals, but only,
moro Socratico, by gentle leading. This I had found from my
experience of working out such a staff at the War Office, a
far easier task. At first the new General Staff had been unreal
and it was only as we got permeated by the spirit, in the

course of our studies of foreign Army Organisation and of our own defects, that it became an affair of spirit and not of letter. Now the Admirals could only be led, if the person who was intrusted with the task had knowledge and experience of this special problem—unless much delay and at least temporary error was to be faced. I certainly should have been merely groping had I been called on to attempt it without five years of training. Would Winston be better off? It was not only the War Staff but the War College and system of naval staff training that had to be dealt with. I did not need to tell him—Asquith—that whatever decision he came to I would do my best, wherever I was, and personally I did not ask for any change. But to me the problem in front was one of the utmost gravity. Germany would now concentrate on the naval situation between her and ourselves. I felt that for more reasons than one I could help here. I brushed aside all notion of the Lord Chancellorship, which Asquith referred to in passing. The interest of the State was the only thing that mattered.

'He asked me to see Winston, first alone and then with him. I did so without mincing matters. Winston was very good—reasoned that if he went there he would work closely with me at the War Office, in the spirit of his father who had always said that there ought to be a common administration. I felt, however, that, full of energy and imagination as he is, he does not know his problem or the vast field of thought that has to be covered. Moreover, though I did not say this to him, I felt that it was only a year since he had been doing his best to cut down McKenna's estimates, and that the Admiralty would receive the news of his advent with dismay. For they would think, wrongly or rightly, that as soon as the financial pinch begins to come, eighteen months from now, he would want to cut down. He is too apt to act first and think afterwards—though of his energy and courage one cannot speak too highly.

'Asquith has taken the whole matter into consideration. That a change must be made is clear. I do not think it is vanity that makes me wish to leap into this gulf. It is the desire to make use of what I have learned in the last five years. I believe I can lead and persuade Admirals and that I have a better chance of success than he will get. If so it is not a question of this person or that—the situation is too grave, and in case Asquith consults you I want you to know what I think. It would be better, if W. does not wish to leave the Home Office, that McKenna should simply exchange with me. But the best would be, I am pretty sure, that W. should go to the War Office.'

After his talk with Haldane and Churchill, Asquith went to Balmoral and there discussed the problem of the Admiralty with the King and Lord Knollys. He then made up his mind that to send Haldane from the War Office to the Admiralty would look too much like a direct snub to the department and that it was important to have the First Lord in the Commons, and he wrote to Haldane:

'I have thought much of the things we discussed at our last talk and I went carefully over the ground at Balmoral with Knollys and the King. They entirely agree as to the need of a change at the Admiralty. The idea of your removal there was naturally very attractive to me, and, as you will readily believe, all my personal prepossessions were and are in its favour. The main, and in the long run, the deciding factor with me, in a different sense, has been the absolute necessity of keeping the First Lord in the Commons. We shall have to encounter there our own little navy men, the experts, such as they are, of the official opposition, and, as our own plans develop, the spokesman of the disgruntled Admirals and the old class of naval specialists. The position can, I am convinced, only be adequately held by a Minister who can speak with full authority, not merely as the head of a department, but as the person primarily responsible for the new policy.

'It is with great reluctance that I have been driven to this conclusion but I know that I can trust you to give not only co-operation but much needful inspiration and guidance to Churchill.'

Churchill assured Haldane that he realized fully the importance of organizing an effective naval war staff and was anxious to have his co-operation in this, and so towards the end of October he became First Lord. When he entered the Admiralty he found Sir Arthur Wilson to be resolutely opposed to the change, and he therefore, wisely, decided to wait until the First Sea Lord's turn of office came to an end early in January, and in the interval he and Haldane got to work. A few weeks later Haldane wrote to his mother: 'Winston and L.G. dined with me last night and we had a very useful talk. This is now a very harmonious Cabinet. It is odd to think that three years ago I had to fight those two for every penny for my army reforms. Winston is full of enthusiasm about the Admiralty and just as keen as I am on the War Staff. It is delightful to work with him. Ll. G. too has quite changed his attitude and is now very friendly to your bear, whom he used to call "the Minister for Slaughter".'

On January 1 Churchill wrote to Haldane: 'I send you herewith a draft memorandum on the War Staff which it is proposed to issue simultaneously with the publication of the appointments. You will see that it is in general terms and that details can be adjusted afterwards. The principles, however, are I think those with which you concur. Without departing from the traditional form and custom of the Admiralty, I have placed the Staff directly under the First Sea Lord, and the War Staff circle with its attendant dignitaries has volatilised into unpretentious Staff meetings and a general admonition to the Chief of the Staff to keep in touch with other Departments. I shall be very grateful for any emendations or excisions which you may care to suggest. But time is pressing, and if you are in general agreement I shall be glad if you will let me know at once. I want to publish on Monday next at the latest. All the parties concerned are red-hot to take up their appointments, and though the secret has been very well kept I expect something will leak out if delay is protracted.'

A week later the new scheme was announced. Churchill made a clean sweep of the Sea Lords. Sir F. Bridgeman became First Sea Lord and Rear-Admiral Troubridge the Chief of the new Naval Staff. Within six months Haldane had left the War Office, and with his successor, Colonel Seely, Churchill established a system of direct liaison. There was no longer any question of the Admiralty being able to meet the requirements of the Expeditionary Force. In this and in his preparation of the Navy for war Churchill did his country very great service, but the way in which the change had been brought about had the effect of making the naval plans appear to be an adjunct to the military plans and for this we were to suffer during the first years of the war.

The French soldiers, with their eyes fixed on the German frontier, had no understanding of the meaning of sea power. They were even disposed to regard their own navy as a means of diverting money which they could spend to better purpose on the army. Sir Henry Wilson, whose dominating personality made him very influential in our War Office at this time, was himself under the influence of Foch, and he believed that our security depended on our creating a conscript army on French lines. He considered the prime function of our Navy to be to help him to make our military assistance to France as prompt and as powerful as possible. In his diary he describes a visit to France early in 1913: 'My talk with Castlenau and Joffre was about Repington's recent articles in *The Times*, where he claims that our Navy is worth 500,000 bayonets to the French at the decisive point. I had written to Fred Oliver that our Navy was not worth 500 bayonets. Castlenau and Joffre did not value it as one bayonet! Except from the moral point. It was realised by these men what a serious statement this was, coming at this particular moment, and it was agreed that it should be thoroughly exposed in the French press. . . . Foch is of exactly the same opinion as regards A'Court's[1] egregious articles as are Castlenau and Joffre, and we talked till midnight.' The result of all this was that as far as the French military leaders were concerned, and they at first dominated the French Government, we went into the war with a military plan only, and they measured our contribution to the war in the number of soldiers we had in France, and so our influence on the strategy of the war was far less than it should have been. Haldane, with his strong views on the importance of the Committee of Imperial Defence, and his desire to see it made into a great general headquarters of the Empire in the event of war, would, if in office, at least have done his best to see that we presented to France not a military plan only but a co-ordinated naval and military plan, which would have made clear to the French soldiers and French Government the meaning of sea power and have made our voice in determining the strategy of the war effective, after the first German rush on Paris had been stayed.

In November 1911 Mr. Balfour resigned the leadership of the Conservative Party, which elected Mr. Bonar Law to be his successor. In a speech at the Albert Hall at the end of the following January the new leader made his declaration of war on the Government. Balfour had refused to oppose Haldane's Army reforms until the Conservative Party could produce something better, and had restrained the Conservative leaders in the Lords from supporting the attacks of the back-benchers. Bonar Law had no such feelings and in his indictment of the Government an attack upon Haldane took a prominent place. Sir Henry Wilson, who was a friend of the new leader of the Conservatives, had primed him in the hope of getting a pronouncement in favour of conscription, but Bonar Law was far too cautious to commit himself to that.

[1] Colonel A'Court Repington.

He said that Haldane claimed to have reduced the cost of the Army, but that in fact when loans were taken into account the cost was about the same as it had been under the last Conservative administration; that Haldane had reduced the Regulars by 20,000 and the auxiliary forces by 30,000 men, and most serious of all he told his audience that the weapons of our army were inferior to those of the armies of other nations and that this was a handicap which no courage could overcome.

Mr. Bonar Law's brief had been hastily prepared or he had not understood it. His financial criticisms were easily answered: the actual reduction in strength of the Regular and auxiliary forces between October 1, 1905, and October 1, 1911, was 27,000, not 50,000, and was more than accounted for by the conversion of 100,000 militiamen, available for home defence, into a Special Reserve of 63,000 available to maintain the Expeditionary Force, and in return the power of the Expeditionary Force had been more than doubled.[1] As to armaments the new rifle and the new field-gun had both been designed under the Conservative Government, and Haldane's part in armaments had been confined to providing a new howitzer. The gravamen of Bonar Law's grave statement on armaments lay in the fact that the Germans had introduced a new bullet which would give their rifle a flatter trajectory than ours. We were in process of following suit. The real answer to Bonar Law came in the war, when, as the Germans admitted, it was our rifle fire which saved us at Mons and at Ypres. It is necessary here to deal with these stale charges, for this attack by Bonar Law killed Haldane's constant efforts to remove army affairs from the sphere of party politics. While Balfour led the Opposition Haldane was at pains to keep him informed as to the major changes he proposed both in organization and in personnel, but with Bonar Law's advent this ceased and his attack was the signal for the

[1]Cf. Appendix II, p. 320.

beginning of that campaign which was eventually to drive Haldane from office. It was taken up with enthusiasm by Mr. Leo Maxse, a fanatical Tory inspired by hatred of Germany, and as editor of the *National Review* he now lost no opportunity of putting Haldane into his pillory.

The Agadir crisis had made relations with Germany, which in May had appeared to be taking a turn for the better, more strained than ever. In November Count Metternich, the German ambassador, had in an interview with Sir Edward Grey summed up the situation as being that it seemed to public opinion in Germany that England had been anxious to get up a quarrel between Germany and France, in which she would join, while on the other hand English people were convinced that Germany intended to make war on England. Attempts were made both at home and in Germany to improve matters. Mr. Lloyd George and Mr. Winston Churchill prepared a memorandum setting out the basis on which, in their opinion, an agreement with Germany might be reached. The terms proposed were acceptance of British superiority at sea, no increase in the German naval programme, no interference on our part with German colonial expansion, and an agreement that neither nation would take part in aggressive plans against the other.[1] This document was given to King Edward's old friend Sir E. Cassel to take to Berlin. Cassel got into touch with the Emperor's friend Herr Ballin and through him with the Emperor and the Chancellor. Cassel returned with a message that the British overtures had been cordially welcomed. The Emperor suggested with the concurrence of his Chancellor, Bethmann-Hollweg, that the Cabinet should send one or more of its members to Berlin for a full and frank discussion of the position. There was a broad hint that the Foreign Minister and the First Sea Lord would be very welcome.

It happened that just at the time when this message reached

[1] Cf. Bethmann-Hollweg, *Reflections on the World War*, p. 48.

England a great coal strike, which was to last for many weeks, had begun, and Sir Edward Grey had at the Prime Minister's request taken charge of the negotiations with owners and strikers. Further, both he and the Prime Minister were agreed that to send the Foreign Minister to Berlin would give the discussion an undesirable appearance of authority. Mr. Churchill had no wish to go. So Grey came to Haldane and said that he had made up his mind that he was the best person for this mission. Haldane demurred and said that if he, who had no official connection with foreign affairs, went, our ambassador in Berlin would certainly feel that there was interference with his functions. He offered, however, to go to Berlin with Grey. Grey pointed out the objections to him and said he would get the ambassador over to arrange matters, and Haldane thereupon agreed and at a Cabinet meeting next day he was formally requested to go to Berlin to carry out informal negotiations, but with full authority to express views and bring back proposals to the Cabinet. After the Cabinet meeting Sir Edward Grey, Mr. Churchill, Lord Haldane, and Sir E. Cassel met and together drafted the following telegram for Cassel to send to Berlin:

'Spirit in which statements of German Government have been made is most cordially appreciated here. New German programme would entail serious and immediate increase in British Naval expenditure, which was based on assumption that German naval programme would be adhered to. If British Government are compelled to make such increase it would make negotiations difficult if not impossible. If on the other hand, German naval expenditure can be adapted by an alteration of tempo or otherwise so as to render any serious increase unnecessary to meet German programme, British Government will be prepared at once to pursue negotiations on the understanding that the point of naval expenditure is open to discussion and that there is a fair prospect of settling it favourably. If this understanding is acceptable the British

Government will forthwith suggest the next step. They think that the visit of a British Minister to Berlin should in the first instance be private and informal.'

This being agreed Haldane prepared to start. He was still chairman of the Royal Commission on the University of London. His interest in higher education was as great as ever and he had just become the first chancellor of the new University of Bristol. He had intended to go to Germany to look into some recent developments in technical education in that country and this he used as a cloak to disguise his mission. It was announced that he was going to Berlin in connection with the work of the Royal Commission, and to give colour to this he took with him as his personal secretary his brother John, then Reader in Physiology at Oxford.

As Haldane had foreseen he did not start under very happy auspices. Unofficial missions of this kind were then rare and neither the German ambassador in England nor the British ambassador in Berlin nor the staff of our Foreign Office looked on them with much favour, while the German Emperor, though very friendly to Haldane, considered it odd that a matter which primarily concerned foreign affairs and the Navy should be entrusted to the Secretary of State for War. The crux of the matter was to induce Germany to relax her naval preparations and Haldane had slight hopes that he would succeed in this. On the eve of his departure he wrote to his mother: 'I start with Johnnie and Sir Ernest Cassel at 9 to-morrow morning. I am now quite prepared, but my mission is a very difficult one and I am far from sanguine of success. Sir E. Goschen, our Ambassador in Berlin, who had been telegraphed for, arrived yesterday and dined here, when Sir E. Grey and I discussed matters fully. He returns to-day to prepare matters for my visit. I met the King yesterday and I go to see him again at six to-night. Naturally he is deeply interested. I find myself the centre of many hopes and wishes, more than I feel that I am likely to be able to satisfy. But it is a memorable task and is well worth while putting all my strength into.'

Haldane has given an account of his mission in his autobiography (p. 238 *et seq.*) and in his *Before the War* (p. 56 *et seq.*), while his official report to the Cabinet, which will be found in Appendix I to this chapter, is published in *British Documents on the Origin of the War* (vol. VI, p. 676 *et seq.*). A more intimate account he wrote to his mother in the train on the way home from Berlin.

'For the last three days I could not write to you—partly for obvious reasons, and partly because every hour and every nerve have been devoted to an absorbing task. But now I will try to make up and post this in London. I have hope now that your prayers have been answered. This is a solemn time, and as memorable as it has been solemn. I have been continuously engaged in the closest and most intimate personal negotiations on a succession of questions going to the root of the cause of peace—not only between Germany and England but over the whole world—and the new atmosphere which has resulted is marvellous. It is too soon to know or be sure of the outcome. But the prospect for the moment is very good, and I seem to have been inspired by a new power. Never once have I lost my nerve or my head, or felt anything but cool and calm, and there has been room at times for a very different experience.

'On Thursday morning (the 8th) we arrived. I saw our Ambassador, who was very helpful in arranging meetings. He had asked the Imperial Chancellor to meet Johnnie and myself at luncheon. Afterwards at 2 he withdrew with the others and left the Chancellor and myself alone. We struck a high tone in a few minutes. I liked and admired the Chancellor and after a short period of reserve he opened his mind to me as I had begun by doing to him. It was not a case of two diplomatists fencing. It was two men trying to meet on common ground to accomplish the highest ideal that was possible to mortals. We spoke intimately for an hour—mainly in German. Unless German had been a second language and thirty years had been spent in learning to understand and admire German things, I could not have succeeded in my task. But the conversation ended wholly successfully. We parted and he went to the Emperor. Next day (Friday) I was summoned to luncheon at the Palace at 1 o'clock. There were the Emperor and Empress and their daughter, and the Chancellor and the Ministers of War and the Navy. I sat in the place of honour by the Emperor, and we all talked partly in German and sometimes in English. Luncheon was short and then the Emperor took me with Admiral Tirpitz, the Minister of the Admiralty, alone into a room. There was a little narrow table. The Emperor put me into his own chair at the head of it and lit a cigar for me, and sat down himself at one side, the Admiral being on the other, while the latter and I began a very difficult negotiation. Admiral T. is a strong and difficult man—a typical Prussian—and he and I fought stiffly. There was perfect politeness but neither of us would move from his position. After two hours of argument and counter-argument—mainly in German—under pressure from the Emperor I got a substantial concession. But I said that while I was glad of it I could not promise them that my Government would think it enough. I left about 5 p.m. for the Embassy where I dictated a secret document, being a précis of the conversation. This I did after each talk.[1] At night I dined with the Chancellor. Kiderlen Waechter—the Foreign Secretary on whom I had called earlier in the evening, and whom I did not trust one inch—was there, and Professor Harnach and some German Foreign Office high officials. After dinner the Chancellor took me aside. He was depressed and so was I. I could see that this great simple man was feeling his difficulties with his own people very great. The Emperor had been delightful to me. I am sure he wants peace most

[1]Included in his diary. Appendix I.

genuinely, but he has Germany to deal with. My only chance was to be very resolute. Next day I got a hint from the Chancellor, through one of his confidential officials, with whom I lunched, that I could best help the Chancellor by being absolutely unbending about naval matters. I went to the Chancellor at 5 o'clock and took this line. He said he would do his utmost. We defined the extent to which I could meet him, and go back to England with hope that the result would be acceptable. We then sat down at a table with paper and pencils all alone, and negotiated the heads of a possible great peace treaty on the very largest scale. This took two hours. We did it in German and in English, so as to avoid misunderstanding. We made it clear that I could only negotiate on the basis of absolute loyalty to English relations with France and Russia, and that our object was to bring them in and make peace and commercial development not only for ourselves but for the whole world. We had maps and dealt with Africa and Asia. I had got it all up, and 25 years of the Bar had equipped and put me on a footing to discuss the points without being embarrassed either by their complication or by the foreign language. He and I indeed helped each other. "Now Excellency," I would say, "I must put on German spectacles and criticise my own point of view from your outlook." And he would laugh. At the end of a splendid interview he rose and took me by the hand and held it and said the moment of his life that he had longed for seemed to have come. If we failed it would be Destiny. But we had, he knew, done all that two men could. We promised each other to spare no effort, I said I would start at once for London. Telegraphed to Asquith and Grey to meet me to-morrow. Besides all this I had to reassure the French Ambassador—I settled a telegram for him to send to the French Premier assuring him of our loyalty and desire to do good for France as well as ourselves. This conversation was in French—where I was not so well off, but I managed.

'I got back to the hotel at 8 last night having finished the day's work—and pretty well tired out. Johnnie has been splendidly helpful and sympathetic and the greatest comfort to me. We were besieged by reporters, whom I would not see and whom he kept off. So great was the excitement in Berlin that an interview with Johnnie, from which they thought we were not really negotiating, sent down the funds in the Bourse. This morning we left. A crowd had assembled to see us start, and cameras and cinematograph instruments recorded the scene. There was a crowd at the station, where we were treated like royalties. The Emperor gave me a little bronze statue for my writing table.

'I did not go to Berlin with power to make a treaty. These affairs are too vast for that. But I went to investigate and discuss whether one could be made. What may be possible with English public opinion in the view of the Cabinet remains to be seen. But my work up to this point has been attended with a measure of success that was neither foreseen nor expected. The second part of my task begins at home to-morrow. The strain has been heavy but I am not tired.

'It is a solemn call this, and come what may I shall feel that the effort has been to do God's work.'

The promise which Haldane's mission held out, and filled both him and his colleagues with hope, was his conviction that Bethmann-Hollweg was quite sincere in his desire for peace and was willing to retard the German naval programme in return for a general and comprehensive agreement with England. Haldane also came home with the opinion that the Emperor wanted friendship with England but there was the doubt that Tirpitz, by playing on his vanity, would burke the essential concessions in the German naval programme. This soon proved to be the case, for when the Admiralty got to work on the new law for the expansion of the German Navy, a copy of which the Emperor had given Haldane, it was discovered that this went much farther than our admirals had anticipated and it became clear that the one price at which substantial concessions could be obtained was a pledge of neutrality in the event of Germany being involved in war, in other words we were to abandon France. This was of course impossible. In the second week of March a glimmer of hope returned. Count Metternich came to see Haldane at Queen Anne's Gate and Haldane wrote hopefully to his mother that night: 'I believe our prayers have been answered, and that the good Chancellor has got the better of Tirpitz and his Admirals. It appears that after all my mission, which seemed to have been wrecked by a German torpedo, will have the results on which we had set our hopes.'

Haldane gave an account of his talk with the German Ambassador in a memorandum to the Cabinet: 'This evening I received a note from Count Metternich expressing a wish to see me immediately, as he had "something of importance and urgency to tell me". I saw him at the Embassy at 10.45. He informed me that he had a communication from the Chancellor in reply to his report that serious exception was taken here to the magnitude of the changes contemplated by the new Fleet Law, and especially to the large increase in personnel. What he had learned he wished in the first place to tell me quite privately and informally. He gathered from Berlin that if the British Government would offer a suitable political formula, the proposed Fleet Law as it stood would be withdrawn. Some Fleet Law there must be, but one of less magnitude would be introduced. I asked him whether he could tell me the extent of the reduction. He replied that he gathered it would be considerable, but that he was not in a position to define it. I gathered that he thought it extended to personnel. I asked whether he wished this communication to be treated as merely between him and me. He said no, he was officially instructed, but he had wanted to see me in the first place to say that time pressed, as a statement would have to be made almost at once to the Reichstag about the Fleet

Law, and the Chancellor wished to be provided with the offer of a formula from us as a reason for not proceeding with his original proposals. I asked whether the formula need go beyond the disclaimer of aggressive intentions and combinations. He indicated that he thought it need not. He added that he was instructed to say that, if, having offered the formula, we were dissatisfied with the naval reductions when they came out, we were to be regarded as quite free to withdraw it; in other words, it was to be conditional on our being satisfied in this respect. I said I would see Sir Edward Grey at once.'

On March 14 Haldane, Grey, and Count Metternich met and drew up the following formula:

'The two Powers being mutually desirous of securing peace and friendship between them, England declares that she will neither make nor join in any unprovoked attack upon Germany, and will pursue no aggressive policy towards her.

'Aggression upon Germany is not the subject and forms no part of any treaty understanding or combination to which England is now a party, nor will she become a party to anything that has such an object.'

This was approved by the Cabinet and went to Berlin. On April 10 the answer came back from Germany that the proposed formula was inadequate. Nothing short of a pledge of unconditional neutrality would do. The new naval law went to the Reichstag and Mr. Churchill immediately prepared his reply to it. So to Haldane's deep distress the hope of a friendly settlement with Germany disappeared.

A few weeks later he wrote to his mother: 'Early this morning Lord Loreburn sent round asking me to come and see him urgently. I went at 9.15 a.m. and he told me that he had just sent in his resignation of the Great Seal and wished me to make the communication to the King. He felt, poor man, too unwell to go himself. The doctors had advised him to resign as his heart was affected. If he did they thought he would recover. I saw the King at 10.45. "Who is to succeed" he asked. I replied that I did not know as the Prime Minister was away. "My choice, if the Prime Minister agrees" said the King, "would be a man who was quite capable of filling three offices, Ambassador at Berlin, War Secretary, and Lord Chancellor. I know one who could do them all easily." This he said with a loud laugh. Asquith returns next week. He has been advised by telegram of the situation.'

Asquith's answer was: 'Ask Haldane who is to succeed him at the War Office.' On getting the Prime Minister's formal nomination he wrote to Asquith:

'MY DEAR A.

'Bonham-Carter and Elibank have told me of your decision and Knollys of the King's approval.

'More than six years ago you fought a hard fight for your old friend over this great office and now you have yourself bestowed it on him. My feeling I will not try to express. You know how deep it is. My mind goes back to the past, to the days when we travelled together to the Law Courts from John Street, Hampstead, days which I am not likely to forget and are very present to me now. I cannot easily write more. I will come to you when you find it convenient to speak of the War Office. There are reasons connected with the Army which make me think that the advantages of taking Seely would much outweigh other considerations.'

Two days later he wrote to his mother: 'Kneeling in front of the King on a cushion yesterday I resigned to him the seals of the Secretary of State for War and received the Great Seal. I then took the oath in his presence, swearing in the Scottish fashion with uplifted hand. Immediately afterwards I went to the House of Lords with the Great Seal and assumed office, taking my seat on the Woolsack as Lord Chancellor and Speaker of the House of Lords. One of the first Peers to follow Lord Lansdowne and Lord Halsbury to congratulate me was Lord Eldon, who spoke of our relationship and of my great-great-uncle his great-great-grandfather. It seems strangely familiar to be in the Great Lord Eldon's place.'

The sequel Haldane tells himself in his autobiography: 'After dinner I slipped away and crossed into New Square to look at the staircase of No. 5, where my old garret had been. I went up the stairs and on reaching what was once my door heard barristers at work late, just as I more than thirty years before used to stay in Chambers to work late. I raised my hand to the knocker intending to ask to see my old room. But I felt shy and returned down the steep stair unobserved.

'It was thus that I returned to my old Mistress, the Law.'

Appendix I to Chapter XII

DIARY OF LORD HALDANE'S VISIT TO BERLIN

I

THURSDAY, FEBRUARY 8, 1912

I arrived in Berlin at 7.30 this morning, and was met at the Friedrichstrasse station by Sir Edward Goschen's motor and the embassy porter. I proceeded with my brother and servant to the Hotel Bristol, which is close to the embassy. I saw Sir Edward Goschen before 10 o'clock. He informed me that he had arranged with the Chancellor that the latter should lunch at the embassy, and that after luncheon I should have a private talk with him *à deux*. Before luncheon I saw Sir Edward, who had in the meantime seen the Chancellor. The Chancellor had asked the question whether I was to talk to him officially, the difficulty being that he, the Chancellor, could not divest himself of his official position, and it would be awkward to talk with me in a purely private capacity. I said I should tell the Chancellor that I had come here officially with the approval of the King and the Cabinet, but merely to talk over the ground, and not to commit either himself or my own Government to any propositions.

At the interview with the Chancellor, which took place at 2 o'clock, and lasted for more than an hour and a half, I began by giving him the message of good wishes for the conversations and for the future of Anglo-German relations with which the King had entrusted me at the audience I had before leaving. He was pleased with this message, and intimated that he would write through the German Ambassador to thank the King. I then said that perhaps it would be convenient if I defined the capacity in which I was in Berlin, and there to talk to him; and I defined it as above intimated. I proceeded to ask whether he wished to make any observations or desired that I should begin. He wished me to begin, and I went on at once to speak to him as arranged in a conversation I had had with Sir Edward Grey before leaving London.

I told him that I felt there had been a great deal of drifting away between Germany and England, and that it was important to ask what was the cause. To ascertain this, events of recent history had to be taken into account. Germany had built up, and was building up, magnificent armaments, and with the aid of the Triple Alliance she had become the centre of a tremendous group. The natural consequence was that other Powers had tended to approximate. I was not questioning for a moment Germany's policy, but this was the natural and inevitable consequence in the interests of security. We used to have much the same situation with France when she was very powerful on the sea that we had with Germany now. While the fact to which I had referred created a difficulty, the difficulty was not insuperable; for two groups of Powers might be on very friendly relations if there was only an increasing sense of mutual understanding and confidence. The present seemed to me to be a favourable moment for a new departure. The Morocco question was now out of the way, and we had no agreements with France or Russia except those that were in writing and published to the world.

The Chancellor interrupted me, and asked me whether this was really so. I replied that I could give him the assurance that it was so without reserve, and that in the situation which now existed I saw no reason why it should not be possible for us to enter into a new and cordial friendship carrying the two old ones into it perhaps to the profit of Russia and France as well as Germany herself. He replied that he had no reason to differ from this view.

In connection with my remarks as to the events of last summer, he interposed that we had military preparations. I replied that no preparations had been made which were other than those required to bring the capacity of the British army in point of mobilisation to something approaching the standard which Germany had long ago reached and which was with her a matter of routine. For this purpose we had studied our deficiencies and modes of operation. This, however, was a purely departmental matter concerning the War Office, and the Minister who did it was the one who was now talking to him and who was not wanting in friendly feeling towards Germany. We could not be caught unprepared, and in Germany they would say that my preparations ought to be matters of routine. They certainly were not evidence of hostility or of any design of attack.

The Chancellor seemed much pleased with this explanation, and said there had been much talk of our fleet and our army, and the steps we had taken, but that he understood the position I had indicated. I said, in reply, that it was a pleasure to me to hear this, and that I hoped I should carry him with me still further in my belief that if Germany had really, which I did not at all suppose, intended to crush France and destroy her capacity to defend herself, we in England would have had such a direct interest in the result that we could not have sat by and seen this done.

He said he did not dissent from this view, nor did he wish to hamper our freedom in such a case. But he wished to propose a formula; the balance of power was a phrase he did not like, though he admitted that the historical considerations I had referred to made it natural that some grouping should take place, and that England should lean towards the weaker side. He had, however, proposed, in his communication to us, a formula of neutrality which might go a long way to help.

I said I cordially agreed with the good intention of his formula, the wording of which was that neither was to enter into any combinations against the other. If this meant combinations for attack or aggression, I was entirely of his mind. But I must put on spectacles in looking at his words, and first of all I would put on German spectacles. How would Germany find herself if, when bound by such a formula, we were so wicked as to attack her ally Austria or to try to grab Denmark, which was of deep strategical interest to her? She would certainly have to combine against us and attack us. Again, suppose Germany joined in an attack on Japan or Portugal or Belgium—he then interposed. 'Or Holland'—but I said I really hadn't all our treaties sufficiently in my head to be as sure about Holland as I was about the others. Or if, I added, Germany were to pounce upon France and proceed to dismember her, what would happen? He answered that these cases were not at all likely, but he admitted that they were fatal to his formula. I asked him whether he would be satisfied with mutual undertakings against aggressive or unprovoked attacks and against all combinations, military and naval agreements, and plans directed to the purpose of aggression or unprovoked attack. He said it was very difficult to define what was meant by aggression or unprovoked attack. I replied that you could not define the number of grains which it took to make a heap, but one knew a heap when one saw one. I did not know what my colleagues would think of such a formula as I had suggested, but it struck me, as at present advised, as not only consistent with all our engagements with other Powers, but as of much more value if it was introductory to substantive clauses about other things. He said that he was inclined to take the same view, but he would like to consider the question. He saw how difficult it was for both countries to make an unrestrictive neutrality agreement which would be consistent with their treaty and moral obligations, but he thought there was something to be said for what I had suggested. The spirit, he said, was everything; and, if there was the real spirit, such words as these might express all that was necessary.

We then passed on to the question of the German fleet, as to which he asked me whether I would like to make any observations. I said I must. He and I had been talking with the most absolute candour and friendliness to each other, and I felt he would regard me as wanting in character were I not very frank with him about the new Navy Law. What was the use of entering into a solemn agreement for concord and against attack if Germany at the same moment was going to increase her battle fleet as a precaution against us, and we had consequently to increase our battle fleet as a precaution against her? This was vital from our point of view, because we were an island Power dependent for our food supplies on the power of protecting our commerce, and for this we needed the two-Power standard and a substantial preponderance in battle fleets. He said that it was absolutely essential to Germany to have a third squadron in full readiness for war. At present, owing to her system of recruiting, for three months in the year she had virtually, owing to the necessity for training recruits, no fleet ready at all. I said I did not contest this; she was quite entitled to have it if she thought it necessary, but the result would be that we should not be able to rely on the two battle squadrons and reserve squadrons which had sufficed hitherto, but that we should be compelled to have five or even six squadrons ready in home waters, perhaps bringing ships from the Mediterranean to strengthen them. He asked me was that necessary if we had a friendly agreement? I said it would be less convincing proof of friendliness if Germany prepared her third squadron, and we should have no option. Still, I said, this was not so serious as the proposal to add a third ship every second year to the German construction programme. This would put us in great difficulties so far as securing the good opinion of the public in England about the value of an agreement. We should certainly have to proceed at once to lay down two keels to each one of the new German additions, and that would cost money and cause feeling. It was true that each country could bear the additional cost without difficulty. They were rich and so were we. If it was for the purpose of the navy our people would not complain, in my opinion, of the addition of another shilling to the income tax, but it would be a great pity. He asked was that really likely to be our programme, the laying down of two additional keels for each German one. I said I had no doubt that that would be the result, and the Government would be turned out if they failed to accomplish it; and therefore some modification seemed to be of the utmost importance, if the agreement was to be a real success.

After a pause he said he would consider this and 'die Sache überlegen'. The conversation up to this point had been largely in German, I taking to English whenever there was a delicate topic, and the Chancellor occasionally speaking English, but nearly always German. In order to avoid misunderstanding we sometimes repeated sentences in the other language. I was impressed by his evident desire to meet us wherever he could, and I derived considerable hope from the manner and emphasis with which he said that he would reconsider the question of the ships. But I must add that he went on to say that the question of the new squadron was vital and that some new ships would be necessary in it. Could I suggest any way out, for they must keep to the plan of a new law? I observed that it was not for me to venture to make any suggestion to his Excellency, but that a spreading out in time of the new programme might make a difference. He said, 'Perhaps, eight or nine years', I added, 'Or twelve, if he could not do better.' He again said that he would take this matter into serious consideration and consult his experts. 'My admirals', he said, 'are very difficult.' 'That was an experience', I observed, 'which we sometimes found in England also.' He then said to me, 'Suppose we were to come to an agreement on the two topics already discussed, what would follow?' I replied that such an agreement would open up a vista of other topics. We were free traders and believed that the more trade Germany developed the more we should develop. He said 'Yes! we each give each other the open door.' I said I wished we could work in the world together a great deal more. He said, 'In Africa, for instance.' I said, 'In Africa particularly.'

He then went over various possibilities in Africa, on which I had been instructed pretty fully by Harcourt and by Grey. He seemed much pleased and I thought a little surprised at our openness to talk over territorial questions in Africa. He never mentioned Walfisch Bay, but when I said that the Island of Timor, to which I thought Germany had a right under the secret agreement, might land us in difficulties with Australia, he added, at once, that he would gladly meet us on that. I said that I could not commit my colleagues on this subject or on anything else further than this, that if we agreed on the two great topics, he would find us in an excellent mood for discussion. He said he would be in an excellent mood for discussion also.

On this I observed that there were one or two little things of which we should then wish to speak, and I mentioned the Bagdad Railway. He smiled and said that he thought he could meet our wishes about that. We discussed it a little, satisfactorily, and then I hinted that there might be commercial enterprises in our sphere of interest in Persia which would possibly be open to discussion as regards German participation, though this must for the present necessarily remain vague.

This brought a very long conversation to a conclusion. He asked me whether, if we could agree on the two first matters, I would like to return to London and take the sense of my colleagues before we talked about the other questions. I replied in the negative. I thought I knew enough of their ideas to be able to do all that we could do at this stage, which was to talk over the ground fairly fully. My instructions were not to bind or commit them, but I knew their intentions so intimately that, with this reservation, I had felt myself in a position to say as much as I had said. I had done my best to express myself to him with the most perfect frankness, keeping nothing back of what was passing in my mind. He said that he had appreciated that throughout our talk, and had liked the conversation all the better on that account; it had been very helpful to him. For two and a half years he had been striving to bring about an agreement between Germany and England. This had been the aim of his policy. He recognised that we desired to preserve to the fullest degree our existing relations with France and Russia; and Germany also had analogous obligations which we would not desire to interfere with. I had said that I could commit nobody in what I had said, and he on his part wished likewise to say that he could commit nobody. He would take counsel over our talk and communicate with me shortly again.

I have reason to think that he went immediately to see the Emperor. There is no saying what difficulties may not crop up. It is evident to me that, as regards others than the Emperor, the Chancellor has not an easy task before him, but I was impressed with what appeared to me to be his absolute sincerity and good-will, and I have confidence that so far as he is concerned he wishes to do his very best. I shall doubtless know much more for better or for worse shortly.

II

FRIDAY, FEBRUARY 9, 1912

I lunched at 1 o'clock with the Emperor at the Schloss. Besides the Empress and Princess Victoria Louise there were present the Chancellor and Admiral Tirpitz and one or two others. After luncheon the Emperor withdrew with me to his study along with Admiral Tirpitz. I found the relations excellent and the atmosphere genial. The Emperor tried, as I did myself, to bring his mind to the standpoint of the other country. After expressing the opinion that an agreement, if it could be come to, would improve things enormously for all of us and indeed for the whole world, and speaking of my conversation with the Chancellor the evening before in terms which showed that he was minutely informed of what had passed, the Emperor invited me to proceed to naval matters. He sat on one side of a table at the head of which I sat, and on the other side Admiral Tirpitz.

I began by saying that I was not a technical expert in naval things and that of course the navy was not my department, but that I understood it would be agreeable to the Emperor to explore the ground with me in this as in previous matters. I might from my want of knowledge use language that was inapt or inaccurate, as indeed might the Emperor himself. But neither of us would be bound, and I might be able to carry back ideas *ad referendum*. A long discussion then ensued, part of it in German, part of it in English, and part in a mixture of both. Admiral Tirpitz and indeed the Emperor himself, said that the original programme was to have a new Fleet Law with a new ship every year of the six; that they had cut it down to three ships in six years beginning in 1912, and it was very difficult to get out of this. Admiral Tirpitz said that he had to take care of the Emperor's position before the German public, and that the three new ships were, moreover, essential for the third squadron, which they desired to introduce for the purpose of having a fleet available all the year round. They could not get the men without the ships. A fundamental law gave them the complement of men only when and if the ships were laid down, and it was therefore necessary to lay down the ships, or at least to get them voted, in order to produce their squadron. I remarked that I did not doubt what Admiral Tirpitz told me, but I pointed out that if we were to enter into an agreement for settling differences and introducing a new spirit into our relations, that agreement would be bones without flesh if Germany began new ship-building immediately. Indeed, the world would laugh at the agreement, and our people would think that we had been befooled. I did not myself take that view, because I thought the mere fact of an agreement was valuable; but the Emperor would see that public opinion would attach very little importance to his action unless the agreement largely modified his ship-building programme.

We then discussed this programme at great length. Admiral Tirpitz struggled for it. I insisted that fundamental modification was essential. The tone was thoroughly friendly, but I felt that I had come to the most difficult part of my task of getting materials fit to bring back for the consideration of my colleagues. The utmost I was able to get to was this: the Emperor was so disturbed at the idea that the world would not believe in the reality of the agreement unless the ship-building programme was modified that he asked me what I would suggest. I said that it was a too technical matter for me to discuss here, but that if he could not drop the new law—which I saw he felt he could not—he might at least drop out a ship. This idea was never abandoned, but Admiral Tirpitz combated it so hard that I said, 'Well, can we not spread the *tempo*?' After much talking we got to this, that, as I insisted that they must not inaugurate the agreement by building an additional ship at once, they should put off building the first ship till 1913, and then should not lay down another till three years after (1916), and lay down the third till 1919. Admiral Tirpitz wanted us to give some undertaking about our own ship-building. He thought the two-Power standard a hard one for Germany, and, indeed, Germany could not make any admission about it. I said it was not a matter for admission. Germany must be free and we must be free, and we should probably lay down two keels to their one. In this case the initiative was not with us, but with them. The idea occurred to all of us on this observation that we should try to avoid defining a standard proportion in the agreement, and that, indeed, we should say nothing at all about ship-building in the agreement, but that if the political agreement was concluded the Emperor should at once announce to the German public that this entirely new fact modified his desire for the Fleet Law as originally conceived, and that it should be delayed and spread out to the extent we had discussed. For the rest, each of us would remain masters in our own houses as far as naval matters were concerned. The Emperor thought the agreement would affect profoundly the tendency in ship-building, and he certainly should not desire to go beyond the three ships. The fact of the agreement was the key to everything. The Chancellor, he said, would propose to me this afternoon a formula which he had drafted. I said that I would see the Chancellor and discuss any further territorial questions with him, and would then return as speedily as I could and report the good disposition which I had found to my colleagues, and leave the difficulties of not being able to stop ship-building more completely, and, indeed, all other matters, to their judgment. I could only assure the Emperor that I had been much struck with the friendly disposition in Berlin, and that he would find a not less friendly disposition in London.

III

FRIDAY, FEBRUARY 9, 1912 (LATER)

After my interview with the Emperor I dined with the Chancellor—Herr von Kiderlen-Waechter was there, but I had no private conversation with him. Indeed, such conversation was unnecessary, for I had thought it prudent to call on him earlier in the evening at his house in the Foreign Office. I had had a quite friendly but not very long talk with him and had touched on politics, but only in general terms, for I had and have the strong impression that the Chancellor did not want him to have a part in the conversation. However, we made friends. At the dinner at the Chancellor's, Baron Stumm, Professor Harnach, Herr Zimmermann, of the Foreign Office, and others were present. After dinner the Chancellor took me into a room with him alone. I saw that he was disturbed by a remark I made as to the difficulty I was sure my colleagues would feel about the smallness of the slackening in German ship-building in the proposals Tirpitz had made to me that afternoon at the Emperor's. I had remarked to the Emperor that I would rather make no observation on them, beyond that I must take them *ad referendum* to the British Cabinet. The Chancellor said that if we could not meet them in their necessity for a new Fleet Law, the idea of agreement must go to pieces (*scheitern*) and that things would grow worse. He had done and was doing his best—what the result of failure would be was matter of destiny (*Schicksal*). I observed that we were now speaking as man to man, that I was as anxious for an agreement as he was, and my colleagues were anxious too. But how would our agreement look if it were followed by more ship-building? And that this was to be so arose from, I did not for a moment say the fault, but the initiative of Germany. He looked depressed.

I then left, for I had to meet M. J. Cambon at 10 o'clock at the British Embassy. With him I had a talk alone. I found him a little nervous, so, without telling him details, I said emphatically that we were not going to be disloyal to France or Russia, that the Chancellor agreed that it would be dishonourable in us if we even talked of departing from the existing agreements, and that we believed a better state of public opinion between England and Germany would benefit France. With that he said he agreed. He suggested that my conversation had no other end than to create a *détente*, as distinguished from an *entente*. I said this was so as regards my conversation. I had not come there to draw up an agreement, or to do more than *tâter le terrain*. But I hoped that more than a *détente* would follow later on—if my very limited mission succeeded. He said he wanted to telegraph the gist of our talk in cypher to M. Poincaré. I said I had no objection, especially if, as he kindly said he would, he would let me see his telegram before it went. This he willingly agreed to, and I saw it the next day and modified it, so that it went in the words of the copy which I have brought with me. As the conversation was in French, this was a useful precaution. Sir E. Goschen also saw him, and I am pretty sure, from a remark of the Chancellor's next day, that he knew that M. Cambon had seen me.

On the Saturday I lunched with Baron von Stumm, of the Foreign Office, who was formerly at the German Embassy in London as Secretary. After luncheon he took me aside and said he had something to tell me. It was that the Chancellor was unhappy over what he had gathered from his talk with me last night; was my impression that my colleagues would consider Tirpitz's concession too small to be accepted by English public opinion? The Chancellor, said Baron Stumm, was not going to let this agreement—which was the dream of his life—founder because of Tirpitz, and it would help him, Stumm thought, if I took a very strong line to the effect that there must be further naval concessions. I took the hint, and when I went, as I had previously arranged with the Chancellor to do, to his house at 5 o'clock, I began by saying that continued reflection had made me even more unhappy than I was after leaving the Emperor's Palace on the previous day. English public opinion would not improbably be unmanageable and, I thought, with reason. He said he saw my point. He would do his best. But the forces he had to contend with were almost insuperable. Public opinion in Germany expected a new law and the third squadron, and he must have these. I said we could not contest Germany's right to do in these matters and indeed in other matters as she pleased. But why not postpone the ship-building for longer and adapt the law accordingly? It was a serious situation. No doubt Germany wanted the third squadron for her recruits, and it was mainly a question of organisation. But it would make her stronger at sea. If an agreement were come to, and it was a success, it would matter much less whether Germany built a few ships more or less. For instance, we did not look closely at how France built. But keep the two-power standard we must, and our people would resent the increasing burden Germany proposed to put on us. It might be fatal to the much-desired *Verständigung*. The Chancellor said he would try. He asked me to consult the experts in London and make a suggestion. I had said, he remarked, that everything was good only on balance, and Germany must for a greater end give up a minor advantage. The new squadron and the new Fleet Law she must have, but it was a question for the experts, on which he did not pronounce, whether a retardation of greater magnitude than Tirpitz proposed might not be possible. I promised to let him know privately the state of feeling here about the Tirpitz proposals on my return.

We then sat down at a table with pencils and paper and went on a voyage of discovery about other matters which are indicated in the notes which I have brought back (printed as appendices). I can only say that the attitude of the Chancellor was that of a high-minded sincere gentleman, and left me nothing whatever to desire. When we parted he held me by the hand and said that whether success or failure crowned the effort which was the greatest object of his life now, he should never forget that I had met him with an openness and sympathy for his difficulties which made the recollection of these days for him a delightful one. I reciprocated his sentiments not less warmly, and said I should now be able to leave next Sunday and lay my impressions before my colleagues.

(*a*) SKETCH OF A CONCEIVABLE FORMULA

1. The high contracting Powers assure each other mutually of their desire for peace and friendship.

2. They will not, either of them, make any unprovoked attack upon the other or join in any combination or design against the other for purposes of aggression, or become party to any plan or naval or military combination alone or in conjunction with any other Power directed to such an end.

3. If either of the high contracting parties become entangled in a war in which it cannot be said to be the aggressor the other will at least observe towards the Power so entangled a benevolent neutrality, and use its utmost endeavour for the localisation of the conflict.

4. The duty of neutrality which arises from the preceding article has no application in so far as it may not be reconcilable with existing agreements which the high contracting parties have already made. The making of new agreements which render it impossible for either of the high contracting parties to observe neutrality towards the others beyond what is provided by the preceding limitation is excluded in conformity with the provisions contained in article 2.

5. The high contracting parties declare that they will do all in their power to prevent differences and misunderstanding between either of them and other Powers.

(b) FURTHER PROPOSALS GIVEN ME IN WRITING BY THE CHANCELLOR

1. England to make no objection to the completion of the Bagdad Railway (e.g., England will not object to the raising of the Turkish customs dues).

2. Thereupon Germany, so far as concerns the Bagdad-Bussorah section, will meet the English wish to have an exceptional position.

3. In the event of England making railways in her zone in Persia she will be willing that Germany should have a participation.

4. Thereupon Germany will agree with England that she will fully recognise the political interests of England in the Persian Gulf and in South Persia. For instance, that England should obtain from Turkey an extensive concession for the Bussorah-Koweit section. Germany gives up claim to that section and will diplomatically assist England to obtain it.

5. Further, Germany will assist England to obtain from Turkey a concession for a harbour in Koweit—a concession similar to that which a German company has at Haidar Pasha.

6. The two contracting parties undertake for the future to exchange views about all questions which may arise, and to endeavour to bring a solution suitable to the reciprocal interests of both parties.

7. Each of the two Powers will make use of its own good and friendly relations to third Powers in order to influence the relations of the other Powers in a friendly sense.

8. Agreement, say, for ten years, with automatic prolongation.

(c) MEMORANDUM

After discussing formulae, we passed to territorial questions. Each of us had a map. The sum and substance of the discussion amounted to this:

Germany would like to have Zanzibar and Pemba. In exchange, she would give us what the Chancellor defined as 'eine sonderbare Stelle' (a special position) in the Bagdad-Bussorah section of the Bagdad Railway.

I replied: 'Nicht nur eine sonderbare Stelle, aber eine kontrollirende Stelle.'

He answered: 'Ich werde Ihren Wunschen entgegen kommen.' He did not wish that this should be done by bringing other Powers into the controlling share. He said that he would arrange that we should have what we desired in a form which he would work out with us.

The other proposals in connection with the Bagdad Railway and Southern Persia appear in the memorandum which he handed to me.

He was anxious to have the piece of Angola reserved for Britain by the secret agreement.

I said that we would like to have the island of Timor.

He agreed to this at once.

I told him that if Germany ever obtained a belt across the Lower Congo—as to which she would have to make a friendly bargain with France as well as with Belgium—we would ask her to let us have the Katanga triangle.

He agreed; but said that he would like very much to have Seal and Penguin Islands, off Angua Pequeña.

I observed that I feared these islands might prove to belong to the South African Union, in which case it would be difficult to exchange them; but I would look into this point.

He replied that he would make no difficulties for us if we could not help him, and I would notice that he had not even mentioned Walfisch Bay, because he knew how difficult our position was with the South African Union.

We went over the map of Africa, but I cannot recall that any further question was raised.

He was thoroughly desirous of meeting our wishes, and said to me: 'I am not here to make a bargain with you. We must look at this thing on both sides from a high point of view, and if you have any difficulties, tell me, and I will see whether I can get round them for you.'

(d) FIRST SUGGESTIONS OF CHANCELLOR— ABANDONED IN FURTHER CONVERSATION ABOUT FORMULAE

1. The high contracting Powers assure each other mutually of their desire for peace and friendship.

2. They will not either of them make any combination, or join in any combination, which is directed against the other. They declare expressly that they are not bound by any such combination.

3. If either of the high contracting parties becomes entangled in a war with one or more other Powers, the other of the high contracting parties will at least observe towards the Power so entangled a benevolent neutrality, and use its utmost endeavour for the localisation of the conflict.

4. The duty of neutrality which arises from the preceding article has no application, in so far as it may not be reconcilable with existing agreements which the high contracting parties have already made. The making of new agreements which make it impossible for either of the contracting parties to observe neutrality towards the other beyond what is provided by the preceding limitations, is excluded in conformity with the provisions contained in article 2.

5. The high contracting parties declare that they will, in the case of either of them having differences with third Powers, mutually give their diplomatic support for the purposes of settling their differences.

Appendix II to Chapter XII

COMPARATIVE STRENGTH OF THE BRITISH ARMY, OCTOBER 1, 1905, BEFORE LORD HALDANE TOOK OFFICE, AND SIX YEARS LATER

ALL RANKS

Strength on October 1, 1905

Regular Forces (vide page 40, General Annual Return), exclusive of Indian Troops on loan and Colonial Troops – – – – – –	263,132
Army Reserve (exclusive of Royal Malta Artillery)	94,342
Total – –	357,474

Militia (United Kingdom) – –	92,672	
„ „ (Reserve Division)	7,657	
	100,329	
Imperial Yeomanry – – – –	25,159	
Volunteers (Great Britain) – – –	252,889	
	278,048	

Total Auxiliary Forces, including Permanent Staff	378,377
General Total – –	735,851

APPENDIX II

Strength on October 1, 1911

Regular Forces (vide page 26, General Annual Report), exclusive of Indian Troops on loan and Colonial Troops - - - - - - 247,973

Army Reserve (exclusive of Royal Malta Artillery) 138,386

$$\text{Total} \quad - \quad - \quad 386,359$$

Special Reserve (all categories), old Militia and Militia Reserve Division 62,801

Territorial Force and Territorial Force Reserve, including Permanent Staff - 268,166

330,967

$$\text{General Total} \quad - \quad - \quad 717,326$$

In October 1905 the 280,000 yeomanry and volunteers had no higher organization, no field-artillery, no field engineers, no transport, and no medical service.

In October 1911 the 268,000 men of the Territorial Force were organized in divisions with establishments in all respects similar to those of the Regular Army.

In October 1905 the 100,000 militiamen were not available for service overseas.

In October 1911 the 63,000 Special Reserve men were available to maintain the Expeditionary Force.

In October 1905 we could mobilize promptly three regular divisions and a cavalry division of three brigades.

In October 1911 we could mobilize promptly six regular divisions to be followed in six weeks by a seventh division and cavalry division of five brigades.

Army Estimates 1905-6, £29,813,000
Army Estimates 1911-12, £27,690,000

Chapter XIII

THE LORD CHANCELLOR VISITS CANADA

1912 to 1913

The months which followed Haldane's appointment to the Woolsack were the one brief period in his life in which he could be said to be popular. The Press almost without exception sang praises of his work at the War Office. The Equity Bar was delighted at his promotion, as were his philosophical friends, while the soldiers were full of regrets at his departure. He attached less value to popular applause than most men, but being human he enjoyed it when it came. His personal friends, Lincoln's Inn, and the generals gave dinners in his honour, the latter an unusual compliment to a retiring Secretary of State for War. Sir John French, who was prevented by an attack of neuritis from coming to the dinner, wrote: 'It had been my intention to express the deep regret felt by the Army at your departure and our gratitude for the splendid work you have done for us. It is the history of all great and far-reaching reforms that their real bearing and their value is rarely appreciated until years after their accomplishment, but I am sure that we can say with perfect truth that the work that you have done in the last five and a half years has placed our military forces in a position far in advance of anything which has ever existed in this country in the way of preparation for war. Personally I feel your loss very deeply and I shall never cease to be grateful for the many lessons you have taught me.' Haig, now in command at Aldershot, wrote: 'I knew we could not expect to keep you forever as Secretary of State, but somehow I had hoped that

322

the evil day would not have come so soon. I expect that you are inundated with letters from officers regretting your leaving us, but I fancy few realise as clearly as I do what the Army owes you. Our German friends say "Every beginning is difficult", but few men could have overcome the awful difficulties which confronted you inside the War Office, when you began your scheme of reform. Everything was done by those who ought to have known better to prevent any progress from being made, how you triumphed and gradually carried everyone with you was truly wonderful. I shall always feel proud that I was one of your humble supporters and was able to look on quietly and admire the genius you displayed in handling the objectors. Your organisation will certainly last and will ever remain a splendid monument to your sagacity and grit.'

The reader may find some difficulty in squaring this account by Haig of difficulties within the War Office with Haldane's own appreciation of the enthusiastic band of reformers and helpers whom he found there. The fact is that a good many of those difficulties were of Haig's creation. He was referring particularly to the formulation of Haldane's system of organization for war in the Field Service Regulations. Haig had charge of the drafting of these, which concerned in great measure the functions of the departments of the Adjutant-General and the Quartermaster-General. These high military functionaries were not disposed to take too kindly to dictation from the General Staff. Haig knew what was wanted and was desperately keen to get a system which would work in war adopted. Being incapable of expressing himself in argument he was apt to be short and even rude with objectors. So a good deal of Haldane's time was taken up with calming the storms which his zealous co-operation raised. These clouds of the past disappeared in the blaze of glory which marked his departure from office.

In July Haldane went to Bristol to pay his first visit to the new university as its chancellor, and there he received a great ovation. His address was concerned with the future of the civic university and a passage in it foreshadows his later union with the Labour Party:

'Elementary education is now the right of all, and since the passing of the Education Act of 1902, an Act the immense advantages of which have always appeared to me to outweigh certain awkward blemishes which have still to be got rid of, the clever boy or girl can generally, by means of a scholarship or a free place, get to the secondary school. But the chances for the poor scholar to get from the secondary school to the University, although they exist, are still far too few. The Labour leaders are quite right when they complain that the prizes of the State are in reality far too much reserved for the upper classes. Where they are wrong, I think, is in the remedy they propose. The State will suffer badly if the level of its civil servants is lowered, and it will be lowered if the qualifications for all positions are lowered to the educational equipment possessed by the youth who has ceased his studies at eighteen. The true remedy is to break down the class barrier by making provision for the youth of eighteen to go on, if he is fit to do so, and to qualify himself more highly. Now here is where the Civic University has a great part to play. It is idle to say, as it is sometimes said, that Oxford and Cambridge include the democracy. Theoretically they do, but not one child of the people out of a thousand has a real chance of becoming an undergraduate there.[1] More accessible Universities are required, and these new Universities, I am careful to add, will only successfully compete with Oxford and Cambridge in serving the requirements of the State if they keep their level very high. A University to be a true University must be a place where the spirit is more important than the letter. In the elementary schools, and to a great extent even in the secondary schools, the teacher is in a position of authority.

[1]In this respect the position at Oxford and Cambridge has changed materially since 1913.

What he says is accepted by the pupil without inquiry. But in a true University where the problems are higher and more difficult, the professor as well as his student is making his voyage of discovery. Both must avoid dogmatic slumber or even supineness. They must in all reality investigate—and be content to investigate. This inevitable feature of the higher work, even where it is primarily educational, has always been recognised by those whose names we reverence most. Lessing meant it when he declared almost passionately that if the Almighty were to offer him the truth in one hand and the search after the truth in the other, he would choose the hand that held the search after truth.'

Relief from the day to day work of a Government department in which inquisitive members of Parliament took more than usual interest and from the tax upon his time of visits to Territorial Army functions left Haldane some leisure for his early love, education. One of his first acts as Speaker of the House of Lords was to steer through the Upper House a Bill for the establishment of the School of Oriental Studies as a school of the University of London. He was still chairman of the Royal Commission on that university, which was drawing to a close, and he gave much attention to the drafting of its report. As chairman of the Privy Council he at once set about implementing his plans for making it a more effective Supreme Court of the Empire, and as it happened one of the first appeals at which he presided was an important Canadian case which lasted several days, and he surprised both his colleagues and the Canadian lawyers by withdrawing to an adjoining room immediately the hearing was over and writing out the judgement in an hour and a half. The report of this achievement which the Canadian lawyers took home with them had an early repercussion. He also set to work to expedite the business of the Supreme Court of Appeal and within twelve months he had succeeded in reducing the delay in time in the hearing of cases by nearly one half, which gave special satisfaction in the dominions. He succeeded in this because by pertinacity and tact he got through an act increasing by two the number of Law Lords. Having in mind, very probably, the experience of his maternal grandfather, who had been driven from the Church of England by the jobbery and nepotism prevailing in early Victorian days in the Lord Chancellor's department over the distribution of Church patronage, he took particular pains to get the best possible advice on the appointments to livings which were within his gift.

When Parliament rose for the summer recess he received an invitation from the Army Council to attend the autumn manœuvres in Cambridgeshire as their guest, and he was particularly delighted when on driving through a brigade resting at the side of the road the men rose and cheered him. 'The army of the day', he wrote proudly to his mother, 'receives me as its father.' As soon as the manœuvres were over he went north to receive the freedom of Dunbar, staying at his old electioneering home Monkrigg, and his old constituents vied with the soldiers in the warmth of their welcome.

When Parliament reassembled in the autumn this pleasant interlude of compliments and congenial work came to an end. The Liberal Party, having secured the Parliament Act, was determined to make the most of the opportunity, and the Home Rule Bill, the Welsh Disestablishment Bill, and the Trades Union Bill were quickly introduced and roused party feeling to white heat. Ministers were shouted down in the Commons and if proceedings in the Lords were more decorous the Chancellor became the natural target of Opposition attack. Lord Roberts revived his campaign for national service and the old charges that the Territorial Army was not fitted either by training or equipment to protect the country against invasion were repeated. Rumours got about that Haldane during his visit to Berlin had proposed to give away parts of the Empire for a very inadequate return, and questions about the visit were asked in the House. The Foreign Office could not, in the national interest, allow a discussion on so delicate a topic, with the result that the guarded answers of the Foreign Secretary were taken to be attempts to cover up the indiscretions of a colleague and Mr. Leo Maxse in the *National Review* began to roll the 'r' in treason, while rumours that Mr. Lloyd George and Sir Rufus Isaacs were concerned in undesirable transactions arising out of Government contracts with the Marconi Company increased the acrimony of party strife.

Haldane had watched sadly the failure of his mission to Berlin to bring an agreement with Germany any nearer. In May Count Metternich had been dismissed from the London Embassy, and this Haldane regarded as a victory for Tirpitz, but he was still convinced that Bethmann-Hollweg desired peace and a rapprochement with England and he took an early opportunity to make himself known to Metternich's successor Prince Lichnowsky. Throughout 1912 the naval competition between the two countries became more and more acute. Germany was going full steam ahead with her new naval law and our Admiralty was, under the direction of Mr. Churchill, replying vigorously. In the summer the Admiralty had decided to withdraw our battleships to home waters from the Mediterranean to meet the growth of the German high seas fleet, and the French at the same time arranged for the concentration of their naval power in the Mediterranean. This left us with a moral obligation to protect the northern coast of France against naval attack by Germany. The international situation was the more strained by the outbreak of the Balkan War in the autumn of 1912 and the unexpected defeat of Germany's protégé, Turkey. In this atmosphere of strain the Kaiser's brother Prince Henry of Prussia came to England and was received by King George V at Sandringham. On December 5 the King told Prince Henry, in answer to an explicit question, that if Germany and Austria went to war with France and Russia circumstances might arise in which we should be bound to come to the help of France.[1] On the same day after consulting Grey Haldane made a precisely similar statement to Lichnowsky, adding that it was out of the question for us to consider a pledge of international neutrality and that an understanding which would recognize Britain's dependence on sea power and put a stop to naval competition was an essential preliminary to an Anglo-German accord.

Early in 1913 there was a brief flicker of hope when Germany re-opened negotiations for the settlement of outstanding colonial questions, and there were hints that an agreement on the new construction of battleships might be reached. Mr. Churchill replied to this in March 1913 with a proposal that both England and Germany should suspend construction for twelve months and take what he called 'a naval holiday'. This produced no response from Germany, and Haldane, whose whole system of military organization was derived from the premises that home defence was primarily a naval question and that if we had an adequate navy the risk of invasion was negligible, supported Churchill consistently in the Cabinet, in opposition to Mr. Lloyd George, who was again on the side of economy. The effect of unrestricted competition in naval armaments between ourselves and the power with the largest and most efficient army in Europe naturally increased both anxiety and anti-German feeling in England and this began to have reactions upon Haldane's position in the country. Mr. Leo Maxse and his followers assumed that Haldane, as the avowed disciple of Hegel and Lötze, was therefore the friend of the Germany of Tirpitz and Bernhardi.

In March 1913 came the state opening of a new session and Haldane's first reading of the King's speech from the Woolsack. The speech was brief but the debates on the address showed that the heat of party feeling was increasing. As the crisis over Ireland drew nearer Haldane had the unpleasant

[1]Trevelyan, *Grey of Fallodon*, p. 230.

task of continually presenting to or defending before a resolutely hostile majority Bills which could only become law by application of the Parliament Act. Lord Roberts campaigned with increasing energy both in the country and in the Upper Chamber and now that Mr. Bonar Law had declared war on Haldane's Army reforms the front Opposition bench reinforced the back-benchers, which they had never done in Balfour's time. So by a strange process, which had no reason behind it, Haldane was signalled out as the whipping-boy of the Liberal Party.

It was probably because of this that Asquith at the end of April asked the King that a vacant knighthood in the Order of the Thistle should be conferred on Haldane and obtained His Majesty's very cordial consent. Haldane replied characteristically: 'My dear A., your letter though full of kindness came to me as a great surprise and caused me some discomfort. I have never loved my peerage, which I took as a duty, and have been delivered by Providence from all aspirations to wear the garments of the senior peers. But this proposal comes not from John Morley or from Rosebery but from you, who have known me intimately for 30 years, and I interpret it as proof of a new token of your affection and a further demonstration of your confidence. Therefore I cannot say no, but I must in honesty add that I think there are others who would have worn the star and collar with more grace.'

The Marconi affair dragged on through the session and added to the embarrassments of the Government. In June Asquith called Haldane into consultation and he interviewed Mr. Lloyd George and Sir Rufus Isaacs with the Prime Minister. Of this he wrote to his mother: '. . . an unpleasant and to me very distasteful business. I hate saying "thank God I am not as other men are" but I am heartily thankful that I have never had any temptation to try and make money by investments. It is apt to be a slippery business. I don't think that in this case there has been more than indiscretion, but the public incited by an opposition out for party gains always believes the worst, and even a small indiscretion may do much harm. Asquith as usual is very calm and judicial but it adds to the difficulties of which he has enough on his hands.'

Early in the year he had received a pressing invitation from the Bar Association of the United States to come as the guest of honour to a meeting which it had arranged with the Bar Association of Canada at Montreal. This first meeting of the American Bar Association in another country was designed to mark the common basis of American and English Law. The invitation to Haldane came from Mr. Kellog, the President of the American Bar Association and was supported by Mr. Taft, Mr. Root, and Mr. Choate, while the Prime Minister of Canada and the leading Canadian lawyers urged its acceptance.

Haldane consulted both the Prime Minister and the King, and both agreed that he should go and that the Great Seal should be put in commission during his absence, which was to be as brief as possible. The King, to mark the importance of the occasion, gave his Chancellor a special message to the conference, signed with his own hand. Armed with this Haldane left England with his sister in the third week of August for what was literally a week-end visit to Montreal. He had a great reception at New York and as an ex-Secretary of State for War was taken to West Point to review the cadets. Thence he went on to Montreal for the great meeting over which the Chief Justice of the Supreme Court of the United States presided. He had, naturally, taken great pains with his address, to which he gave the title 'The Higher Nationality'. It contained two particularly noteworthy passages. In the first of these he dealt with the reinforcement of the authority and power of the law by the development of ethical habit within a community:

'Besides the rules and sanctions which belong to law and legality, there are other rules, with a different kind of sanction, which also influence conduct. I have spoken of conscience, and conscience in the strict sense of the word, has its own court. But the tribunal of conscience is a private one, and its jurisdiction is limited to the individual whose conscience it is. The moral rules enjoined by the private conscience may be the very highest of all. But they are enforced only by an inward and private tribunal. Their sanction is subjective and not binding in the same way on all men. The very loftiness of the motive that makes a man love his neighbour more than himself, or sell all his goods in order that he may obey a great and inward call, renders that motive in the highest cases incapable of being made a rule of universal application in any positive form. And so it was that the foundation on which one of the greatest of modern moralists, Immanuel Kant, sought to base his ethical system, had to be revised by his successors. For it was found to reduce itself to little more than a negative and therefore barren obligation to act at all times from maxims fit for law, universal maxims, which because merely negative, turned out to be inadequate as guides through the field of daily conduct. In point of fact that field is covered, in the case of the citizen, only to a small extent by law and legality on the one hand, and by the dictates of the individual conscience on the other. There is a more extensive system of guidance which regulates conduct and which differs from both in its character and sanction. It applies, like law, to all the members of a society alike, without distinction of persons. It resembles the morality of conscience in that it is enforced by no legal compulsion. In the English language we have no name for it, which is unfortunate, for the lack of a distinctive name has occasioned confusion both of thought and of expression. German writers have, however, marked out the system to which I refer and have given it the name of "Sittlichkeit". In his book, *Der Zweck im Recht*, Rudoph von Jhering, a famous professor at Göttingen, with whose figure I was familiar when I was a student there nearly forty years ago, pointed out, in the part which he devoted to the subject of "Sittlichkeit", that it was the merit of the German language to have been the only one to find a really distinctive and scientific expression for it. "Sittlichkeit" is the system of habitual or customary conduct, ethical rather than legal, which embraces all those obligations of the citizen which it is "bad form" or "not the thing" to disregard. Indeed regard for these obligations is frequently enjoined merely by the social penalty of being "cut" or looked on askance. And yet the system is so generally accepted and is held in so high regard, that no one can venture to disregard it without in some way suffering at the hands of his neighbours for so doing. If a man maltreats his wife or children, or habitually jostles his fellow-citizens in the street, or does things flagrantly selfish or in bad taste, he is pretty sure to find himself in a minority and the worse off in the end. Not only does it not pay to do these things, but the decent man does not wish to do them. A feeling analogous to what arises from the dictates of his more private and individual conscience restrains him. He finds himself so restrained in the ordinary affairs of daily life. But he is guided in his conduct by no mere inward feeling, as in the case of conscience. Conscience, and for that matter, law overlap parts of the sphere of social obligation of which I am speaking. A rule of conduct may, indeed, appear in more than one sphere, and may consequently have a two-fold sanction. But the guide to which the citizen mostly looks is just the standard recognised by a community made up mainly of those fellow-citizens whose good opinion he respects and desires to have. He has everywhere around him an object-lesson in the conduct of decent people towards each other and towards the community to which they belong. Without such conduct and the restraints which it imposes there would be no tolerable social life, and real freedom from interference would not be enjoyed. It is the instinctive sense of what to do and what not to do in daily life and behaviour that is the source of liberty and ease. And it is this instinctive sense of obligation that is the chief foundation of society. Its reality takes objective shape and displays itself in family life and in our other civic and social institutions. It is not limited to any one form, and it is capable of manifesting itself in new forms and of developing and changing old forms. Indeed the civic community is more than a political fabric. It includes all the social institutions in and by which the individual life is influenced—such as are the family, the school, the Church, the legislature, and the executive. None of these can exist in isolation from the rest; together they and other institutions of the kind form a single organic whole, the whole which is known as the Nation. The spirit and habit of Life which this organic entirety inspires and compels are what, for my present purpose, I mean by "Sittlichkeit". "Sitte" is the German for custom, and "Sittlichkeit" implies custom and a habit of mind and action. It also implies a little more. Fichte defines it in words which are worth quoting, and which I will put into English: "What to begin with", he says, "does 'Sitte' signify, and in what sense do we use the word? It means for us, and means in every accurate reference we make to it, those principles of conduct which regulate people in their relations to each other, and which have become matter of habit and second nature at the stage of culture reached, and of which therefore we are not explicitly conscious. Principles, we call them, because we do not refer to the sort of conduct which is casual or is determined on casual grounds, but to the hidden and uniform ground of action which we assume to be present in the man whose action is not deflected and from which we can pretty certainly predict what he will do. Principles, we say, which have become a second nature and of which we are not explicitly conscious. We thus exclude all impulses and motives based on free individual choice, the inward aspect of 'Sittlichkeit', that is to say morality, and also the outward side, or law, alike. For what a man has first to reflect over and then freely to resolve is not for him a habit in conduct; and in so far as habit in conduct is associated with a particular age, it is regarded as the unconscious instrument of the Time Spirit."

'The system of ethical habit in a community is of a dominating character, for the decision and influence of the whole community is embodied in that social habit. Because such conduct is systematic and covers the whole of the field of society the individual will is closely related by it to the will and spirit of the community. And out of this relation arises the power of adequately controlling the conduct of the individual. If this power fails or becomes weak the community degenerates and may fall to pieces. Different nations excel in their "Sittlichkeit" in different fashions. The spirit of the community and its ideals may vary greatly. There may be a low level of "Sittlichkeit"; and we have the spectacle of nations which have even degenerated in this respect. It may possibly conflict with law and morality, as in the case of the duel. But when its level is high in a nation we admire the system, for we see it not only guiding a people and binding them together for national effort, but affording the most real freedom of thought and action for those who in daily life habitually act in harmony with the General Will.'

In the second passage he extended his view to the development of a like ethical habit in international relations:

'Grotius concludes his great book on War and Peace with a noble prayer: "May God write", he said, "these lessons—He Who alone can—on the hearts of all those who have the affairs of Christendom in their hands. And may he give to those persons a mind fitted to understand and respect rights, divine and human, and lead them to recollect always that the ministration committed to them is no less than this, that they are the Governors of Man, a creature most dear to God."

'The Prayer of Grotius has not yet been fulfilled, nor do recent events point to the fulfilment being near. The world is probably a long way off from the abolition of armaments and

334

the peril of war. For habits of mind which can be sufficiently strong with a single people can hardly be as strong between nations. There does not exist the same extent of common interest, of common purpose, and of common tradition. And yet the tendency, even as between nations that stand in no special relation to each other, to develop such a habit of mind is in our time becoming recognisable. There are signs that the best people in the best nations are ceasing to wish to live in a world of mere claims, and to proclaim on every occasion "Our country right or wrong". There is growing up a disposition to believe that it is good, not only for all peoples but for all nations, to consider their neighbours' point of view as well as their own. There is apparent at least a tendency to seek for a higher standard of ideals in international relations. The barbarism which once looked to conquest and the waging of successful war as the main object of statesmanship, seems as though it were passing away. There have been established rules of International Law which already govern the conduct of war itself, and are generally observed as binding by all civilised people, with the result that the cruelties of war have been lessened. If practice falls short of theory, at least there is to-day little effective challenge of the broad principle that a nation has as regards its neighbours' duties as well as rights. It is this spirit that may develop as time goes on into a full international "Sittlichkeit". But such development is certainly easier and more hopeful in the case of nations with some special relation, than it is within a mere aggregate of nations. At times a common interest among nations with special relations of the kind I am thinking of gives birth to a social habit of thought and action which in the end crystallises into a treaty, a treaty which in its turn stimulates the process which gave it birth. We see this in the case of Germany and Austria, and in that of France and Russia. Sometimes a friendly relationship grows up without crystallising into a general treaty. Such has been the case between my own country and France.

We have no convention excepting one confined to the settlement of old controversies over specific subjects, a convention that has nothing to do with war. None the less, since in that convention there was embodied the testimony of willingness to give as well as to take, and to be mutually understanding and helpful, there has arisen between France and England a new kind of feeling which forms a real tie. It is still young and it may stand still or diminish. But equally well it may grow, and it is earnestly to be hoped that it will do so.

'Recent events in Europe and the way in which the Great Powers have worked together to preserve the peace of Europe, as if forming one community, point to the ethical possibilities of the group system as deserving of close study by both statesmen and students. The "Sittlichkeit" which can develop itself between the peoples of even a loosely connected group seems to promise a sanction for International Obligation which has not hitherto, so far as I know, attracted attention in connection with International Law.'

The idea in this passage is familiar enough to-day, but coming from such an authority in 1913 it attracted widespread attention. The address was not only very warmly received by the great gathering to which it was given, but was very widely circulated throughout Canada and the United States, and compliments upon it poured in. Mr. Kellog wrote: 'I can say without reservation that no speech within my recollection has made such a profound impression and received such universal commendation as yours. It has been printed and circulated to all members of the American Bar Association and I am constantly receiving enquiries for copies. I have watched with a great deal of interest the comments of the leading journals and they have been highly commendatory. In coming to America and delivering this speech you performed a great service to both countries, and I am very sure we shall all realise the lasting benefit of closer relations which have been so greatly facilitated by your efforts.'

Haldane sent a copy of the address to Bethmann-Hollweg, who answered: 'Accept my warmest thanks for your address at Montreal and for the kindly words which accompanied it. I had already read extracts from your speech in the newspapers. I admire the clearness with which you develop the necessity that the mutual relations of nations should be governed by the principle of "Sittlichkeit". What we have had to experience during the past years in the Balkans teaches us above all that the principle is far from being widely acknowledged. But on the other hand the Great Powers have shown through the attitude they have assumed towards the Balkan War, that with them too the principle is a guiding thread of action, it at least begins to make a pressing demand which cannot be overlooked.

'If I had the happiness of finding myself of one mind with you on these points in February 1912, it has been to me a still greater satisfaction that our two countries have since then had a number of opportunities of working together in this spirit. I hold the optimistic view that the great nations will be able to progress further on this path and will do so.

'Anyhow I shall as far as it is in my power devote my energies to this cause and I am happy in the certainty of finding in you a devoted fellow worker.'

This letter confirmed Haldane's conviction that Bethmann-Hollweg sincerely desired an understanding with England and understood the conditions in which it could be obtained. He refused to abandon hope that the German Chancellor's influence would prevail, while he was equally resolved to support Churchill's naval programme until such time as Germany renounced or postponed the application of her Naval Law. There was in fact a marked *détente* towards the end of 1913 in the strain upon our relations with Germany, but this was in the main due to our increasing absorption in Irish affairs rather than to any real improvement in Anglo-German feelings.

It is ironical that this speech, which created such an impression abroad, became one of the sticks which his enemies at home used to beat him. He had used German words, he had quoted German philosophers, and it was in reference to this that a friend said of him, 'Germany is his spiritual home', which, applied as it was meant to be applied to the Germany of Hegel, Fichte, and Lötze, was true. This statement provided one of those tags which the Press loves to take out of its context and tack on to a public figure. It was put into Haldane's own mouth and applied to a very different Germany.

Chapter XIV

WAR

1914 to 1918

From his triumph at Montreal Haldane returned to the dust of a very dusty arena. The Marconi affair dragged on and the Opposition naturally made the most of it, but it was Ireland which was the real centre of unrest. It had become clear that the Government intended to use the Parliament Act to force through the Home Rule Bill in the session of 1914. Shortly before Haldane left England Mr. Bonar Law had said: 'I can imagine no length of resistance to which Ulster may go in which I shall not be ready to support them.' Shortly after his return mass meetings were organized in all parts of Ulster to sign a covenant pledging the signatories 'to use all means which may be found necessary to defeat the present conspiracy to set up a Home Rule Parliament in Ireland'. Thereafter Ulster proceeded actively and openly to create an army of its own, a proceeding which was answered on the other side of the border by the creation of 'National Volunteers'. In this highly dangerous situation the King sought to bring the leaders of the Government and of the Opposition together and with some success. A number of secret and informal conferences took place, in which Haldane did his best to help in the building of a bridge, and in November and December he had talks with Mr. Redmond, which left him with the hope that a settlement was in sight.

In December he wrote to his mother: 'The situation is anxious and difficult but far from hopeless. This wild talk of civil war has no foundation except in the passions it arouses.

The problem has been narrowed down to the terms on which Ulster can be excluded from Home Rule. Redmond, who is really very responsible, is prepared to advocate to his people that Ulster shall be excluded as the price of peace. He will do all in his power to restrain his wild men. I wish I could be sure that Carson will do the same. Asquith is calm and resolute and is showing himself to be a real leader. I have in these days come to greatly admire the King. He has shown himself to have far more of his father's qualities of tact and judgment than I supposed. He is being bombarded by the Tory extremists with all sorts of suggestions. He is to dismiss the Government and appeal to the people, refuse assent to the Home Rule Bill and other wild ideas are thrust upon him. He remains quite calm, is sure of his constitutional position and is being of real service in seeking a way out.'

With the opening of the new session of Parliament these hopes of any early settlement vanished. In introducing the Home Rule Bill once more on March 9, 1914, Asquith announced that he was willing to include an amendment giving Ulster the right to exclusion for six years. This was as far as Redmond was prepared to go. Carson immediately refused the compromise and demanded what he called 'a clean cut' combined with a threat of resistance to anything less. This at once renewed the talk of civil war.

Throughout the autumn and winter of 1913 uneasiness in the Army had been growing. There is no doubt that the majority of the officers sympathized with Ulster and, while many of those who were Ulstermen and a few English enthusiasts were ready to go to any lengths, the majority were greatly perturbed and honestly perplexed at the prospect of having to decide between conscience and duty if the Army received orders to coerce Ulster. Sir Henry Wilson, an Ulsterman, who was a whole-hearted supporter of Carson, was in the War Office as Director of Military Operations, and he was also a personal friend of Mr. Bonar Law, whom he kept informed of his views of what was happening in the Army. The Conservative leaders openly declared their conviction that the Army would refuse to enforce Home Rule upon Ulster, and there were not wanting active propagandists to tell the soldiers that the day was nigh when such orders would be issued to them, information combined with broad hints that if they resigned or were dismissed they would be reinstated by the Conservatives.

Early in March 1914 the Government was informed that plans were afoot to seize arms and ammunition at some of the more isolated stations in Ulster. It then instructed the War Office to reinforce the garrison of Ulster to an extent sufficient to prevent this and at the same time arrangements were made to concentrate the constabulary, who were scattered in small posts. In transmitting the necessary instructions to Sir Arthur Paget, who was commander-in-chief in Ireland, the Army Council warned him that the movements of troops into Ulster might provoke disturbances and directed him to take the necessary precautions. He was also authorized to inform his officers that those whose homes were in Ulster would be allowed to apply for leave of absence during the period of operations and would, if they took such leave, be reinstated subsequently; that any other officer who was not prepared to carry out his duty should say so at once; such officers would be dismissed. The Conservative Press had expressed the opinion that it was the intention of the Government to apply Home Rule to Ulster by force of arms. The very unusual terms of the Army Council's communication together with Sir Arthur Paget's manner in making the communication to his officers, and the fact that Mr. Winston Churchill, as First Lord, had ordered the 3rd Battle Squadron to Lamlash, in the Isle of Arran, where it would be within a couple of hours of Belfast Lough, seemed, very naturally, to support this opinion and most of the officers of the Regular Army expected to be faced with an order to take part in civil war. After due consideration of the offer made to them Brigadier Hubert Gough, then commanding the 3rd Cavalry Brigade at the Curragh, and the great majority of his officers informed Sir Arthur Paget that they were prepared to be dismissed.

The news of this caused wild excitement. The Liberal Press called the action of General Gough and his officers mutiny. They had in fact been placed in a dilemma in which they should never have been placed, and had accepted an offer made to them by superior authority. The Conservative Press hailed with delight this confirmation of its view that the Army would not act against Ulster. Many of Haldane's old friends amongst the generals came to him for advice and help, and in particular the two members of the Army Council most concerned, Sir John French, the Chief of the Imperial General Staff, and Sir Spenser Ewart, the Adjutant-General. Haldane advised them that they should admit frankly that a mistake had been made in asking officers what their action would be in hypothetical contingencies. To this both agreed and he assisted in the drafting of a memorandum, on which an Army Order approved by the Cabinet was based, forbidding such action and also forbidding any officer or soldier to ask for assurances as to the orders which he might be required to obey. To this was added the statement that it was the duty of every officer and soldier to obey all lawful commands requiring him to support the civil power. When presented with this order General Gough asked whether the duty to support the civil power meant that, if the Home Rule Bill became law, the Army would be required to enforce it upon Ulster. Colonel Seely,[1] the Secretary of State for War, knew that this was not a question which had been considered by the Cabinet and that the military measures which were proposed were not intended for that purpose. He therefore added to the Cabinet's memorandum a paragraph stating that the Government had no intention of using the power of the Crown 'to crush poli-

[1] Now Lord Mottistone.

tical opposition to the policy or principles of the Home Rule Bill'. The memorandum with this addition was initialled by Colonel Seely, Sir John French, and Sir Spenser Ewart. The Government at once repudiated the addition as being in contradiction to that part of the Army Order forbidding officers to ask for assurances as to orders which might be given them. Colonel Seely, Sir John French, and Sir Spenser Ewart thereupon tendered their resignations.

Sir John French came to Haldane in great distress and sought his help in putting his action in the proper light and Haldane drafted for him the following letter to Asquith:

'MY DEAR PRIME MINISTER,

'I have read what you said on Friday afternoon in the House of Commons. I may say that any notion of an officer bargaining about his orders is as repugnant to me as it is to you and I may add that General Gough expressed the same view to me at the interview with him on Monday. I understood General Gough only to ask for a document, as something which he might have in his hands to enable him to allay dangerous misapprehensions and excitement in his brigade. I handed it to him in the belief that it represented the considered opinion of His Majesty's Government. In doing so I conceived that I was simply explaining what I took to be, and to have been throughout, the intention of the Government not to use the army for the purpose of coercing opinion in Ulster or undertaking active operations there.

'What you said on Friday I have carefully considered and I think that the intimation which you conveyed to the House of Commons is substantially just what I meant to convey to General Gough, not in a process of bargaining, but as an explanation of what I feared he and other responsible Generals might have misinterpreted. It is a real pleasure to me to be able to convey to you that what you have said satisfies my own sense of what I owe to the Army and to myself and I believe that it will satisfy others.

'Nothing could be more unfortunate in the best interests of the army than the creation of an impression that the word of a member of the Army Council or indeed of any officer could be lightly set aside after it had served its immediate purpose. It was this consideration that prompted me and the Adjutant-General to tender our resignations and we wish to remove any impression in the mind either of the public or of the army that we have been actuated by any desire to embarrass His Majesty's Government.'

Haldane suggested that Asquith should read this letter to the House and that French and Ewart should then withdraw their resignations.

When this draft had been sent off to Asquith, Haldane wrote to his mother: 'I have been labouring for peace and I am in hope that it will now result. The devotion of the soldiers to their old chief is touching. I think they felt that their honour was safe in my hands and I did all that I could to guard it and to save French and Ewart from the consequences of an honest mistake. There has been much misunderstanding and muddle and who is to blame it is hard to tell. There are I think a few of the soldiers, not many, who are letting themselves be used as the tools of the Tory extremists, but the vast majority are gravely distressed at a situation which should never have arisen. Anyhow you can be assured that there never has been any plan for using military force to coerce Ulster.'

Asquith's answer to Haldane's draft for the letter for French arrived on March 30:

'MY DEAR H.

'I have carefully read the draft letter. I need not say, with the utmost disposition to make any terms with French, that are compatible with our Parliamentary position. But I am satisfied we could not possibly survive any recognition, express or implied, of the Gough treaty, and it is equally clear that French will not remain except upon that footing.

'I fear this is an impasse from which there is no escape, much as it is to be deplored. You have done your part to find an accommodating formula and I gather from Bonham Carter[1] that you cannot do more.

'I see no way out of the imbroglio but for Seely to go also and I propose myself, for a time to take his place. Churchill who is here is entirely of the same opinion.'

So the resignations of Seely, French, and Ewart were accepted and Asquith became Secretary of State for War. The question of the constitutional position of the Army was thus settled, but the settling of it had made the problem of Ulster more acute than ever. The opposition, well primed by Sir Henry Wilson, professed to have definite proof of the Government's intention to invade Ulster in force and bitter debates took place in both Houses.

Speaking in the House of Lords on March 23, when the excitement was at its height, Haldane said: 'Naturally the Government have given a good deal of attention to the possibility of an outbreak in Ulster and to the possibility of interference with the ordinary liberty of the subject. With that situation and with the strongest desire to avoid anything that might lead to a conflict great care has been taken. No orders were issued, no orders are likely to be issued and no orders will be issued for the coercing of Ulster. So far as public opinion is concerned it will be left to make itself manifest, but if there is anything which amounts to a menace against the cause of law and order that must be dealt with.'

The sentence, 'No orders were issued, no orders are likely to be issued and no orders will be issued for the coercing of Ulster' was seized upon and paraded as a contradiction of the statement Grey had made in the Commons on the previous day to the effect that no government could abdicate its right

[1] Sir Maurice Bonham Carter, Asquith's private secretary.

to use all the forces at its disposal in defence of law. Read in conjunction with the sentence which followed no one could maintain seriously that there was any contradiction, but as is usual in times of political excitement the sentence was taken from its context and made to appear to be a surrender by the Government. Therefore when the report of his speech came to him for revision before its publication in *Hansard* Haldane, unwisely as he afterwards admitted, inserted the word 'immediate' before the word 'coercing'. This provoked another storm and he was charged in the House of Lords with having altered the meaning of what he had said, and his explanation was labelled as prevarication or as a legal quibble. The animosity of the Opposition was concentrated upon him, and he was marked down for attack by the backbenchers and by a section of the Conservative Press. Questions were again asked in the House about his visit to Berlin in 1912 and there were again broad hints and, in some cases, positive statements that he had gone to Germany on his own initiative and, without any authority from the Cabinet, had proposed a bargain with that country which was against our interests. A trickle of anonymous letters, which was before long to become a torrent, began and Leo Maxse's vituperation increased with every issue of the *National Review*. It was a curious development that at the very time when his assailants were using every weapon which came to their hand the generals, of whom the Opposition were posing as champions, were coming to Haldane for advice and comfort.

It is not less curious that six months later, a week after the first battle of the Marne, when the Expeditionary Force which Haldane had created had saved France, frustrated the German plan of campaign in the West, and raised high our hopes after the depression of the retreat from Mons, there was no relaxation of the venom with which he was pursued by his political opponents. On September 15 the motion that the Home Rule Bill should be placed on the Statute Book, its application to be suspended till peace was restored, when the Government promised an amending Bill, came before the House of Lords. Lord Londonderry then said:

'I spoke to some of my colleagues on this bench and to some of my colleagues in the House of Commons and I said: "I put no trust whatever in the statements or in the political honesty of His Majesty's Ministers." Why did I say that? I did so because my mind went back to the most extraordinary performance, which I have ever known in this House, when the noble and learned Viscount on the Woolsack, secretly hoping that it would not be noticed, altered from *Hansard* an important statement in his speech as reported in *The Times*. Since then I have never had any confidence whatever in the political honesty of His Majesty's Ministers. More than that I say that a more extraordinary action by anyone occupying the Woolsack has never taken place in your Lordships' House and I go further and say that if I thought any of my friends behind me could have been guilty of such an action I should be ashamed to be a member of the Unionist party.'

This kind of vituperation has, of course, its place in the ordinary party game and is harmless in ordinary times, but when it is continued into times of national crisis and has the effect of depriving the country of the services of a man preeminently fitted to serve it, its consequences are tragic. The Curragh incident passed into the background but Ulster still occupied the front of the stage and another crisis arose when a cargo of 30,000 rifles and 3,000,000 rounds of ammunition for the Ulster volunteers was successfully landed in the fourth week in April. Fortunately just at this time the Opposition again offered to negotiate. These negotiations dragged on with little prospect of success, and as a final effort the King summoned a conference at Buckingham Palace, which ended in failure on July 24, three weeks after the murder of the Archduke Franz Ferdinand and his wife at Serajevo and the day following the presentation of the Austrian ultimatum to

Serbia. A major issue was at that very time driving the Irish problem from the political stage.

It is an example of the complete absorption of our political world with Ireland that throughout this period there is but one reference to Germany in Haldane's papers. The improvement in Anglo-German relations had continued during the summer. Our fleet had paid a ceremonial visit to Kiel during the Kiel Regatta and had been received very warmly. The first hint of trouble appears in a letter from Haldane to Grey dated July 5:

'MY DEAR E.

'Lichnowsky who has just come back from Berlin came to see me yesterday. He appears to be very worried about the state of opinion in Germany. Austria he says is in a white heat of indignation over the murder of the Archduke and is contemplating drastic action. I asked him if he meant by this war, and he replied that that would depend on Serbia, but that Austria felt strongly that Serbia must be publicly humiliated. The general feeling in Berlin was, he said, that Serbia could not be allowed to go on intriguing and agitating against Austria and that Germany must support Austria in any action she proposed to take. There was naturally apprehension in Germany that Russia would support Serbia and that led him on to say that he had heard the opinion expressed in authoritative quarters that we had entered into a naval treaty with Russia.[1] I told him that that was nonsense and advised him to see you at once and tell you what he had told me. He brought me a letter from Ballin, which was the reason of his visit and Ballin too takes a pessimistic view and evidently thinks that Austria may drag Germany into trouble.'

[1] In April Grey had agreed that our naval attaché in Russia should enter into conversations with the Russian naval staff and this became known in Germany, but there was nothing proposed of the nature of a naval treaty.

Simultaneously with the arrival of the news of the Austrian ultimatum to Serbia the following letter arrived from Count Alexander Hoyos, who had known Haldane when he was on the staff of the Austro-Hungarian Embassy in London in 1911, and was, in July 1914, in the Austro-Hungarian Foreign Office:

'DEAR LORD HALDANE

'I venture to write to you with Count Berchtold's knowledge in the serious crisis which my country is passing through because I learned to value your sense of justice during my stay in England and feel sure that you will judge of the difficulties which have driven Count Berchtold to the step he has taken with impartiality and be able to realise, apart from European politics and the present groupment of powers, in an unbiassed manner, that no other way was open to us but to try and force Serbia to renounce her ambitions and to suppress the agitation against us in her country.

'When Bosnia and Herzegovina were occupied by Austria-Hungary in 1878 Europe recognised that she was the only country capable of dealing with a most difficult administrative and political problem. The two provinces are inhabited by a population of roughly 2 million souls of which 800,000 are orthodox Serbs, 700,000 Mahommedans and the rest Catholic Croats. It was always our aim not to make any difference between the different races and religions and to govern the country as justly and impartially as possible. That is one of the reasons why the Mahommedans have not left the country but are increasing, whereas they were wiped out in all other Balkan states as soon as Christian rule began. We have kept perfect order in the country and for many years racial and language questions did not exist, really not until King Peter came to the throne of Serbia.

'When we annexed the two provinces in 1908 a storm of excitement burst over Serbia and found a strong echo in Russia. We had a bad platform from an international point of view on that occasion, because we had been obliged to surprise Europe and violate an international treaty, no one however in Europe, except the Serbian Government, thought of disputing our right of keeping the two provinces we had held for 30 years and the whole of Europe understood our point of view, when at the end of the crisis we had to force Serbia formally to renounce any claims on Bosnia and to give us friendly assurances for the future.

'We then gave our new acquisition a very liberal constitution, so liberal that, to quote an example, the press laws are less stringent than they are in France, and have since done our best to let free and constitutional institutions take root in the country. I may mention that at the present moment the working majority in the Bosnian diet consists of Serbs, Croatians and Moslems, all of whom are loyal, as is the vast majority of the population.

'Unfortunately this state of things does not suit our Serbian neighbours. They, on the contrary, for some years have done their best, by the aid of schoolmasters, pamphlets, and secret societies, to foster an agitation, which is to bring about a revolution in Bosnia, Herzegovina and our other Southern Slav provinces, as soon as Serbia thinks the moment come to realise her ambition.

'The Balkan war and the unexpected success it brought the Serbian army has strongly increased this agitation, has sharpened its methods and has above all things convinced the Serbian man in the street, officer or civilian, that Austria was too weak to interfere in the Balkan struggle and that she will fall to pieces as soon as the great day dawns when Russia decides to plant her flag on the Carpathian mountains. It is this false atmosphere, this utter disregard for plain facts or realities in Belgrade which chiefly brought about the murder of our heir apparent in Sarajevo.

'The assassins all came from or had been in Belgrade, three of them have confessed, independently one from the other, that they received bombs and revolvers from a Serbian officer belonging to the Panserb secret society, Narosus Odbrava, and that Serbian frontier guards and customs officials helped them to smuggle the bombs while crossing the border and to get to Sarajevo safely. About 70 people were in the plot and our poor Archduke had six more bomb throwers and assassins waiting for him in case he escaped the first two.

'And behind all these deadly intrigues looms Russia as the protector of the Southern Slavs, as the missionary of militant orthodoxy in Galicia and Hungary, as the aggressive force, whose political aims and ambitions coincide with those of Serbia and also with those lately to be traced in Roumania. All to destroy Austria-Hungary to bar any interference in the future, when Russia decides to go to Constantinople and further. That is how matters really stand and that is why we can hesitate no longer but must try and break through the chain of iron that is being forged to bind and destroy us.

'The Russian Minister in Bucharest described the situation very well when he said to a colleague: "Nous avons mis déjà un couteau dans le ventre de l'Autriche et nous en aurons bientôt un autre."

'A well-known Russian historian, Professor Mistrofanoff, published an interesting article the other day, in which he told the Germans that Russia could never be friends with them as long as they stopped her taking Sweden, Galicia and Constantinople.

'These of course are not the views of a statesman but of a professor, yet they are very symptomatical for the trend of thought in Russian nationalist circles and prove how danger-ous Russian dreams must become for the peace of Europe.

'All these symptoms have been watched here carefully for some time, the murder of the Archduke brought a slow and steady development to a hasty climax and if we are now tak-ing matters in hand seriously, even at the risk of a general European war breaking out, we do so fully conscious that our country's existence is in danger and that Austria would be signing her own death warrant, if she continued passively enduring while her enemies are scheming to break her up as old iron.

'I trust and hope that this will be realised in England. Many I know who have suffered from the uncertainty of the political situation of the last 2 years will blame us for disturbing the peace of Europe, but they should consider that this uncertainty cannot cease as long as Russia and her friends in the Balkans remain convinced that we are going to pieces and that they will get a large share when this happens. It is this false impression which creates the unstable atmosphere from which we have all suffered in the last years.

'And lastly Englishmen should realise what the whole world would look like if the Russian daydreams came true, if Russia held the Balkans and Constantinople in undisputed sway and need fear no one in her back and flanks, when once she followed the example of Alexander the Great and turned her eyes towards India.

'These are world wide problems and I can't help hoping that their vital importance for Europe, for our culture and western tradition, will be realised in England.

Believe me, my dear Lord Haldane,
Yours very sincerely
A. Hoyos.'

Haldane's note on this letter ran: 'This is very serious. Berchtold is apparently ready to plunge Europe into war to settle the Serbian question. He would not take this attitude unless he was assured of German support. Hoyos' letter is clearly intended to prepare us for the ultimatum and is an attempt to scare us into neutrality with the Russian bogy. The one hope is that Bethmann-Hollweg's influence in Berlin will prevail.'

On July 24 Grey proposed that Germany, France, and Great Britain should confer with the object of mediating in the Austro-Serbian quarrel, and the next day Herr Ballin arrived in London and on that night he dined with Haldane, Grey, Morley, and Miss Haldane at Queen Anne's Gate. Ballin was evidently very anxious and his visit was probably another effort on the part of the Central Powers to gain our neutrality. Both Grey and Haldane were then still hopeful that the proposed international conference would find a solution, but both of them told Ballin independently that if Germany attacked France we could not remain neutral. On July 27 Grey came to stay at Queen Anne's Gate and Haldane then gave up all other work and devoted himself to easing the strain on his friend.

On July 28 Germany refused Grey's offer of a conference and Austria declared war on Serbia. Haldane then gave up all hope of peace. His comment was: 'The German General Staff is in the saddle.'

The next night Asquith, Grey, and Haldane dined together at Queen Anne's Gate and talked till 1 a.m. The three were agreed that nothing but a miracle could keep us out of war. When Asquith left Haldane scribbled a note to his mother: 'The declaration of war by Austria against Serbia has made the situation very critical. The Prime Minister was here with Grey and myself till one this morning. It is a time for calmness and decision. We are making all preparations.[1] If we fail in nerve it may be our turn next, if we are firm we may bring things quickly to a close.'

The three friends were in fact in advance of the opinion of the majority of the Cabinet and of public opinion. The man in the street was asking himself why he should be involved on behalf of 'a lot of Serbian murderers'. It became clear that

[1]The Cabinet had agreed with Mr. Churchill's proposal that the Fleet, which had been assembled for a trial mobilization, should be kept together and on the 29th the Cabinet authorized the issue of the warning order to the Services for the initiation of the precautionary measures to meet an immediate prospect of war.

the one thing which would unite the great majority of the
Cabinet and the opinion of the country would be the invasion
of Belgium by Germany, which was resisted by Belgium.
Haldane was well aware that if Germany attacked France she
would invade Belgium in force, but it was by no means certain that Belgium would fight, and there was a considerable
body of opinion in the Cabinet which saw no reason why we
should defend Belgium if she did not propose to defend herself. The issue was partly cleared by Belgium, which ordered
mobilization on August 1, and by the news which arrived on
August 2 that there were large movements of German troops
towards the Belgian frontier. While Grey and Haldane were
at dinner at Queen Anne's Gate that night a telegram was
brought to Grey announcing that Germany had presented an
ultimatum to Belgium demanding the free movement of
German troops through Belgian territory. Haldane was convinced that the invasion of Belgium west of the Meuse in
force was an essential part of the German plan and he convinced Grey that the only safe course for us was to order
immediate mobilization. The two then walked across to
10 Downing Street and there had a long talk with the Prime
Minister, who agreed that mobilization should be ordered.
In this he was boldly anticipating the agreement of his
Cabinet, which, while probable, was not certain. But a decision of this kind was easier for a British Prime Minister than
for the head of a Continental government. The order for the
mobilization of a Continental army sets in motion a machine
which, once started, can hardly be arrested, and it is therefore
true to say that the order for the mobilization of a Continental army means war in ninety-nine cases out of a hundred.
In our case an expeditionary force has not merely to be
mobilized but to be transported overseas, and mobilization
entails no risk of frontier collision. Asquith could therefore,
if the need arose, persuade his Cabinet that no irrevocable
step had been taken. He therefore agreed to the proposal of

HALDANE AND GREY WALKING TO NO. 10, 1914

Haldane, who then pointed out that, as Prime Minister he would be fully occupied on August 3, and suggested that he should send his former War Minister to the War Office with authority to order mobilization. Asquith agreed and handed Haldane a note which ran:

'C.I.G.S.   WAR OFFICE
                         WHITEHALL S.W.1

'The Cabinet approves of mobilization. Please put the necessary machinery, messages, etc., in order. The proclamation will be made tomorrow.

                              H. H. A.
                              3. Aug. 14.'

With this in his hand Haldane re-entered the War Office on the morning of August 3, assembled the Army Council and told them to proceed with the necessary preparations for a general mobilization.

In the meantime General Wilson had been busy. It was he who had worked out the plan for the co-operation of our army with the French army in the event of war, and he had always assumed that the two armies would mobilize at the same time. France had begun mobilization on the afternoon of August 1, and Wilson was gravely perturbed at our delay. He therefore got into touch with the leaders of the Opposition, informed them of what he knew of the hesitations of the Cabinet, and urged them to bring pressure on the Government. The result was a meeting of the leaders of the Opposition, which Wilson attended, and a letter on August 2 from Mr. Bonar Law to Asquith promising the support of the Opposition in resisting German aggression.

On August 3 the news that Belgium had rejected the German ultimatum and that King Albert had appealed to King George decided the majority of the waverers in the Cabinet, only Lord Morley and Mr. Burns resigning, while Grey's great speech in the House that evening carried opinion with him. We were resolved to resist an attempt to violate the neutrality of Belgium.

From the House of Commons Haldane went back to the War Office, where he found two letters waiting for him. The first was from Field-Marshal Lord Nicholson, whom he had made the first Chief of the Imperial General Staff:

'DEAR LORD HALDANE

'You have been going through such an anxious time that I have not written before, but now I gather that a decision has been arrived at which to my mind is worthy of the Government and the Empire. If so I feel strongly that you ought to go back to the War Office though you can ill be spared from your present high appointment. But "inter arma silent leges".'

The other, in pencil, was from Haig at Aldershot: 'I hear that you have returned to the War Office. I hope that you will stay there. There is no one who can in this crisis do for us there what you can do.'

Late that night Haldane wrote from the War Office to Asquith;

'MY DEAR A.

'Everything here is going smoothly. No fuss nor flurry. The proclamation goes out to-morrow and Wednesday (August 5) is the first day of mobilisation. I have been thinking about you. As Prime Minister you will have no time to spare for the War Office and I think you should hand over the seals at once. I am willing, if you wish it, to stay on in my old office, and some of my soldier friends have been urging this upon me. In my opinion you should make Kitchener your War Minister. He commands a degree of public confidence which no one else would bring to the post. I have just had a long talk with Sir John French and we agreed that the 5 cavalry brigades and six divisions of the Expeditionary Force should be sent over at once. They can all be assembled by August 20.'

At the very time when Haldane was writing this note scribblers in Fleet Street were at work on an attack upon him. The news that he had re-entered the War Office had got about and at once there was a clamour, led by the *Daily Express*. This pro-German, this friend of the Kaiser, this man who had said that his spiritual home was in Germany, was seeking to worm his way back into the War Office, and the abuse was coupled with a demand that Kitchener should go to the War Office.

Actually Asquith agreed with Haldane that Kitchener should be War Minister and at the Prime Minister's request Haldane sounded Kitchener on the subject. On August 4, on the same day, again at Asquith's request, Haldane arranged for a war council on the 5th to be attended by the leading generals, and it was Haldane who invited Kitchener, Roberts, French, Ian Hamilton, Wilson, with Haig and Grierson, the two commanders-designate of the 1st and 2nd Army Corps, to be present.

At the council there was much discussion as to where and in what strength the Expeditionary Force should go. Haldane urged that it should be sent to France complete, and, as strongly, that it was too late to make any change in the plan which had been worked out by our General Staff with the French General Staff. On this latter point the council was agreed, but on the dispatch of the whole six divisions he was in a minority. Kitchener did not share the view, which Haldane had held consistently, that with a predominant fleet the risk of invasion was negligible, and one of his first acts as War Minister was to send the 4th division to the East coast. So at a further meeting of the War Council on August 6 it was decided that no more than four divisions should be sent at first to France.

Meantime the gossips had been busy. Haldane was responsible for delaying our mobilization, he was against the prompt dispatch of the whole of the Expeditionary Force. So Balfour, as a friend of Haldane, was urged to bring pressure on him, and on August 4 he wrote:

'MY DEAR HALDANE

'The fact that we worked together upon the sub-committee of the Defence Committee up to Feb. 9 this year, combined with the fact that the Unionist Party are most anxious to aid to the very best of their ability the Government in the present crisis, emboldens me to write to you on the subject of the Expeditionary Force.

'As you are aware, I was altogether opposed, as a matter of general policy, to completely denuding these islands of regular troops. I certainly have no predilections for a policy of military adventure on the Continent; but surely there are almost overwhelming reasons at this moment for giving all the aid we can to France by land as well as by sea.

'(1) As regards Germany, we have burnt our boats. We have chosen our side and must abide by the result.

'(2) The sort of British force that we could send, after leaving 2 divisions at home, is, no doubt, a very small fraction of the troops immediately available for field operations in the North East of France.

'(3) If Germany could be "stalemated" in her advance through Belgium and North East France, the position becomes very perilous with the menace of Russia on her eastern frontier.

'If, on the other hand, the Germans are in sufficiently overwhelming numbers to inflict on France a crushing defeat, the whole future of Europe may be changed in a direction which we should regard as disastrous.

'(4) Is it not a fundamental principle of strategy in a crisis of this particular kind either to keep out of the conflict altogether, or to strike quickly, and strike with your whole strength?

'I know you will forgive me for troubling you with this

note; but the circumstances are unique and a course which would otherwise be unjustifiable will, I know, be forgiven.

Pray believe me yrs very sincerely

ARTHUR JAMES BALFOUR.

'P.S. Do not trouble to answer this. It is enough if you will consider it.'

To this Haldane replied on August 6:

'MY DEAR BALFOUR

'After War Council this evening we sanctioned the immediate despatch of the Exped. Force of 4 Divisions and the Cavalry Division. There has not been much delay, as mobilization could not take place early—they should be on the transports on Sunday. All this is of course very private. We have telegraphed to Belgium that this force is starting.

Yours very sincerely

HALDANE.'

This complete misconception of Haldane's attitude and actions, even by men who knew him and should have trusted him, would be comic had not its results been tragic. The ignorant abuse and ridiculous charges which poured into him at the instigation of the *Daily Express* need no more than mention. Such things are inevitable in times of great popular excitement, and Haldane was far from being the only one to suffer from them. But what is not excusable is that these attacks were permitted, if not actually encouraged, by those who, if they had given a little thought to the matter, must have realized that they were rendering ineffective the services of an organizer of proved ability at the very time when those services were most needed. A word from Mr. Bonar Law would have damped down the campaign of the *Daily Express*, just as a word from Balfour damped down the exuberance of his backbenchers when they were disposed to challenge Haldane's Army reforms. An immediate result of the campaign was that, very naturally, it lessened in Kitchener's eyes the value of Haldane's advice and made him more disposed to go his own way than to profit by the work and experience of his predecessor. Kitchener came into the War Office after a long career of great distinction in Egypt, South Africa, and India. Of the Army at home, of its organization and of its problems he knew little, and most of those soldiers who knew these things went off to France. He came into the War Office with a clearer vision than any one else of the vastness of the task with which the nation and the Empire was confronted when it was involved in war with the greatest military power in Europe, and he determined from the very first to prepare for that war on a scale which transcended anything which any one else had conceived as likely to be needed. He determined to expand our little Expeditionary Force of six divisions into seventy divisions, and to prepare for a war which would last three years. It is true to say that his vision in the greatest crisis in our history saved us. But it is equally true to say that it would have saved us with less effort and, very probably, more quickly if he had been willing to build on foundations which had been well and truly laid.

His experience in the South African War with units raised by patriotic citizens had not been a very happy one. He was aware of the criticism of Haldane's Territorial Army, of which he had no personal knowledge, and he distrusted the Territorial Associations in the belief that the influence of county magnates would be used to get military appointments for their friends. He therefore decided to create the new armies, which became known as Kitchener's armies, under his direct control. In other words he decided to improvise as he had done on a much smaller scale in Egypt, and improvisation was the very thing which Haldane's scheme was designed to avoid.

Haldane did his best to explain to Kitchener the system which he had devised and how the Territorial Army should be used to expand the Regular Army, but Kitchener had

HALDANE AND KITCHENER ENTERING THE WAR OFFICE
AUGUST 5, 1914

made up his mind and would not be moved. Having stated his case and having failed to establish it, Haldane loyally supported the War Minister in every possible way, while he watched sadly, his Territorial Army being pushed more and more into the background. There is not to-day any one acquainted with the problem who is not convinced that if Kitchener had used Haldane's system as it was meant to be used, and if the same assistance in the provision of regular officers and non-commissioned officers had been given to the Territorial Army as was given to the Kitchener army, the expansion of our military forces would have been far more orderly and more rapid than was the case. It is, at the least, probable that we should have had available in April 1915 sufficient troops to have made the Dardanelles campaign a success. In spite of the fact that in the first year of the war they were the Cinderella of the Army, the Territorials came triumphantly into their own, and the final proof that Haldane was right and Kitchener wrong is that in the reconstruction of our Army after the war, with all its experience behind us, the Territorial Army became officially the means of expanding our military forces.

Meantime the campaign of vituperation against Haldane gathered weight. Apart from mere ignorant abuse the charges made against him were that as Secretary of State for War he had been aware of Germany's preparations and intentions and had concealed this information from his colleagues in the Cabinet; that he had without informing the Foreign Office engaged in an intrigue with Ballin and other German friends; that he had gone to Berlin in 1912 on his own initiative, and there proposed a bargain with Germany detrimental to our interests, and that as Secretary of State for War he had reduced the Regular Army and particularly the artillery. The latter charge gathered weight as the progress of the war made apparent the increased importance of artillery, and it was repeated long after the war was over. In fact Haldane's reforms had not resulted in the reduction of a single gunner or of a single gun, and had greatly increased the gun-power of the Expeditionary Force. In proof of this I attach as an appendix to this chapter a statement prepared in the War Office after Haldane had left it.

The bottom would have been knocked out of most of these charges if Haldane's correspondence with Ballin and the official documents relating to his visit to Berlin in 1912[1] had been published. Haldane quixotically refused to make the Ballin letter public, on the ground that it was private correspondence and that he would not consent to its publication without the consent of the other party, which it was impossible to obtain. Once war was declared there could have been nothing detrimental to national interests in the publication of the documents relating to the 1912 visit. But it was against the traditions of the Foreign Office and it might possibly have led to demands for the publication of other papers, which it would not have been convenient at that time to make known. In any event publication was refused at the time when it would have been useful and Haldane was not the man to press for it in his own interests. A somewhat jejune summary of the documents was published by the Foreign Office on August 26, 1915, after the mischief had been done, and was followed on September 6 by this memorandum:

'Some misunderstanding appears to have arisen in certain quarters with regard to the position of Lord Haldane in connexion with the Anglo-German negotiations of 1912, an account of which was recently issued by the Foreign Office. Lord Haldane did not accept the formula which was proposed to him, when he was in Berlin, by the German Chancellor. He could not, however, refuse to submit the formula to the Cabinet, and it was so submitted. The rejection of the formula was made on the authority of the Cabinet and with Lord Haldane's approval.'

[1]Appendix I, Chapter XII.

Without the means of answering the attacks upon him, Haldane felt that they not only weakened his own position, but were embarrassing to the Government, and therefore he went to Asquith in September 1914 and offered to resign. Asquith, who was always contemptuous of Press attacks, and was apparently unaware that they, or at least the more serious of them, were credited by responsible people, laughed at the idea of taking serious notice of the campaign, and persuaded Haldane to join a munitions committee of the Cabinet, which he was setting up to assist Kitchener.

The work of the higher courts of appeal was to a great extent in abeyance and attendance on the Woolsack in the House of Lords left Haldane with time at his disposal, and this he devoted to relieving the strain on his friend Grey, as he had done ever since the Foreign Minister came to his house on July 27. On two occasions during the late autumn and early winter he took over the Foreign Office for short periods, in order that Grey might go to his birds in Northumberland for a much needed rest.

Haldane could at this time, in the eyes of his critics, do nothing right. A story got about, and was seriously credited by the Conservative leaders, that during the second of the periods in which he had acted as Foreign Minister he had ordered the release of a ship laden with copper, which had been detained at Gibraltar by Grey's orders, and that this ship had found its way to Germany. Lord Derby fortunately repeated this story to Mrs. Asquith, who told Grey of it, and he was able to stamp it as a lie.[1]

Living in this atmosphere of poison gas, relieved only by the letters of congratulation which he received from the soldiers, naturally affected Haldane's spirits. He felt that he could not pull his weight in the Cabinet and was not in the least surprised at the dénouement when it came. It came in May 1915, when circumstances forced Asquith to reconstruct his

[1]Trevelyan, *Grey of Fallodon*, p. 274.

Government. At the Prime Minister's request all the members of his Government placed their resignations in his hands, and when the negotiations with the Conservatives for the formation of a coalition were begun it was found that Mr. Bonar Law insisted as an essential condition of the co-operation of his party that Haldane should have no part in the new Government. With real regret Asquith agreed on the ground that on no other terms was a coalition possible. So on May 26 Haldane handed back the Great Seal to the King. The slight to him was made the more pointed in that the Conservatives did not demand the Lord Chancellorship for themselves, and Haldane was succeeded on the Woolsack by another Liberal, Lord Buckmaster. Grey was furious and wished to resign, but was persuaded by Asquith that it was his duty to his country to remain.[1]

Haldane took his ejection from office philosophically and retired to Cloan, grieved chiefly at the distress which these events caused his mother. Indignant letters from his soldier friends in France and from many others poured in, and the King's reply to the attacks, as it was to be a little later when similar attacks came from the same quarter upon Kitchener, was to award Haldane the Order of Merit.

Three days after he had ceased to be Lord Chancellor he wrote the following account of his part in the Cabinet crisis:

'I wish to put on record the circumstances under which, on Wednesday last the 26th May, I resigned the Great Seal into the hands of the King.

'On Monday 17th the Prime Minister sent round a circulation box to his colleagues in the Cabinet to say that he had come to the conclusion that we ought all to resign in order that a new Government might be formed on a national basis. The decision came as a surprise to the whole of us, but we learned the reason later. Lord Fisher had resigned as First Sea Lord, and the Admiralty were likely to be exposed to criti-

[1]Trevelyan, *Grey of Fallodon*, p. 276 et seq.

cism because of differences of opinion between him and Churchill about the Dardanelles expedition. Besides this Lord Kitchener was being attacked about munitions of war. It was said that he had failed to supply the Army in France with what it needed and had asked for. The Opposition had in consequence, so we gathered, threatened an attack, and the only way to stave this off was to form a new Administration which should include all parties. A group of newspapers was attacking Kitchener. For months past these papers had been attacking me on various grounds. The main ground was that I was supposed to have leant in the past to ideas of friendship with Germany and to have been duped. The other was that I had reduced the strength of the Army. Neither of these allegations was true. But for a long time these assertions had been made so widely and persistently that I was well aware that a multitude of people believed them. I had in the winter before drawn the attention of the Prime Minister to their mischievous effect in time of war, and pointed out that they were serious in such a time, and ought not to pass unnoticed. I did what I could to meet them myself, but I warned him that in the end the general interest might make it better that I should not remain in the Government. Neither he nor Grey thought them important enough for official denials.

'The facts, so far as Germany is concerned, were briefly these. When I took office as War Minister in 1906 I was deeply concerned at the outlook. In Germany, which I know well, there were two dangerous parties. One which wanted peace but believed that England, France and Russia were secretly combining to ring Germany round, and perhaps try to crush her. Another which believed the German Army was invincible, and which really wished for war and a German triumph. For the rest the bulk of the people of Germany always seemed to me to be decent peace-loving people, but I knew that they would follow their flag if it was threatened. In England, on the other hand, the bulk of the population hated spending money on armaments, and would have turned the Government out in 1906, had it even talked of increasing expenditure on the Army. On the other hand the great majority of the diplomatic class were anti-German, and could not refrain from showing it in trifles. The Germans knew well how these disliked them. The war party in Germany cited the fact as evidence of the hostile attitude of England. I set myself with all my energy to meet the situation. I tried on every opportunity to speak in a friendly way of Germany. I was invited in August 1906 to visit the Kaiser at Berlin, and I did so, first paying King Edward, who was at Marienbad, a visit. My diaries kept for him of this visit in 1906 are probably among the records at Windsor, and the most important of them is, I think, among my own papers.[1] I succeeded in breaking down what was at first a certain reserve at Berlin, and ultimately made, as I believe, an impression of good will and friendliness. The authorities even gave me access to the Prussian War Office, and to much information about the organisation of the German Army, which afterwards proved of value to us. From this time friendly relations sprang up between the German Ambassador in London and myself. The German press began to be a little less hostile to England, and I was able to tell Grey, from time to time, what I found. When the Kaiser came to visit King Edward at Windsor three years later I was there, and acted as the go-between in delicate negotiations about the Baghdad railway. At no time did I take any step without the full assent of Grey and the Foreign Office. My sole purpose was to get rid of the friction which had existed and in my view was a source of peril. Meantime I was reconstructing the Army and supporting the development of naval strength in Home waters.

'In 1911 there was a crisis about the Agadir incident. So uncertain did the prospect look at one time that I asked and obtained permission to spend the money requisite for perfect-

[1] Cf. pp. 192-200.

ing our mobilization arrangements. The Expeditionary Force was made ready. Since 1906 conversations had taken place with the French General Staff about joint plans for defence against the possible invasion of France by Germany. Grey had spoken of this in January 1906, after the Morocco incident, and had commenced the discussions which the two General Staffs carried on. I had consulted Sir John French and asked him to prepare himself for the possible command of our troops in France. With my assent he had devoted much time and thought to preparation against a calamity which we hoped would be averted, but for which we were bound to be ready. The examination of the question was afterwards continued in the Committee of Imperial Defence. The result was that in 1911 we were nearly as well prepared as we were in 1914. Since 1911 the work had been steadily carried on. We dared not do more than we did. In the first place to do so would, as far as we could judge, have precipitated war at a time when Russia was unready. In the second place Parliament would have interfered and stopped us. Indeed it was with the utmost difficulty that I had been able to get the minimum of money with which I could work, and I had to resist repeated efforts to cut down the Army.

'In 1912 relations with Germany continued to be strained, though war had been averted. By desire of the Cabinet and with full instructions from Grey I went to Berlin on behalf of the Sovereign and the Government to hold conversations there. These are recorded in the précis made at the time and printed by the Foreign Office for the Cabinet.[1] I therefore do not repeat them here at length. I had full and friendly conversations with the Kaiser and with Bethmann-Hollweg. I was able to be frank because I had been friendly. I told them that their new shipbuilding programme would inevitably lead to our laying down two ships for every one of theirs—a result which happened. I also told them that we could accept no

[1] Cf. Appendix I, Chapter XII.

formula of neutrality which could tie our hands if Germany threatened to attack France in which we had a deep interest, although we were not bound by treaty to her. I added that actual treaties might compel us to intervene were Japan, Belgium or Portugal threatened, and that therefore I must reject the formula of the unconditional neutrality of both nations whatever war might arise. Subject to this I said we desired a new friendship with Germany into which we might carry our existing friendships with France and Russia, to the profit of all four powers. But I added that, if they persisted in their new fleet law, the British public would be cool about such an agreement, if accompanied by a new German Fleet law imposing heavy naval burdens on us. In the result the Emperor and the Chancellor, although I believe thoroughly sincere at the time in desiring good relations, found that they could not stop the Fleet law. Admiral Tirpitz, whom I saw, was too strongly entrenched. Although this proposal failed we none the less made progress with ideas for territorial arrangements in Africa and elsewhere. Negotiations as to these sprang up between the two Foreign Offices and the relations between these offices became excellent, and continued so through the Balkan difficulties and right down to the outbreak of war. My mission at least helped to this result, and it considerably increased the nascent desire for friendly feeling on both sides. Later on the Emperor appears to have been captured by the military party, but at this time I am certain that he had not yet been captured. Like Bethmann-Hollweg, he was opposed to the idea of war. The fear which arose later out of the movement for Slav independence, the fear of a ringing round of Germany by a group of powers with aspirations different from those that were hers, appears to have influenced the Kaiser's choice. He always left on my mind, when I talked with him, the impression that, along with a desire for peace, there existed in his mind a desire to succeed his relative Frederick the Great in his rôle of a mighty war lord. The two motive forces, fear and ambition, probably united in finally determining his choice. I hold him deeply responsible for the war, for I am satisfied that he could have averted it. The war parties, such as they were, in Russia, France and England, counted for much less than did the war party in Germany. Still they were there, and their voices in the press, a fertile source of international mischief, hampered the efforts of those who sought to make the German people realize how unreal was the ground of Germany's fear. But the main obstacle was the attitude of those of whom I have spoken in Germany herself.

'After 1912 Grey did all, to the best of my judgment, that a man could do. He had the task of preserving the confidence of France and Russia, as well as of gaining that of Germany; during the Balkan difficulties he laboured with a single purpose, that of keeping the great powers in unison.

'I have never been myself pro-German in any other sense than that I knew and admired German literature and German thought, and the German power of organisation. My only doubt now is, whether I should not have pressed more strongly for the realisation of the perilous character of the situation, in the days before 1911. Whether I could have done any good I do not know. It must be remembered that Grey had not then got the confidence of France and of Russia as he got later, and as it was desirable that he should get it. Of this I am pretty certain that we could not have made naval or military preparations for war on a larger scale than we did without precipitating the very situation we desired to avoid. As it was we ran some risks, I think unavoidably.

'About the work I endeavoured to accomplish in connection with the Army I say nothing. The details lie open for the public judgment.

'But that there has arisen in the mind of certain people misunderstanding of the course I pursued, both as regards Germany and the Army, there is no doubt. I have written these notes to show that the things that have been said and written about that course are based on a radical misinterpretation.

HALDANE.'

In this note Haldane gives his reasons why more could not be done in the way of military preparation than was done. To these it may be added that the size of the Expeditionary Force was conditioned then, as it is to-day, by the Cardwell system, which regulates the number of battalions, batteries, and squadrons on home service. The Expeditionary Force could only have been increased by the introduction of conscription and this was at the time both politically impracticable and militarily dangerous. As to its equipment and organization, the *Official History of the War* declares that 'in every respect the Expeditionary Force of 1914 was incomparably the best trained, the best organised, and the best equipped British Army which ever went forth to war'.[1] Defects in our preparations became apparent as the war progressed, and of these one of the gravest was that we had made no attempt to organize industry to maintain the Army in the field. This was due to the fact that hardly any one except Kitchener had believed that the war would be prolonged. Financiers and economists were agreed that Europe could not stand the strain of a long struggle, while military opinion, not only in this country but in others, held that the exhaustion of modern battle would result in the speedy collapse of one side or the other. The Germans had laid their plans to defeat the armies of France in forty days. Sir Henry Wilson records in his diary an interview which he had with General Berthelot, the head of the Operations Section at Joffre's headquarters, in September 1914, after the first battle of the Marne: 'Berthelot asked me when I thought we should cross into Germany, and I replied that unless we made some serious blunder we ought to be in Elsenborn in four weeks. He thought three weeks.'[2]

[1] *Official History of the War: France and Belgium 1914,* 1933 edition, p. 10.
[2] *Field-Marshal Sir Henry Wilson,* Callwell, vol. I, p. 177.

Not even Kitchener had foreseen a war in which the guns would be firing, not in the occasional battles which had occurred in previous wars, but every day and every night. True a Russian, M. Bloch, had predicted the deadlock of trench warfare, but this happened to be one lucky shot in a review of the future of war containing many other predictions which the event proved to be wrong. For example, he said, 'In the war of the future shell, which is much less effective than shrapnel, will be employed less than formerly. Shrapnel will be the chief weapon of artillery.' Haldane had taken the best available military advice as to the equipment of his Expeditionary Force and had acted upon it. His General Staff had advised against providing it with heavy artillery on the ground that this would hamper its mobility, while artillery opinion in 1914 was strongly in favour of shrapnel as against high explosive for field artillery. The public, which knew nothing of these things, was naturally enough disposed to blame the War Minister who had claimed to have prepared the Army for war, when surprises came for which we were not ready.

This was one reason why there was no effective rally to his side when the popular frenzy against any man who had had, or was supposed to have had, friendly relations with Germans, was directed against him. There were other reasons for this. One of them was his personality. I have said that the only time in his life when he enjoyed any general popularity was during the few months which followed his retirement from the War Office. He never sought popularity, and he was not the type of man to whom it came naturally. He was held in high esteem in his own constituency and by his group of personal friends, but he never attracted any considerable following within his own party or from the general public. He had never been a good party man, and a large body of Liberals remembered that he had endeavoured to get Rosebery to oust Campbell-Bannerman, and that he had been active in the campaign to force C. B. into the House of Lords. Many

Liberals looked askance at his imperialism, and the majority of them knew little and cared less about Army reform, save as a means of reducing Army estimates.

Haldane's two loves, philosophy and education, made no general appeal. When he spoke on a matter on which he felt deeply or in which he took a real interest, his words were apt to tumble over one another, and his arguments were often involved. He was never a maker of phrases. The only sport in which he took any interest was his shooting in the Perthshire hills. A love of horse flesh is a political asset, but Haldane's devotion to his dogs had no like appeal. He had none of those little human weaknesses and foibles which often endear a leader to his followers. The Aristides of politics are rarely popular. Mr. Lloyd George could come through the Marconi affair and bob up smiling, but when Haldane was accused of being a pro-German down went his name on the oyster-shell.

The British public is never deliberately ungenerous, and the prime reason for the success of the attacks on Haldane was that the public did not understand what he had done for them. He was in the public mind associated chiefly with the creation of the Territorial Army and the Officers' Training Corps. On behalf of both he had stumped the country. But now Kitchener occupied the front of the stage and Kitchener's armies had relegated the Territorial Army to the background. Haldane's real work for the Army, and through it for his country, had been done within the War Office. He had set himself in 1906 to create a force which should be in all respects complete and be able, in case of need, to come to the help of France in the shortest possible time. Actually the Expeditionary Force was at its place of concentration in France in fifteen days. When Haldane entered the War Office he found that it would have taken two months to prepare a much smaller force for embarkation. The rapidity with which we mobilized and transported our Expeditionary Force in 1914 completely surprised the Germans, who were not aware that our men were at Mons until they came into contact with them. Our presence at Mons saved the French armies from envelopment. Within three weeks the same Expeditionary Force decided the issue in the first battle of the Marne and foiled the long-prepared German plan of campaign in the West. Haldane's organization of the Expeditionary Force had saved us. There have been, and probably will be for a long time, arguments whether the Expeditionary Force was sent to the best place. For the place chosen Haldane had but a very indirect responsibility. There had been no doubt that prompt aid to France was essential and it was Haldane who made it prompt. But that was by no means the whole of Haldane's work. Of the rest the man best qualified to speak shall tell. When the Armistice came Haldane at once wrote to Haig to congratulate him, and he received the following reply:

'Tuesday 19th Nov. 1918.

GENERAL HEADQUARTERS,
BRITISH ARMIES IN FRANCE.

'MY DEAR LORD HALDANE,

'There has been so much going on here that I have not been able to attend to my private correspondence. I therefore hope that you will forgive me for not writing to thank you sooner for your most kind letter.

'I appreciate very much indeed your kindly remembrance of my work with you at the War Office. For me that time will always stand out in my memory most prominently because the organisation of our Army *for war* dates from then. Until you arrived at the War Office no one knew for what purpose our Army existed! And I feel sure that all the soldiers who in those strenuous years were working in the War Office will bear witness to the all-important service which you then rendered to the British Army in the Empire. You then sowed the seeds which have developed into the tremendous instrument which has vanquished the famous German Army and brought about a victorious peace. And where would we be to-day without the Imperial General Staff which was your creation and the Field Service Regulations (Part II. Organisation) which you forced through in spite of opposition from Army Council and Treasury?

'I and many soldiers with me, are greatly distressed at the ungenerous treatment which you have received during the critical phase in our country's history; and I hope the day is not far distant when the invaluable services you have rendered to our Empire may be adequately recognised.

'With heartfelt admiration for the way in which you have done your duty and ignored all the spiteful criticisms of the Press, which has attacked you, and again many thanks for your very welcome congratulations on what the British Army has done.—Believe me, Yours very truly,

D. HAIG.'

Haldane had in fact, when he retired from the War Office, extended the organization of the General Staff not only to the whole Regular Army, but also to the Territorial Army and to the Empire, and he had provided for the whole Empire, before the event, a system of organization for war. In the past we had invariably improvised such a system and arrived at one which would work by the costly experience of trial and error. Haldane's system not only enabled the dominions to organize their forces uniformly with our own, and far more rapidly and effectively than would without it have been the case, but it stood the test of the greatest strain in our history, and is to-day substantially the same as it was in 1914. Of none of these things was the general public aware.

Upon the Foreign Office communiqué on Haldane's mission to Berlin in 1912, published at the end of August, Haldane had some correspondence with Grey and in reply to a letter from him he wrote:

6 Sept. '15.

'MY DEAR EDWARD,

'It is good of you to have written as you have. I was wearied when I wrote to you by articles which appeared in the papers (some of them enclosed in the usual anonymous letters) distorting the meaning of the F.O. Communiqué. But such articles are not to be wondered at in a time of excitement such as this. Anyone who has identified himself with efforts and utterances, such as mine have been for years past, ought to accept the inevitable gently.

'I have spent a really happy August, immersed in studies which had for long been interrupted, and from which I hope to produce some result before long. I have read pretty hard and time has flown.

'I despair of getting the figures as to German absorption and wastage in Russia properly worked out. The General Staff organization which ought to be at work simply does not exist. There are fragments for which individual ministers are responsible, but there is no one to co-ordinate the work. I am in communication with Hankey, the Press Bureau, the General Staff and the Actuaries, but they appear to be incapable of getting to work together, and the confusion is disconcerting. General Staff work is a thing which requires training and watching over, and no one takes sufficient interest in it to insist on the co-ordination of the necessary elements.

'However, the Germans in Russia must now be getting used up by a fairly rapid process.

'What the Balkan States are doing, and whether they are making any progress towards convergence I suppose that even you do not know.

'We must stick to hope in Wordsworth's sense, and hold to the obligation of high courage.

'The success or failure of the new German loan is going to be a very interesting question.

'This fine weather is admirable for you, and I hope you will have a real rest. After the middle of Sept. I shall aim at running up to London for a day or two.

Ever yours,

HALDANE.'

We have here a hint of what might have been had Haldane remained in our councils during the war. He knew, as no other civilian with like influence knew, the supreme importance of a well-organized General Staff in the higher direction of war, and he saw at once how impossible it was for Kitchener to direct effectively without its aid. I have spoken of the absence of any organization of industry for war as one of the main defects in our preparations. The other was the lack of any organization for the higher direction of war. Haldane had always conceived of the Committee of Imperial Defence being adapted for this purpose. This defect might well have been remedied more speedily and effectively than it was if he had been able to bring his experience and counsel to the Cabinet. Therefore his dismissal from office was far more than a personal injustice, it was a national tragedy.

He remained quietly working at Cloan, to be howled at whenever he made, as he did occasionally, a brief appearance in public. The work to which he turned can best be dealt with in the next volume. We leave him at that work, quietly confident that when the men who knew came back from France they would bring with them his justification. It came first when Haig, after leading the victory march past the King at Buckingham Palace, walked across to Queen Anne's Gate and there handed to Haldane the volume of his dispatches inscribed:

'To Viscount Haldane of Cloan—the greatest Secretary of State for War England has ever had. In grateful remembrance of his successful efforts in organising the Military Forces for a War on the Continent, notwithstanding much opposition from the Army Council and the half-hearted support of his Parliamentary friends.

HAIG, F.M.'

Appendix to Chapter XIV

CHANGES IN THE ROYAL ARTILLERY

1906 TO 1912

LORD HALDANE came to the War Office in December 1905 and left in the spring of 1912. The dates taken as representing the period of his administration are the 1st January 1906 and 1st January 1912 as regards the actual strength. As regards establishments the years taken are 1905–6 and 1912–13. The figures are as follows:

No reduction of Establishment.

Establishment (including India), 1905–6
Horse and Field Artillery, 29,878
Garrison Artillery   22,851

1912–13
H. and F.A.   30,070
R.G.A.   18,738

No reduction of Strength.

Actual Strength, January 1906
H. and F.A.   30,540
R.G.A.   23,923

January 1912
H. and F.A.   31,245
R.G.A.   18,406

On the same dates the strength of the Army Reserve was :

1 January 1906

H. and F.A.	8,185
R.G.A.	4,965

1 January 1912

H. and F.A.	17,570
R.G.A.	7,456

Large increase of Strength, including Reserves.

There was also on 1 January a force of 6,005 Field Artillery Special Reservists which did not exist in 1906. Thus the strength of the Horse and Field Artillery, including the Regular Reserve, increased from 38,725 to 48,815, not including the 6,000 Special Reservists, while the strength of the Garrison Artillery, also including Reserves, fell from 28,888 to 25,862.

The reduction in the Garrison Artillery was due to two causes. To the extent of about 500 it represents the transfer of the fortresses of Halifax and Esquimalt to the Canadian Government. The rest arises from a thorough revision of coast defences at home and abroad carried out by a joint Naval and Military Committee appointed by the *Unionist* Government in 1905. This Committee swept away a large mass of ancient heavy guns from our fortifications and remodelled them on the basis of a smaller number of modern guns of more rapid fire and greater power, with consequent economies in gun crews.

As regards Horse and Field Artillery, the batteries in existence at the beginning of 1906 included sixty-seven which had been added immediately before and during the South African War. None of these batteries were specially earmarked for training drafts or reinforcements. There were ninety-nine field batteries at home of which sixty-six belonged to the first line force of three army corps, and of those only forty-two could be mobilized with the necessary ammunition columns and parks, even by stripping all the others bare. It was urgently necessary to increase the available men in the shortest possible time. Lord Haldane earmarked the thirty-three batteries not included in his Expeditionary Force of six divisions as training batteries for Regular and Special Reserve recruits, the Special Reserve doing six months continuous training and afterwards an annual refresher course. This rapidly turned out men of valuable quality for work with the ammunition columns. To make a quick start some nine or ten thousand men of the old Militia Artillery were put through a special course of training to fit them for field duty. In 1909 so much progress had been made that Lord Haldane was able to add six howitzer batteries to the Expeditionary Force and to reduce the number of training batteries to eighteen, thus leaving nine spare batteries surplus to the first line. At the same time the numbers of the Field Artillery Special Reserve were reduced to about 6,000 and a larger number of Regular Reservists provided by introducing a proportion of men serving three years with the Colours and nine in the Reserve.

By 1910 Lord Haldane was able to announce in his memorandum on the estimates that the whole of the Field Artillery, now seventy-two batteries, of the Expeditionary Force could mobilize. In addition to this there had been created over 150 Territorial horse and field batteries, some of which, by replacing Regular batteries in India and elsewhere, had already[1] proved of the utmost value.

No reduction of Cadres.

Of the total number of seventeen horse and 105 field batteries of Regulars existing at the end of 1905 not a single battery has been reduced; though most of the men were removed from training batteries to make room for recruits, there was no reduction in the total number of officers, and the whole of the equipment and ammunition of these batteries was also retained undiminished.

[1] In 1914.

INDEX

INDEX

INDEX

K1